Singapore
Off center

A Photographic Exploration

Scott Shaw

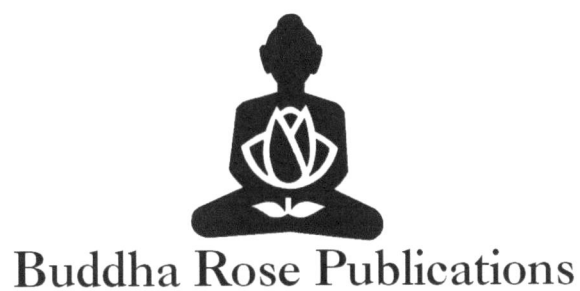

Buddha Rose Publications

Singapore Off Center
Copyright © 1984 by Scott Shaw
www.scottshaw.com
All Rights Reserved

No Part of this book may be reproduced
in any manner without the expressed written
permission of the author or the publishing company.

First Edition

ISBN-10:　1-877792-60-8
ISBN-13:　978-1-877792-60-1

Photographed with a vintage Leica camera.

Printed in the United States of America

10 9 8 7 6 5 4 3 2 1

Singapore
off center

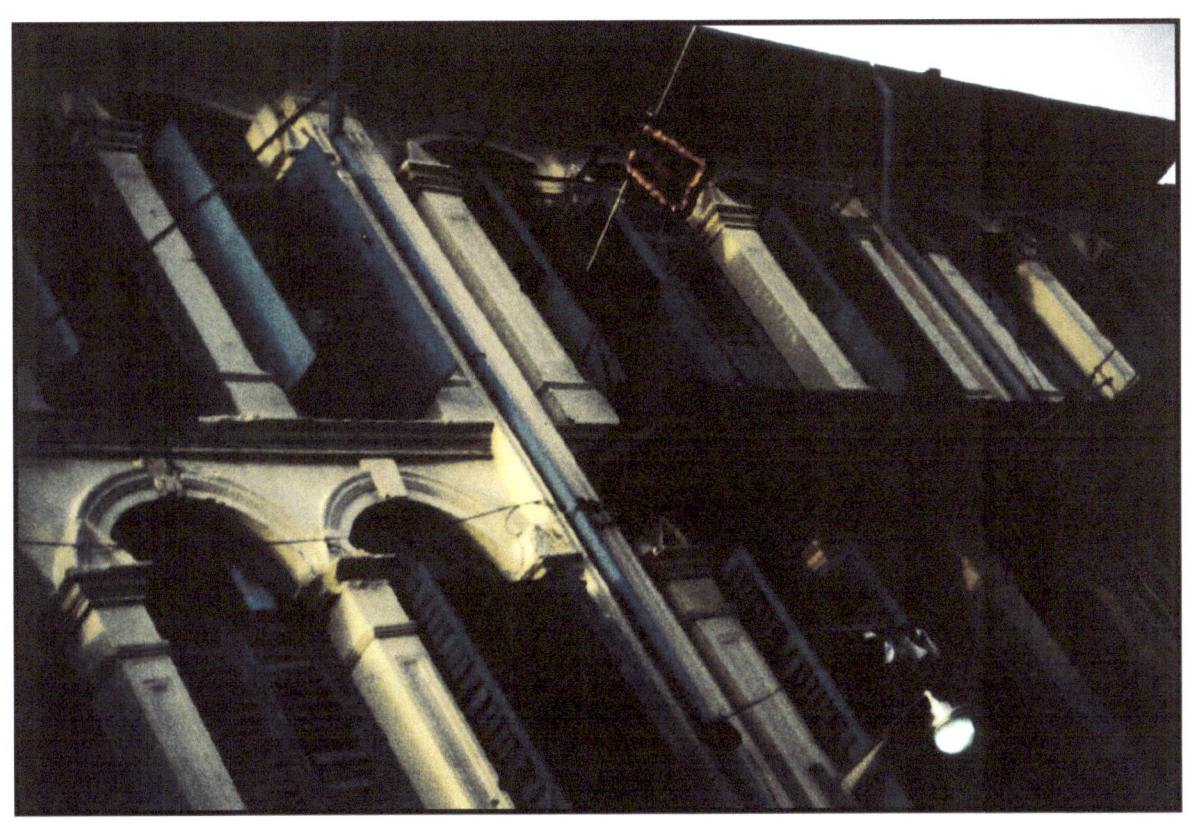

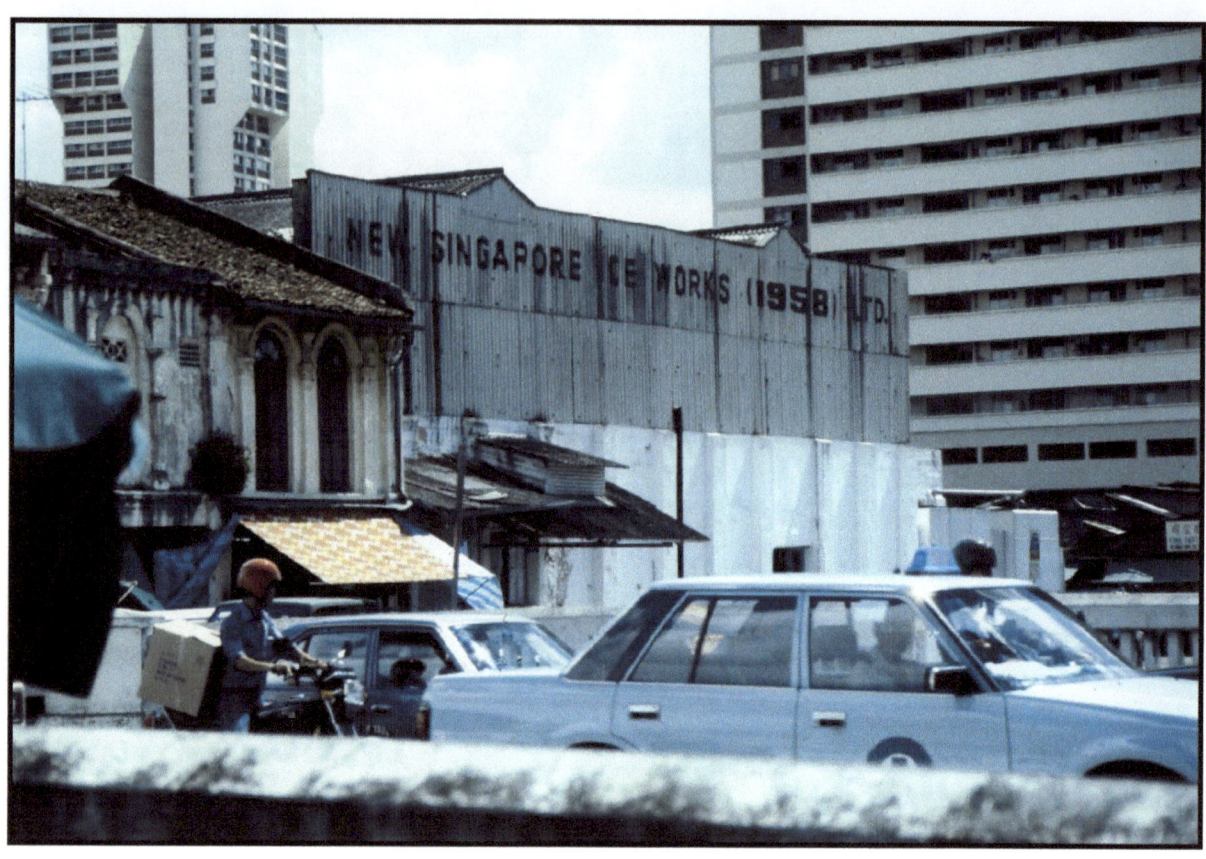

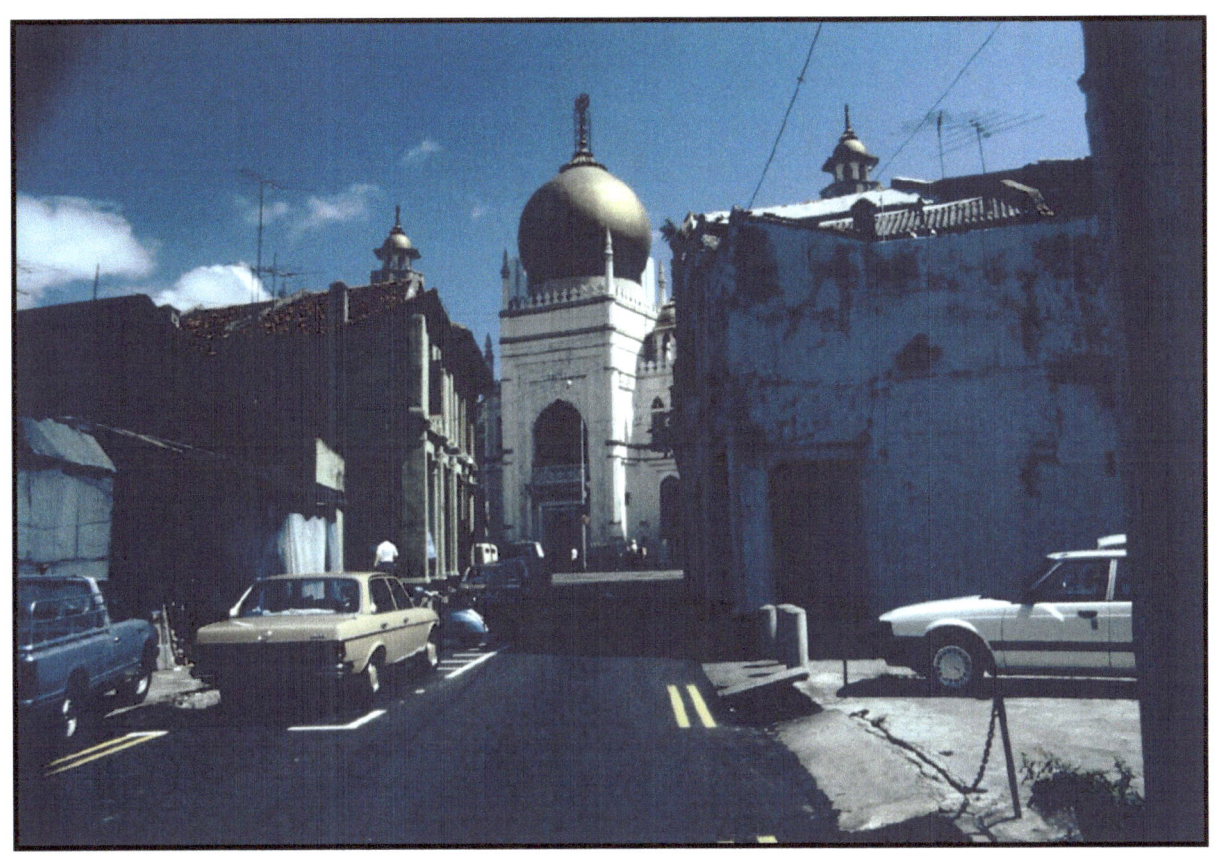

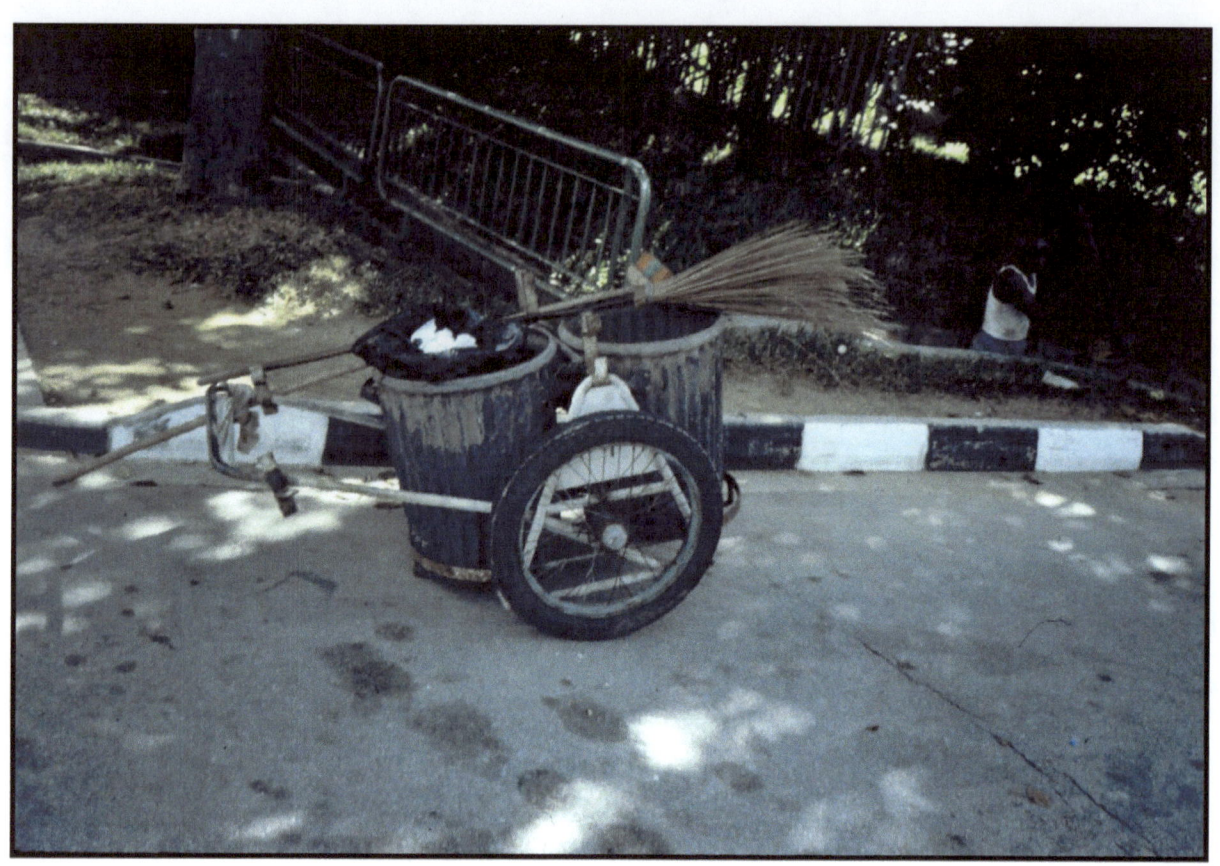

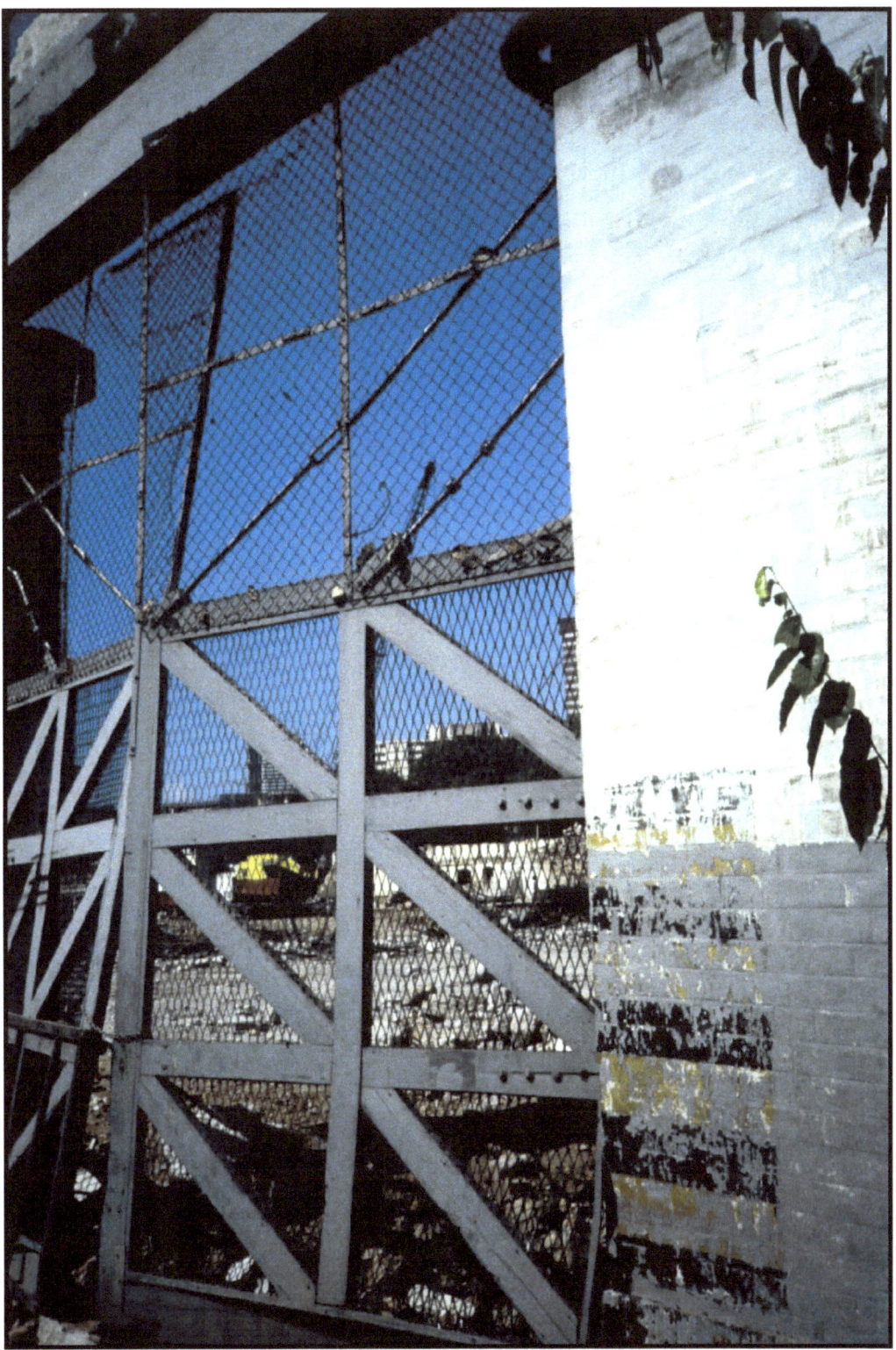

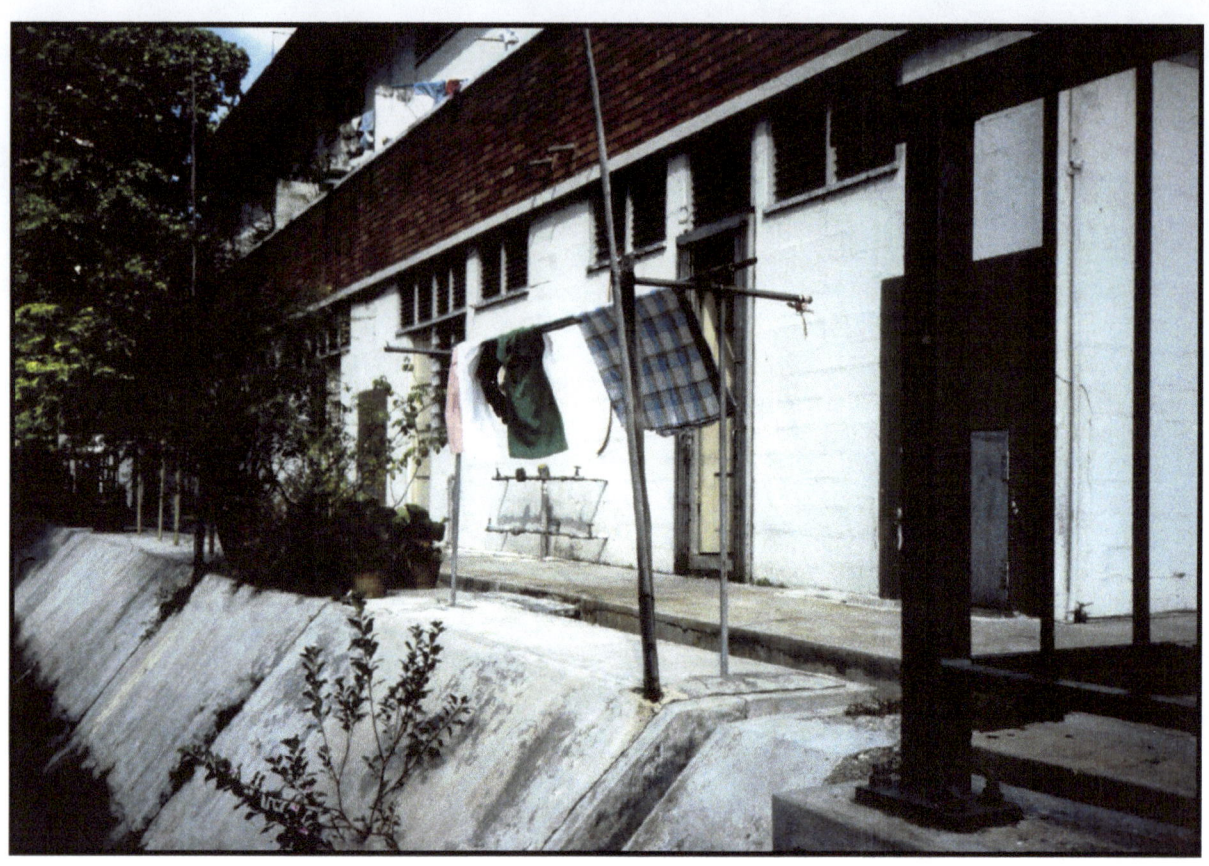

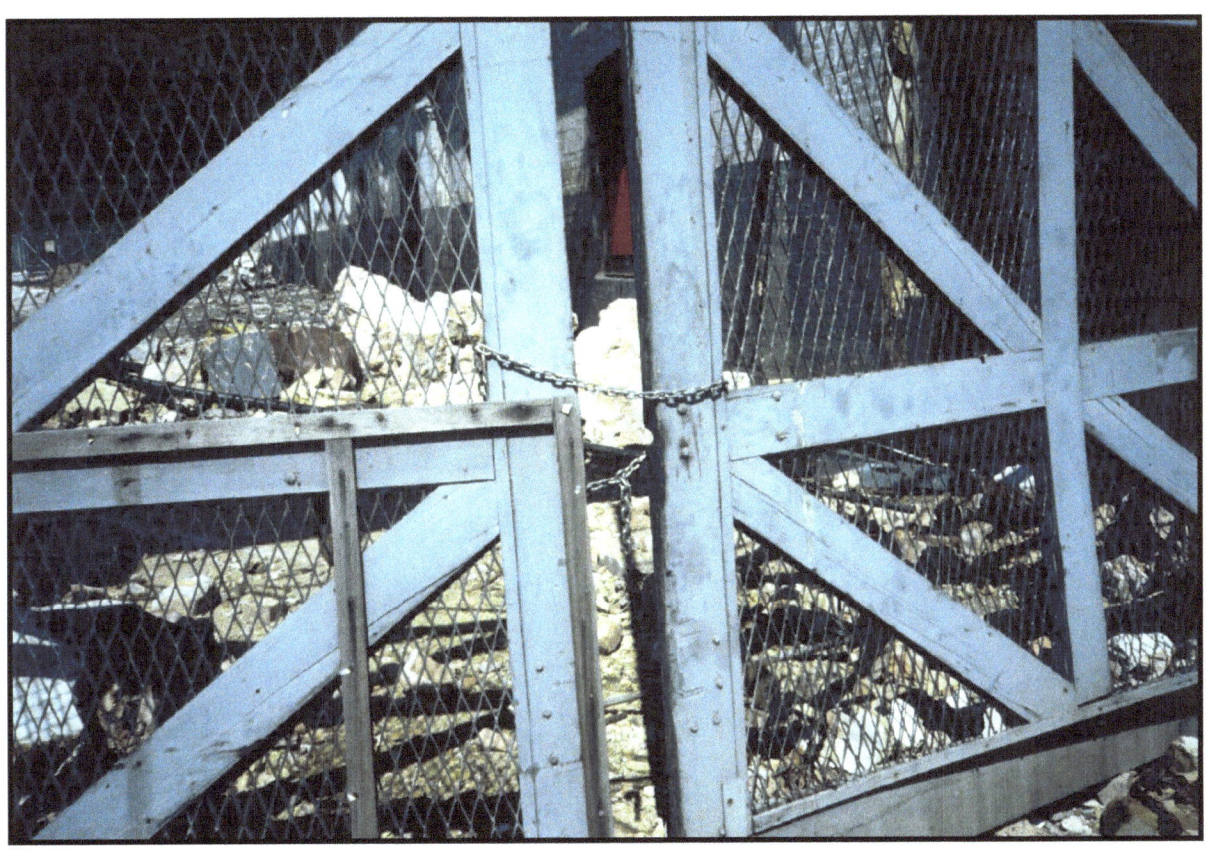

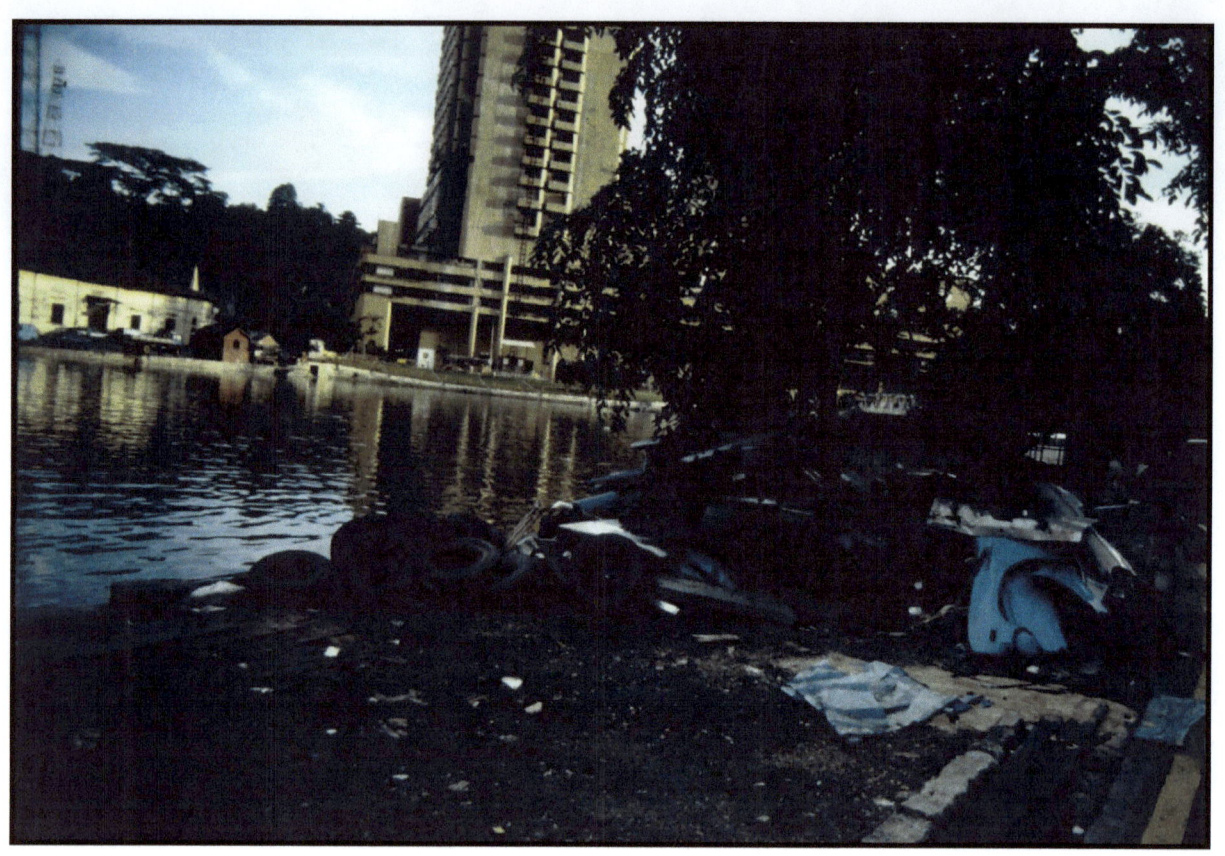

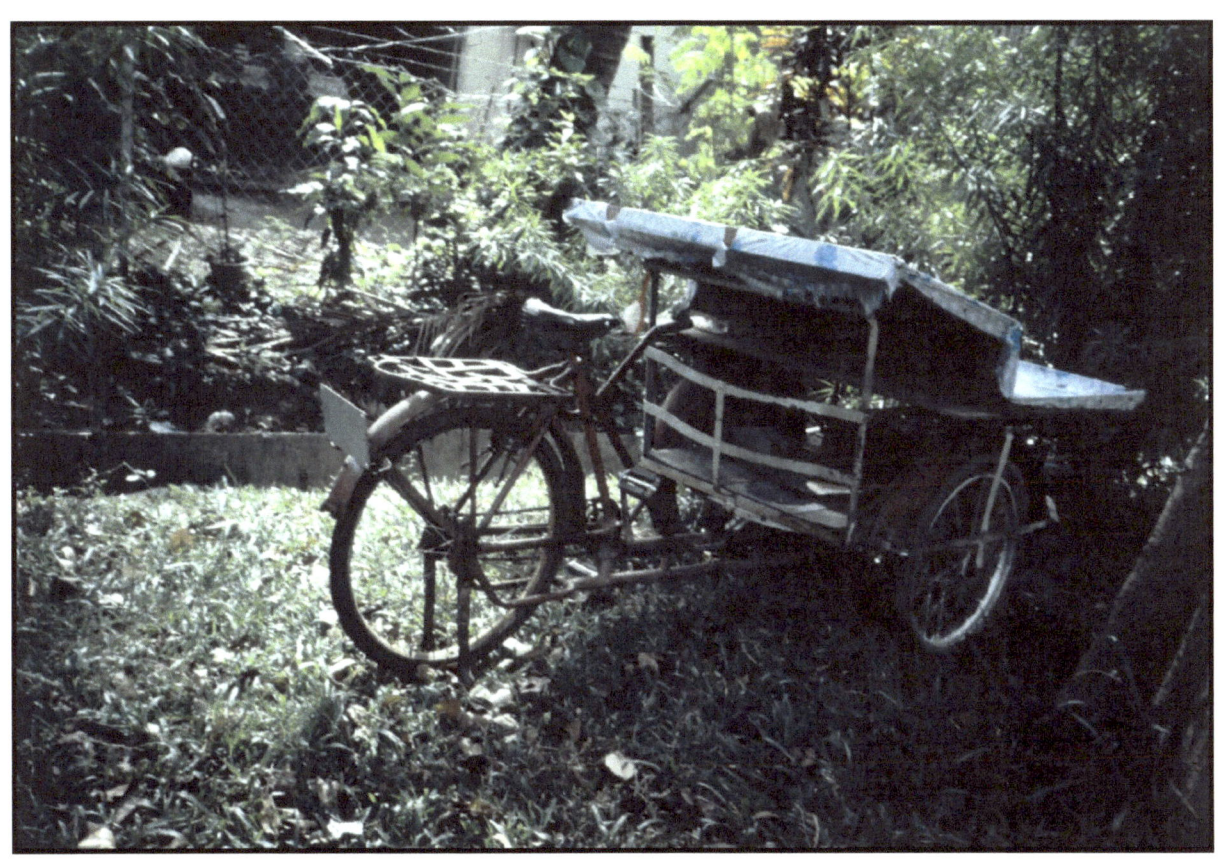

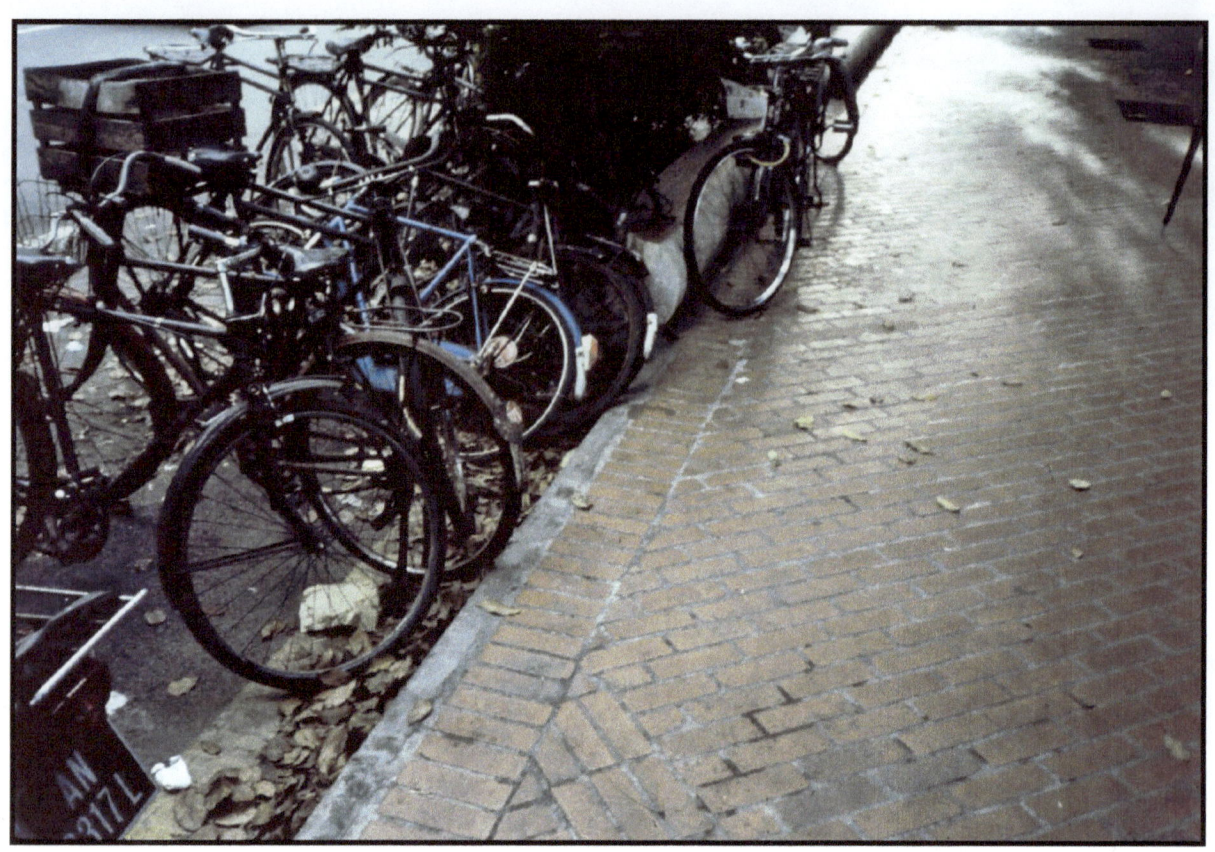

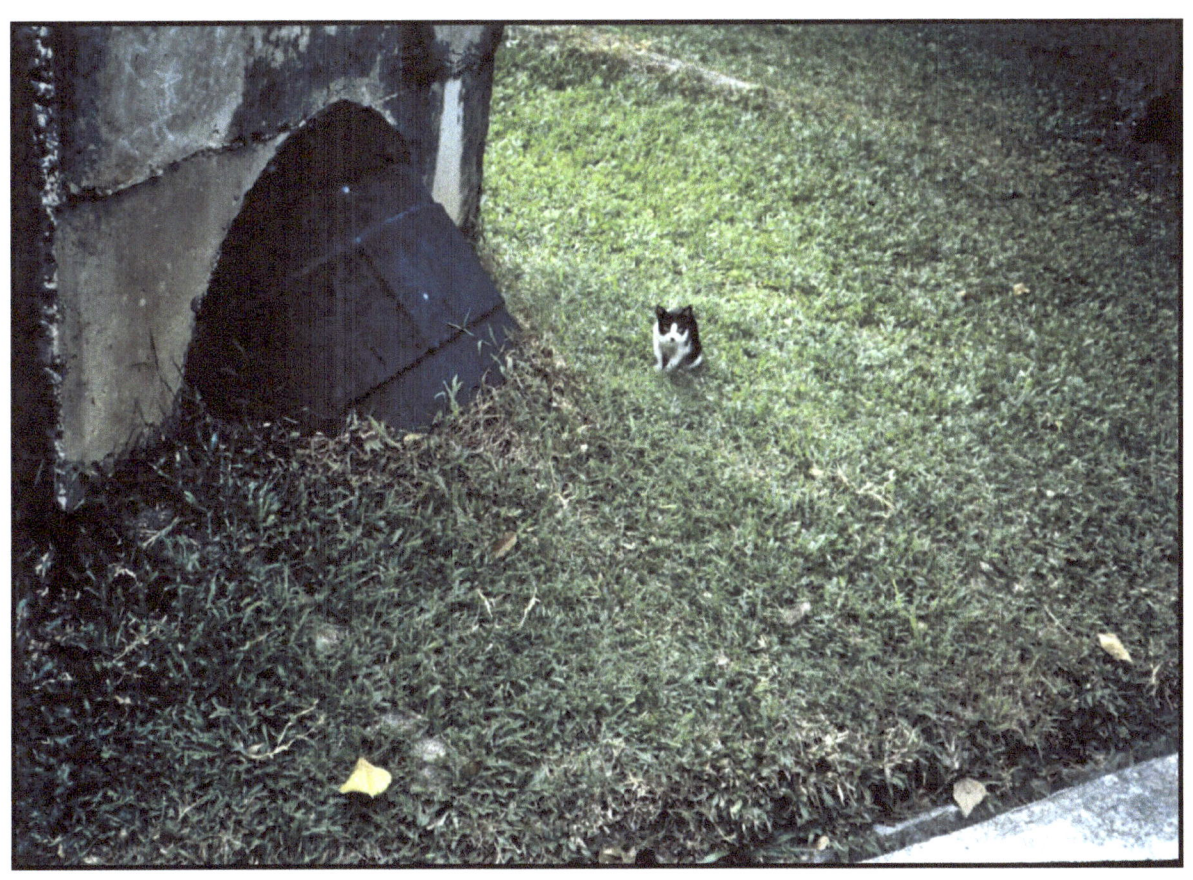

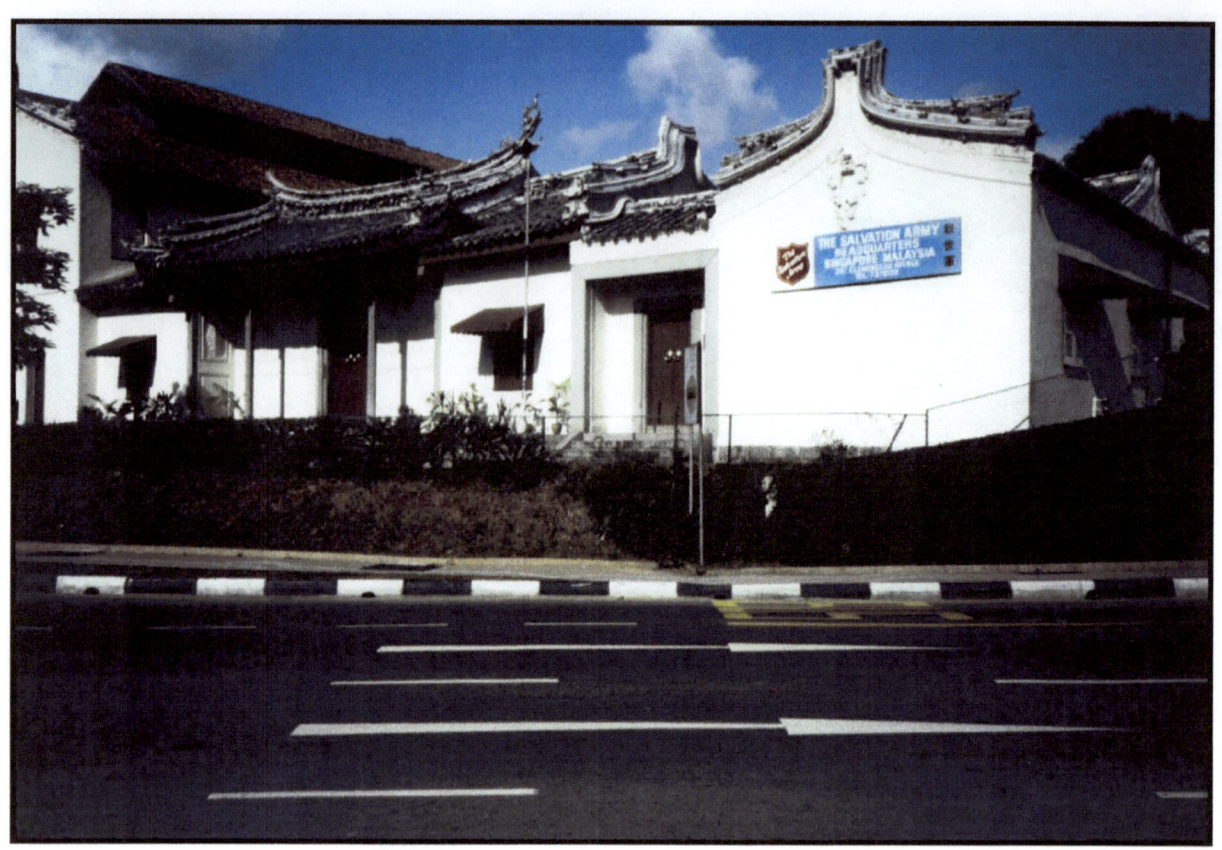

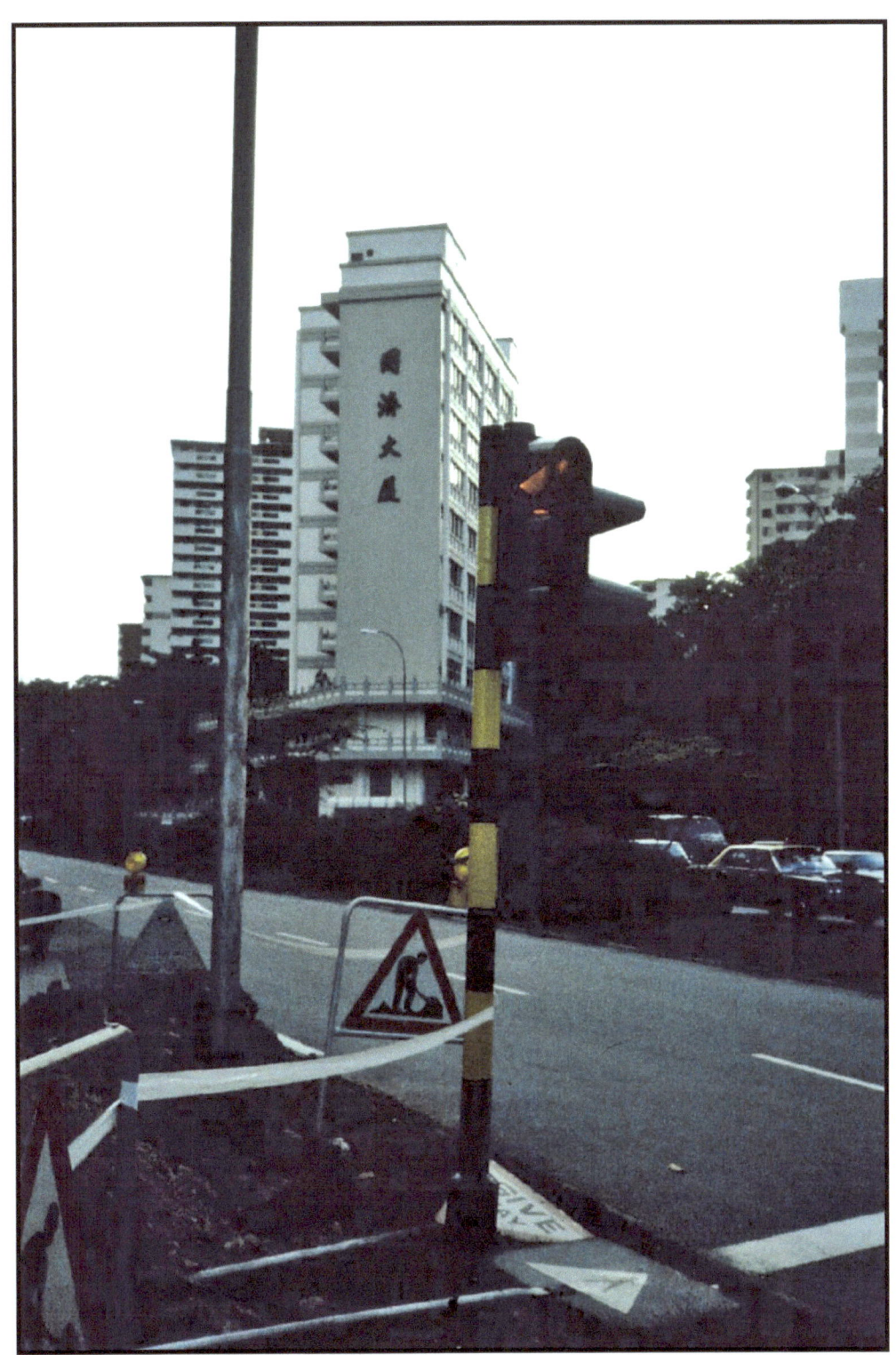

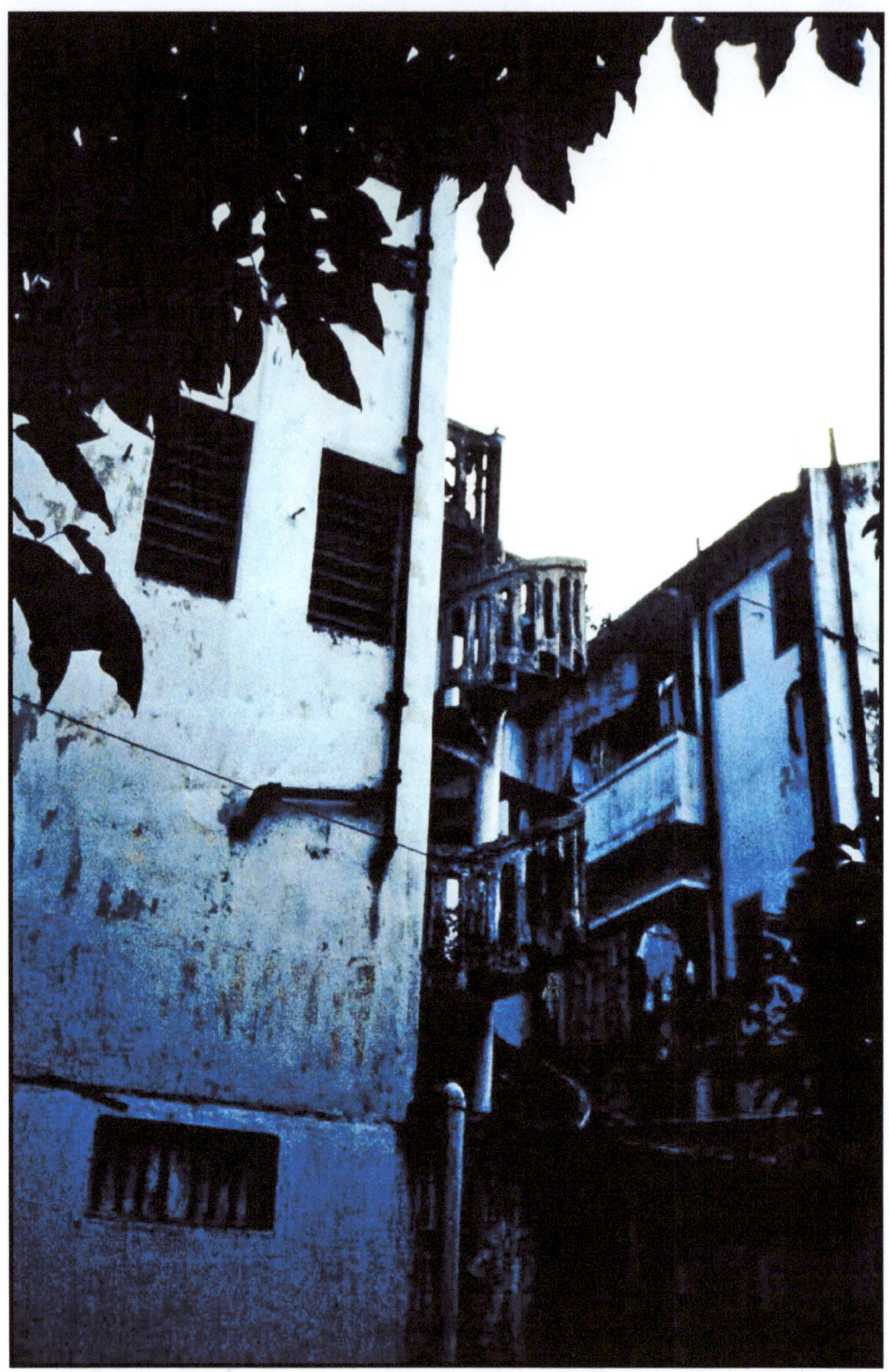

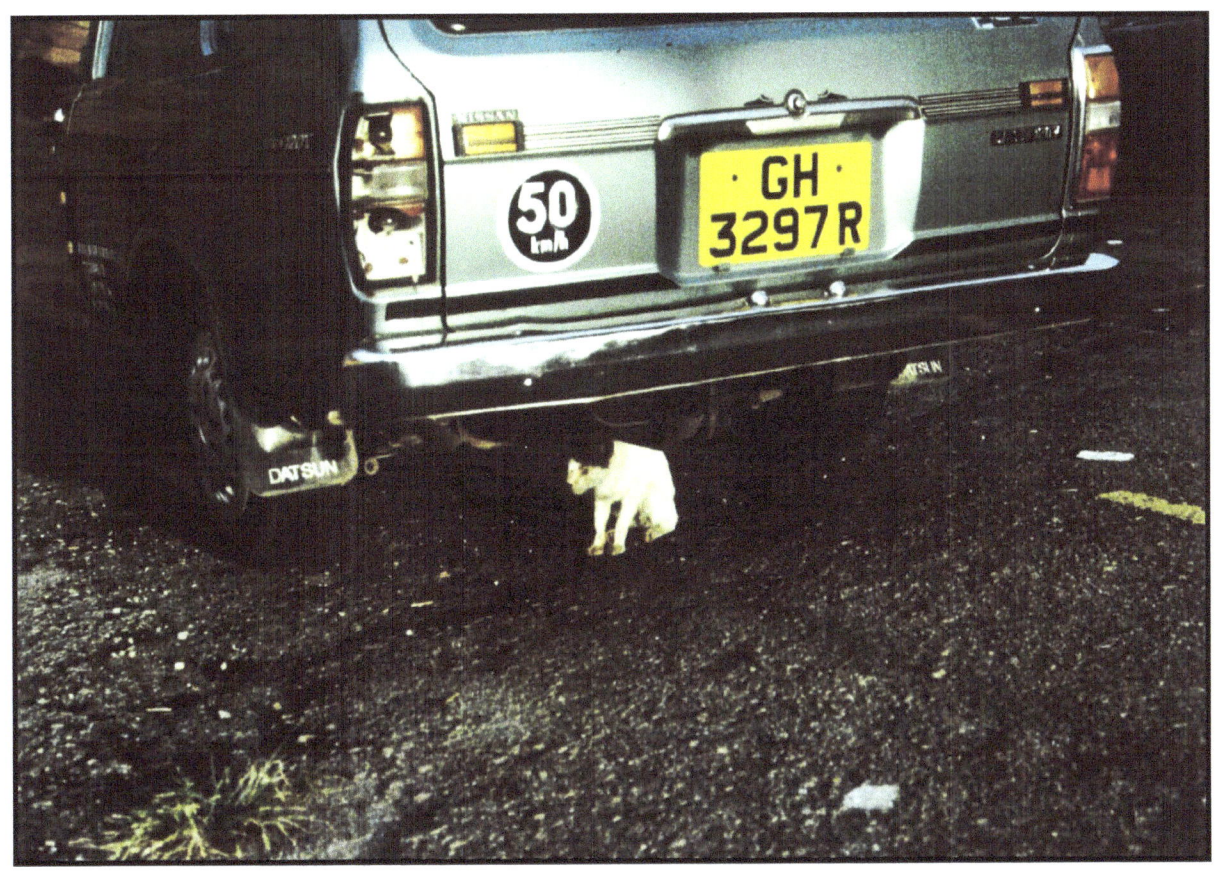

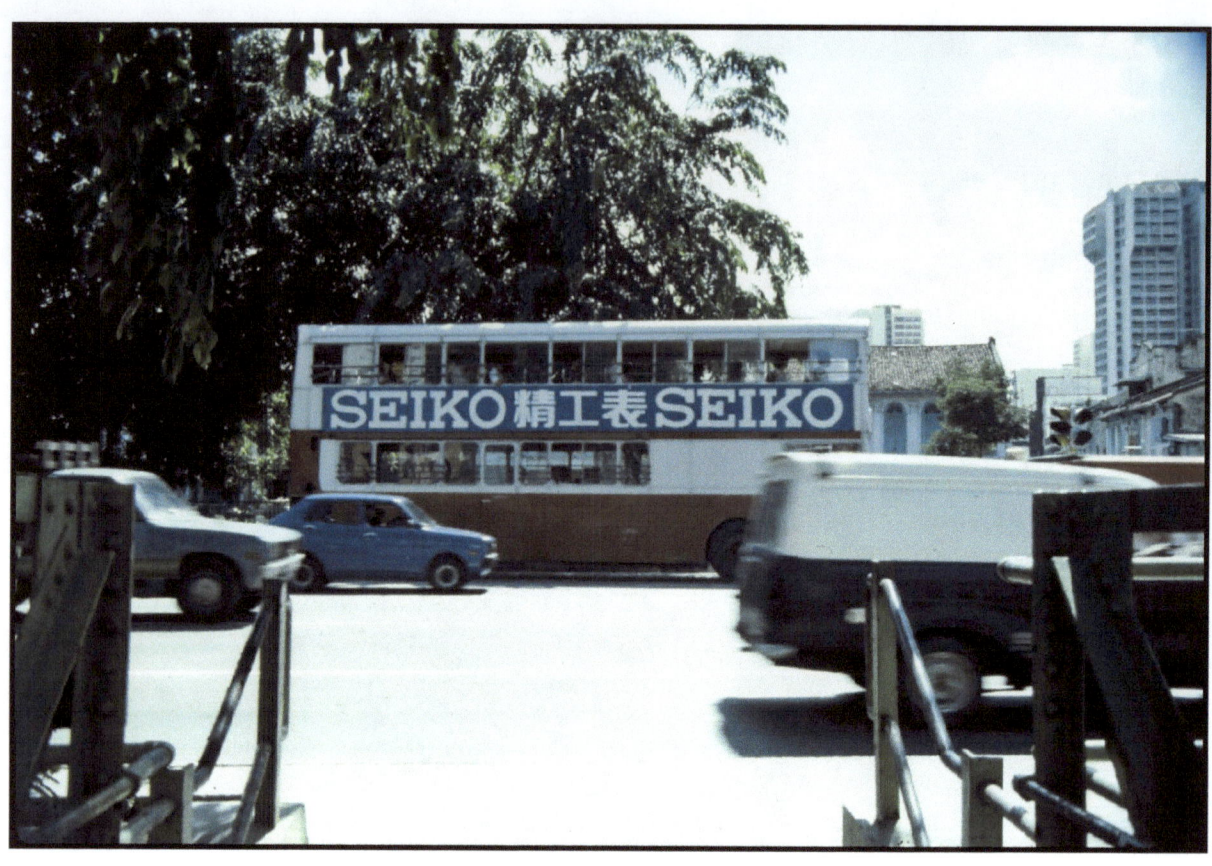

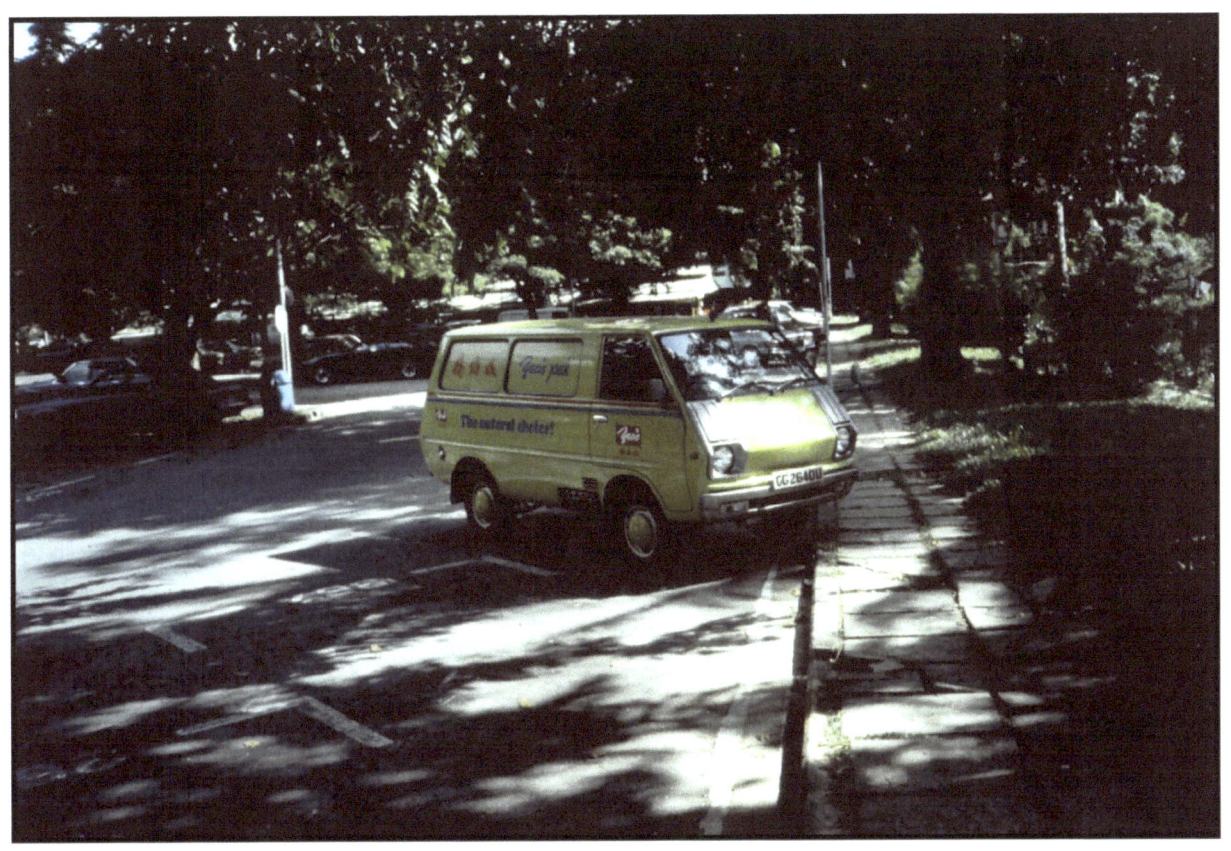

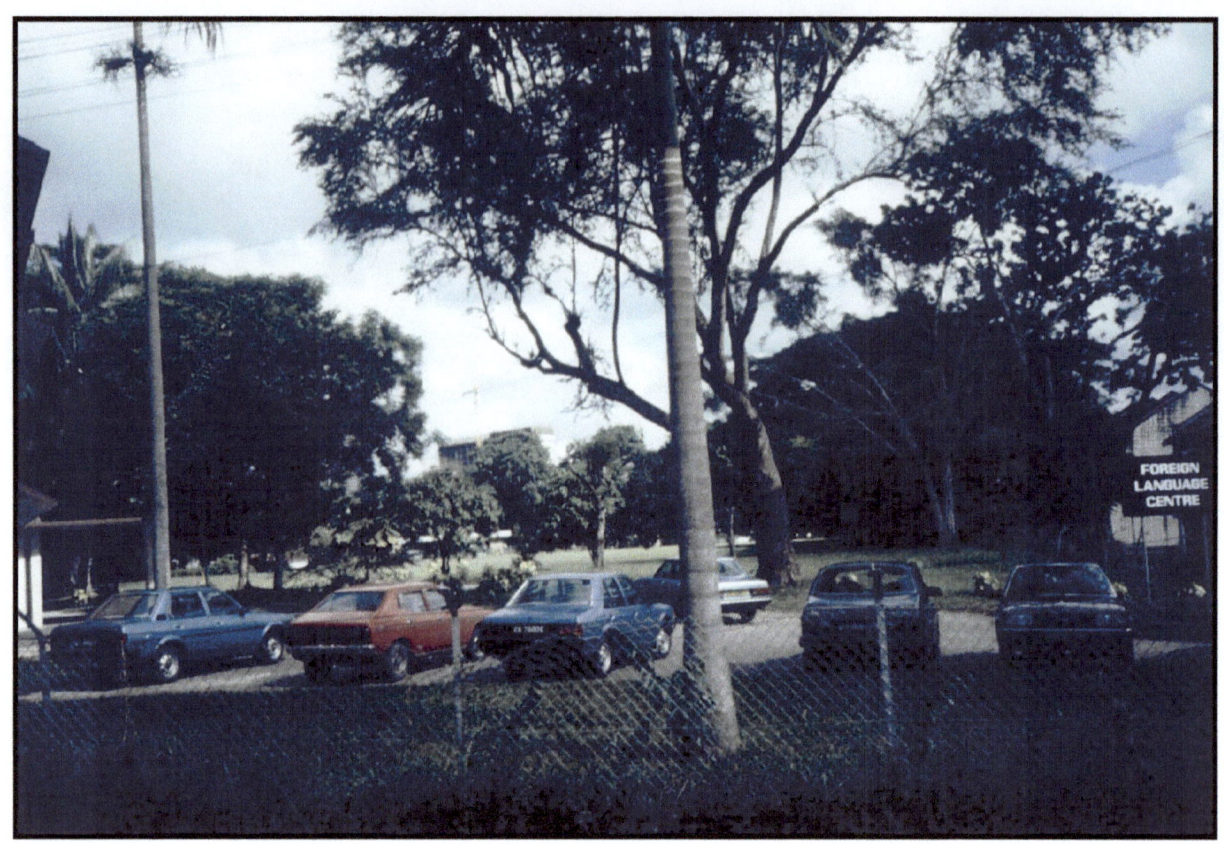

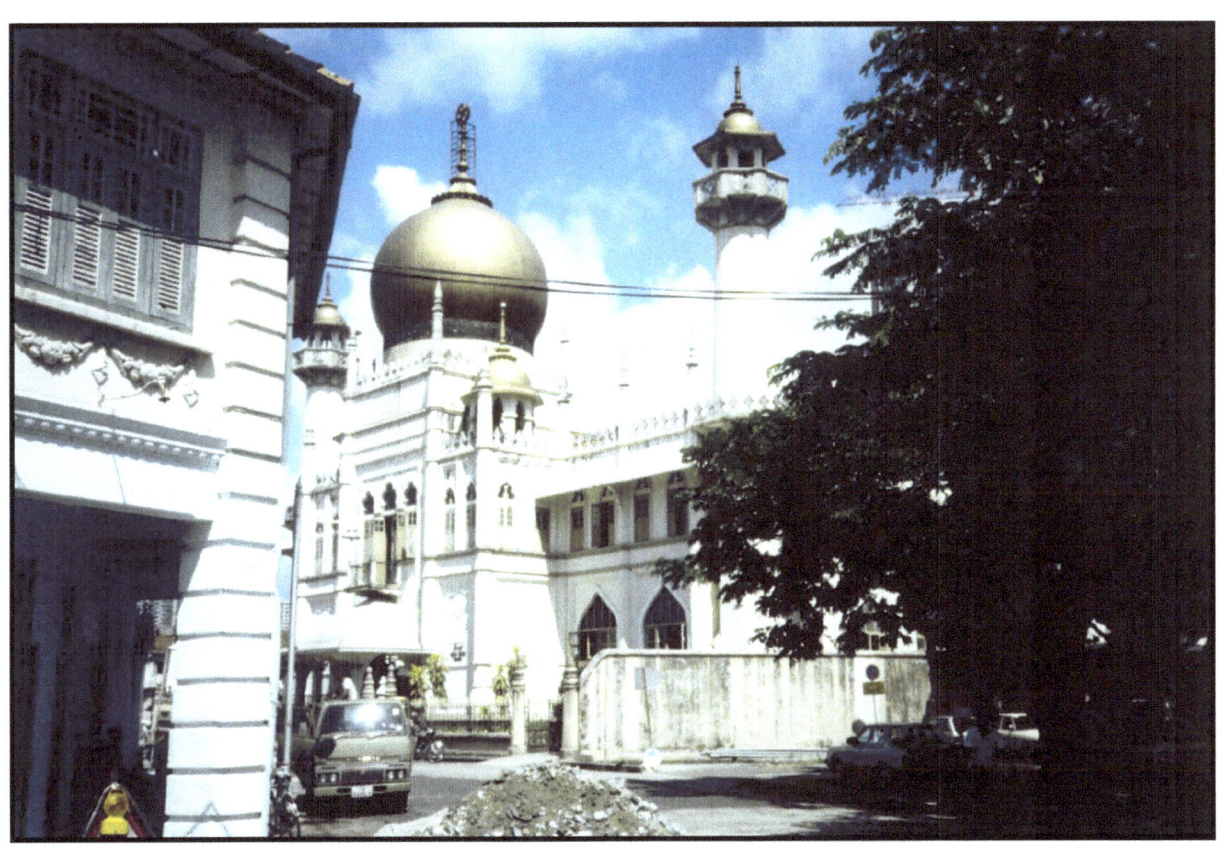

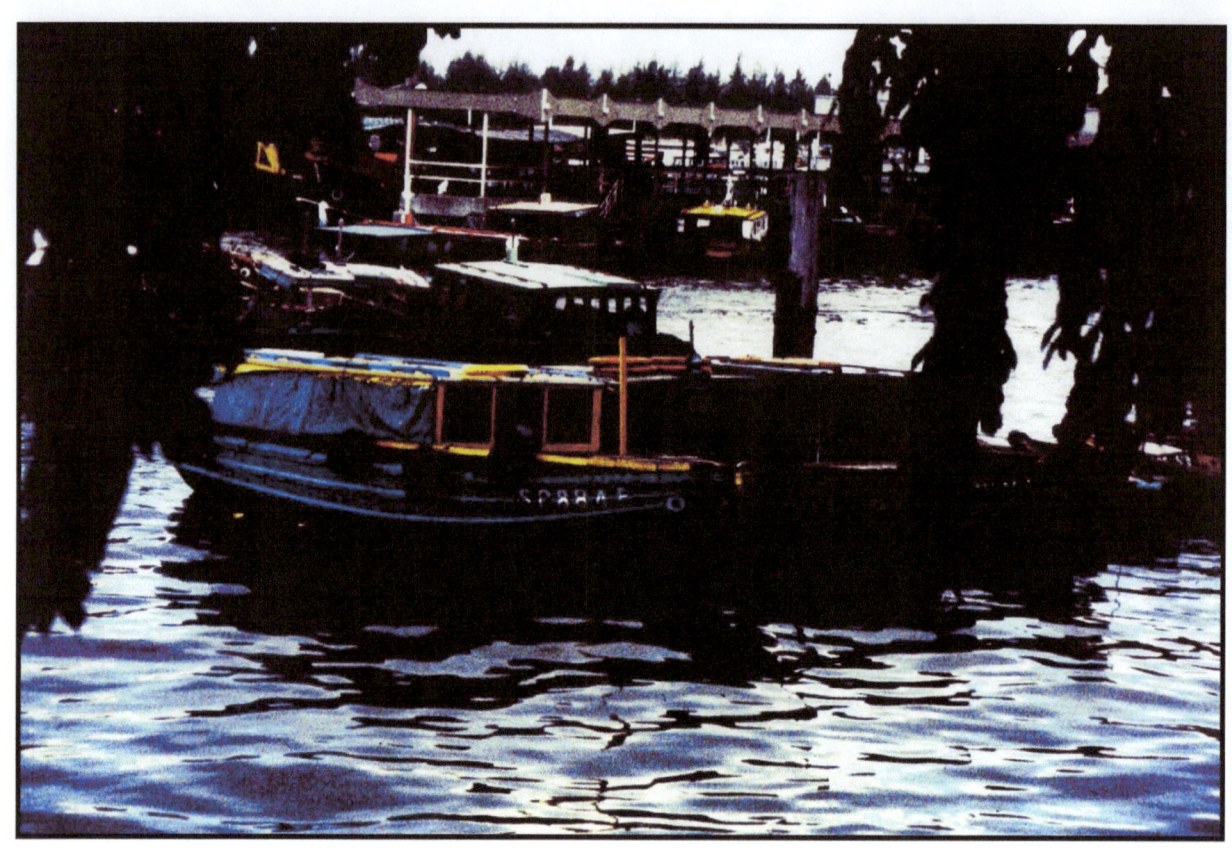

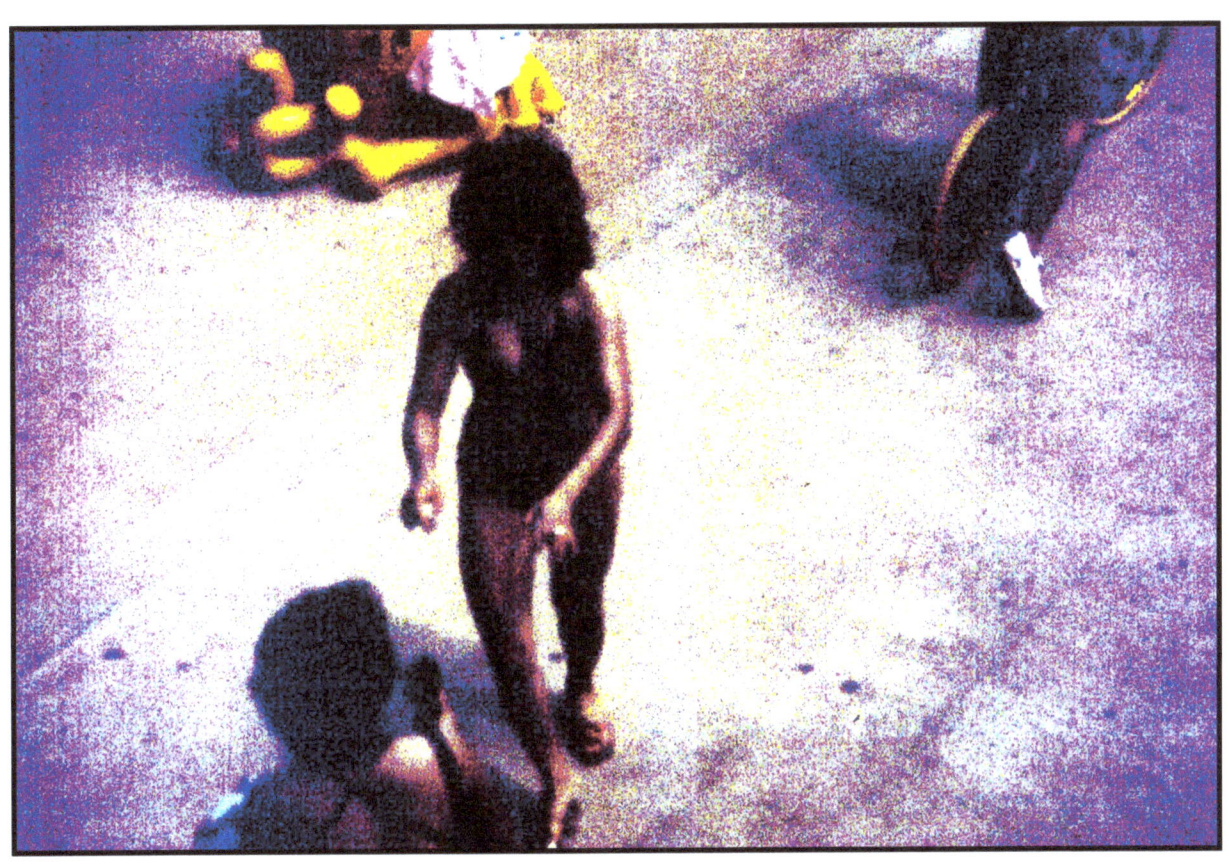

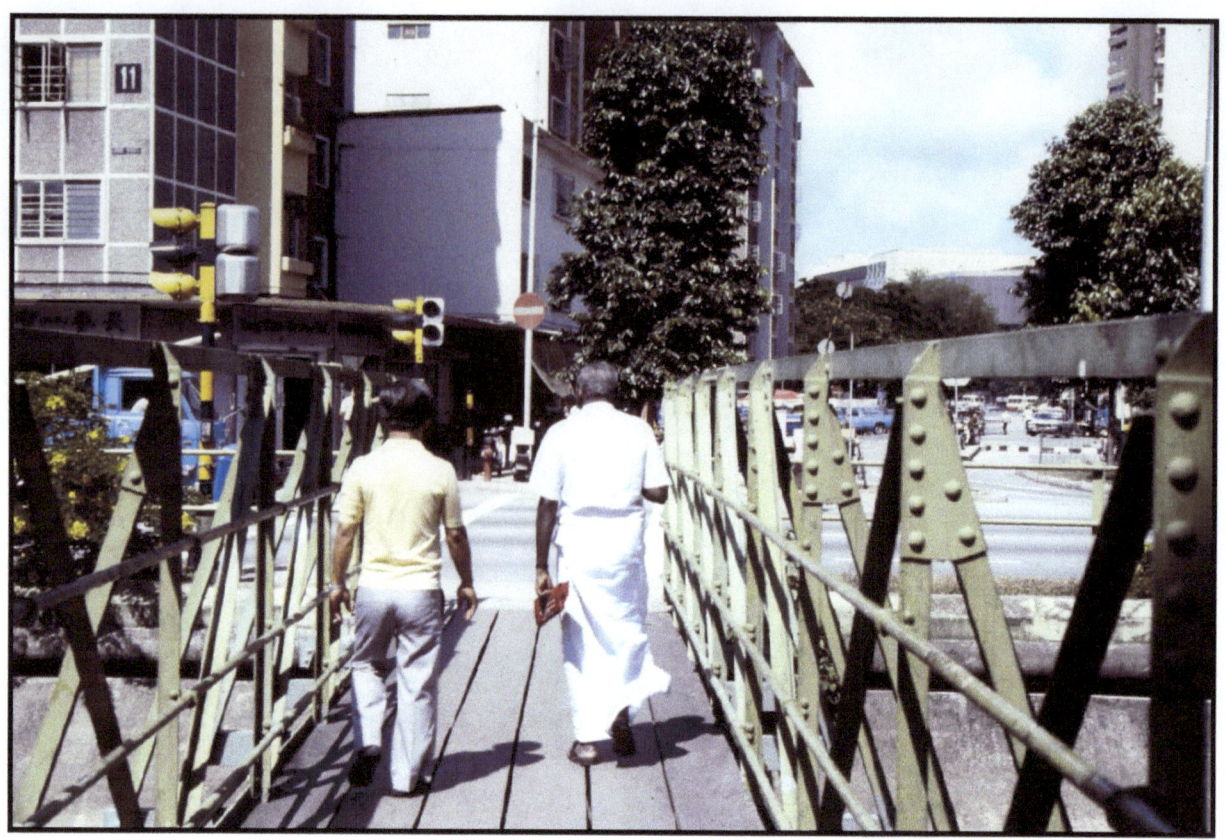

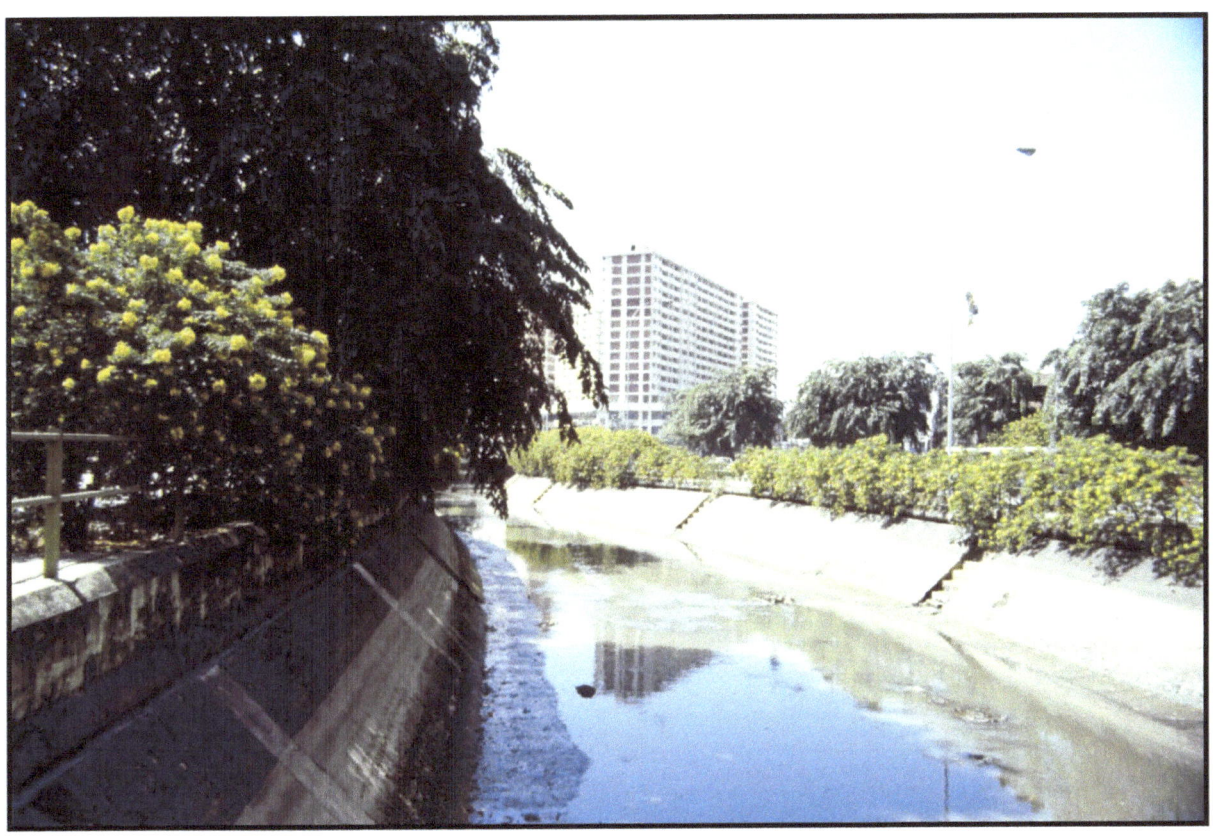

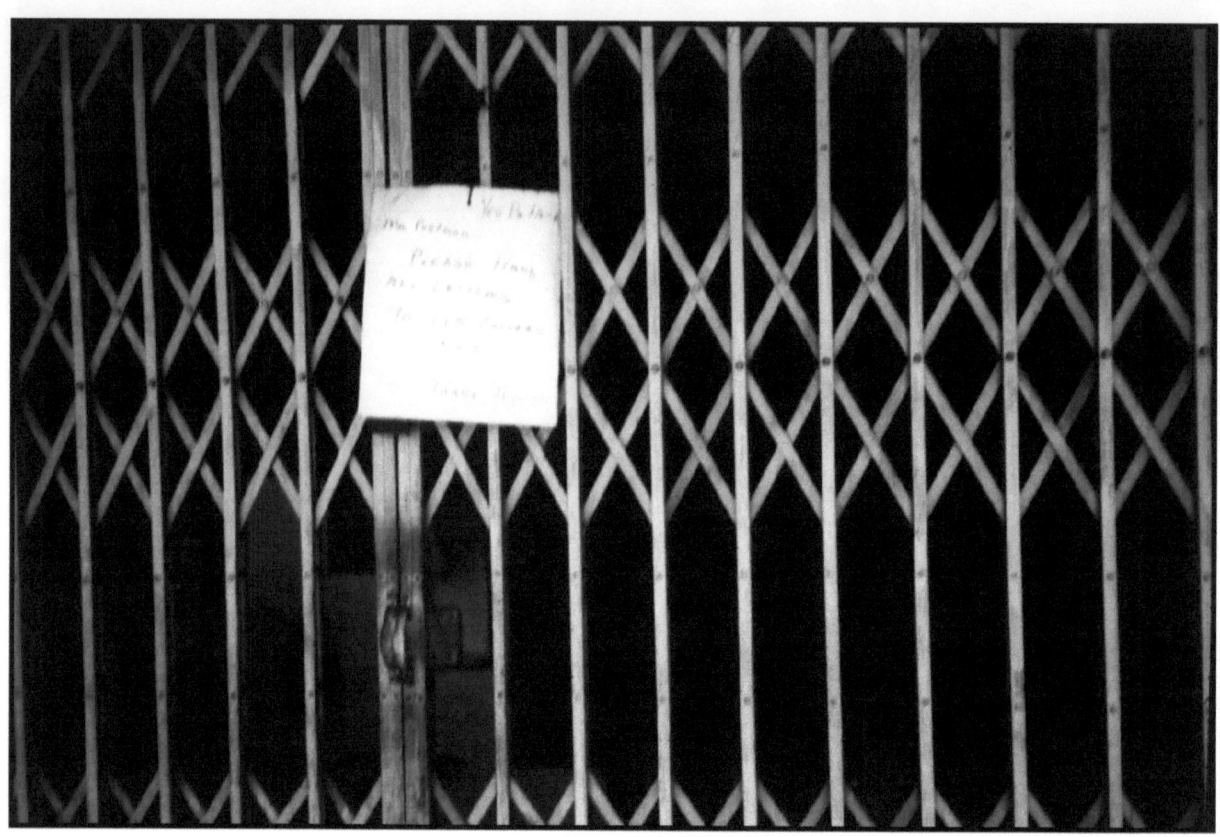

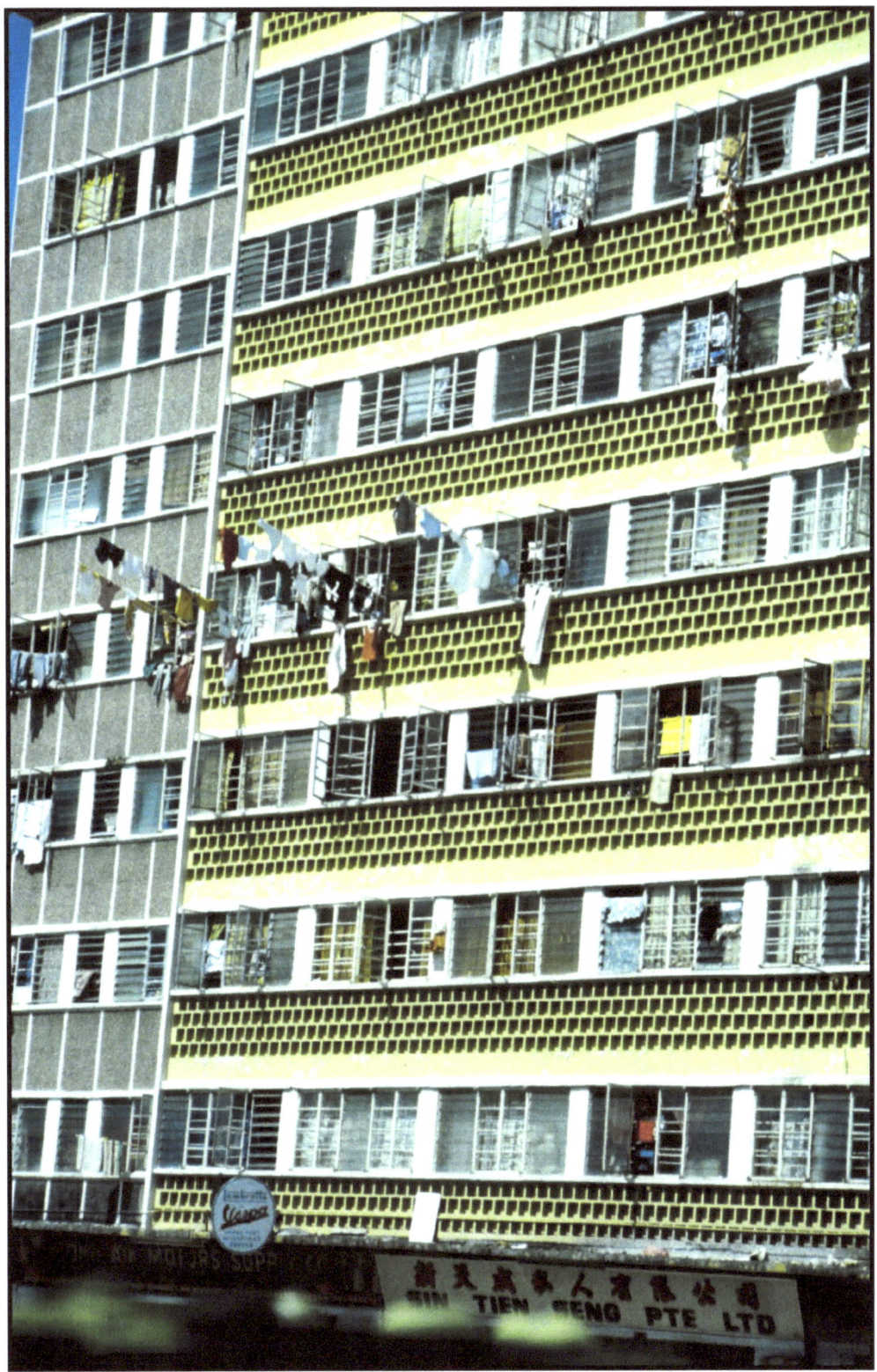

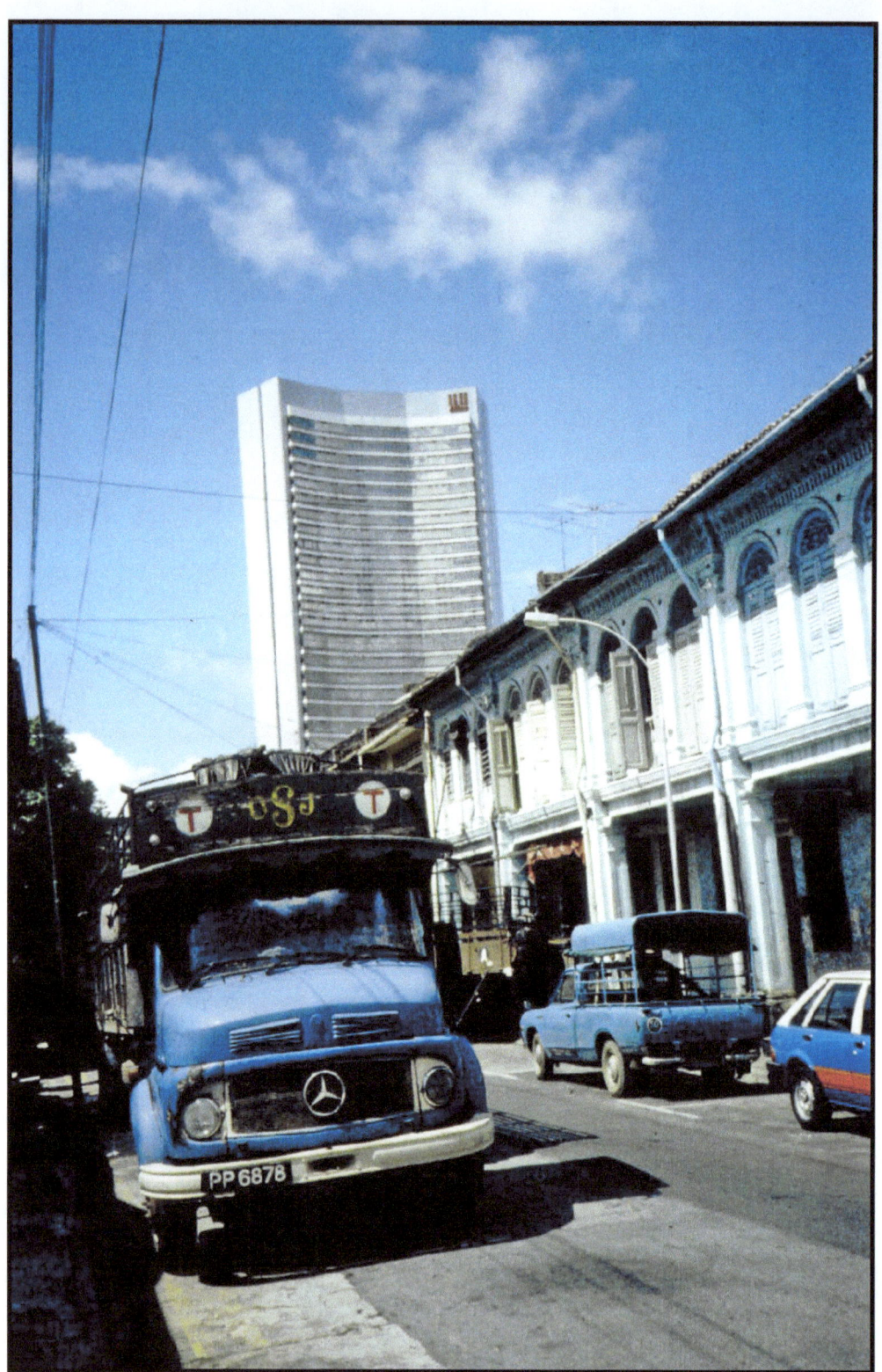

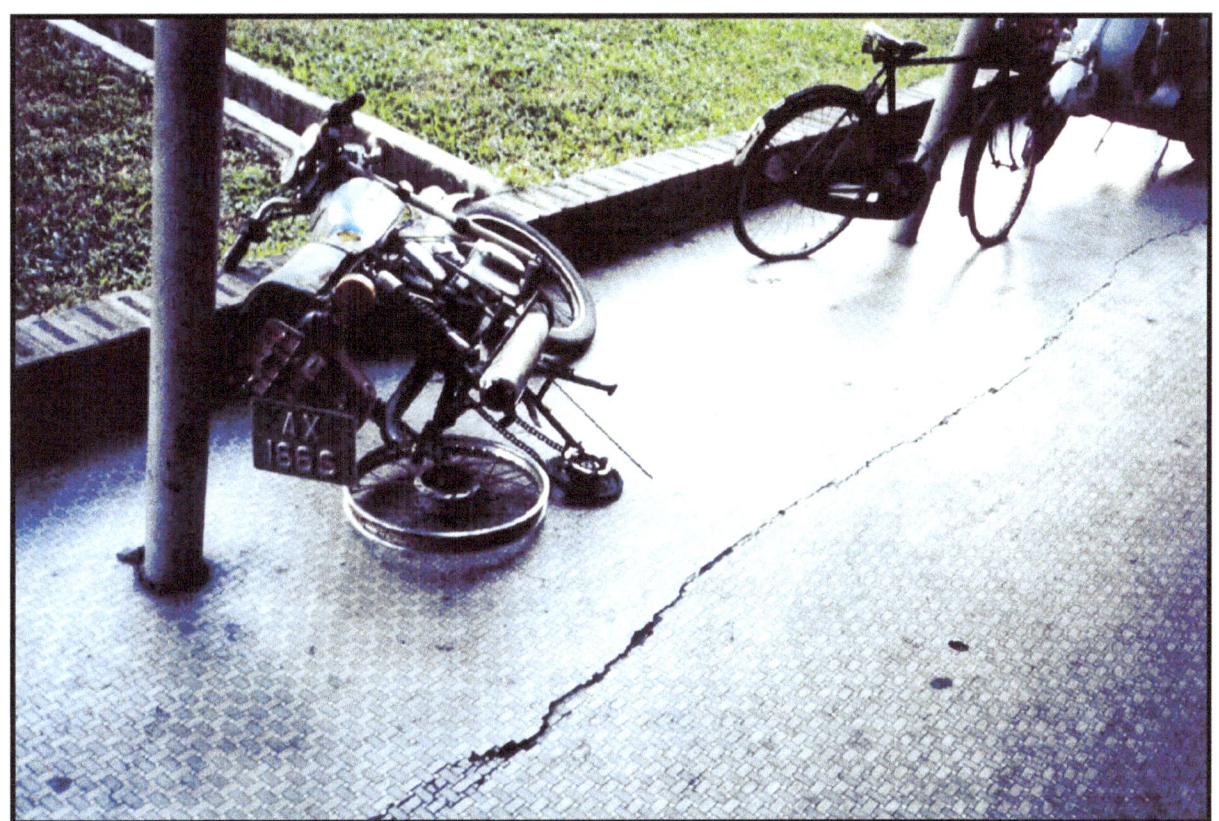

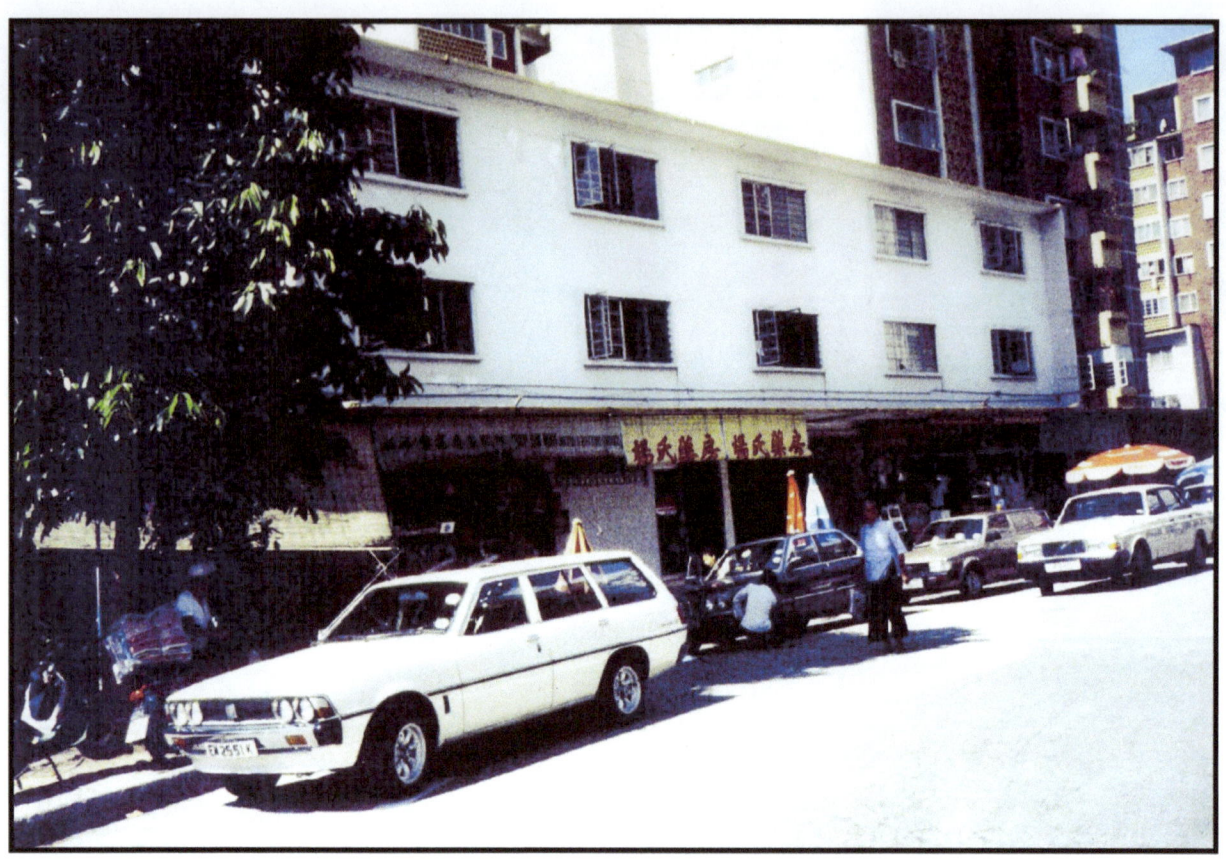

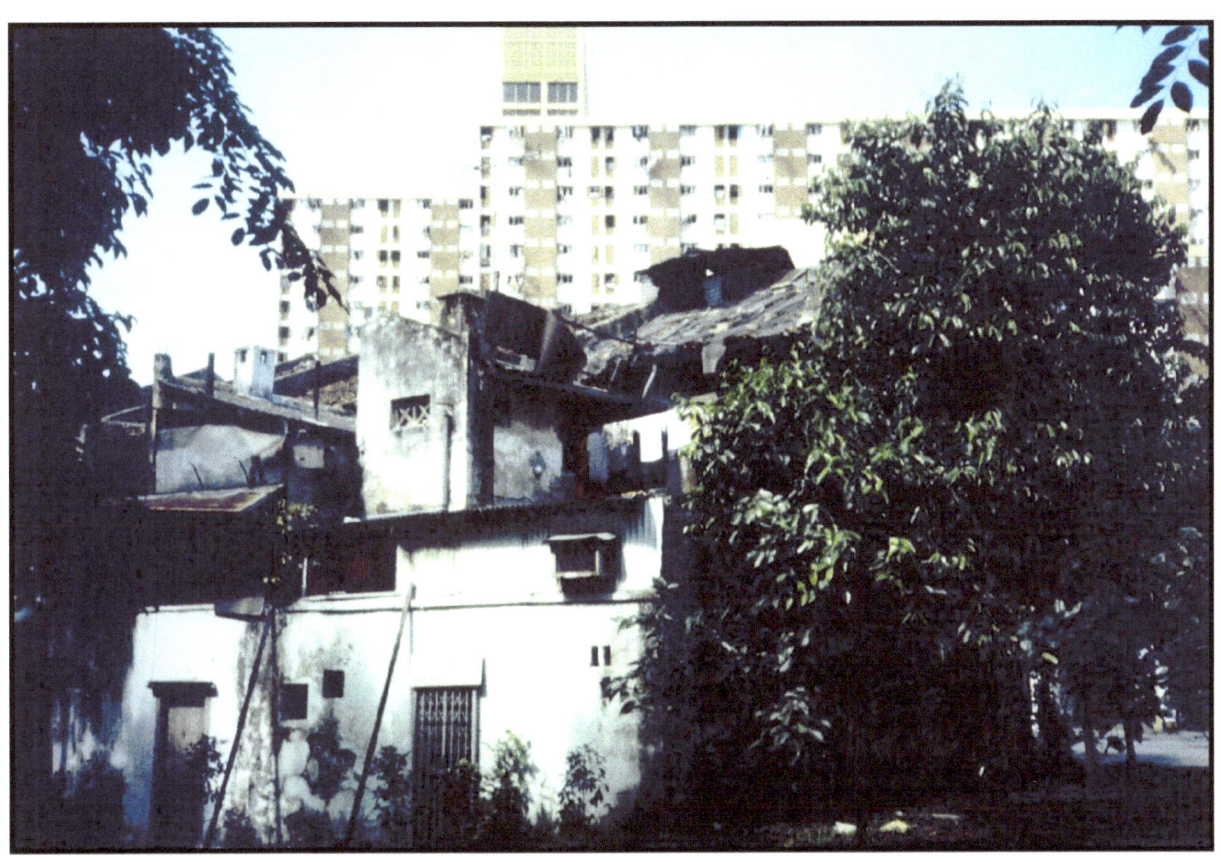

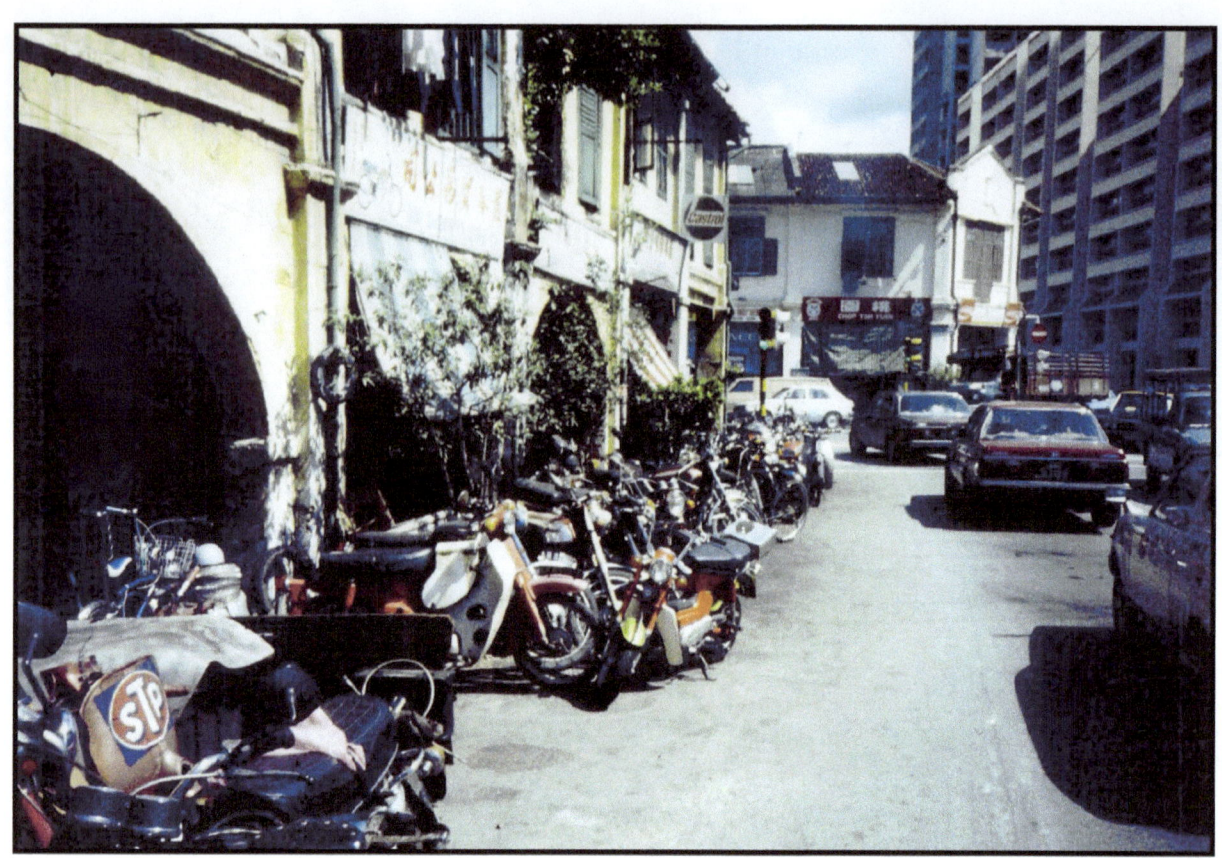

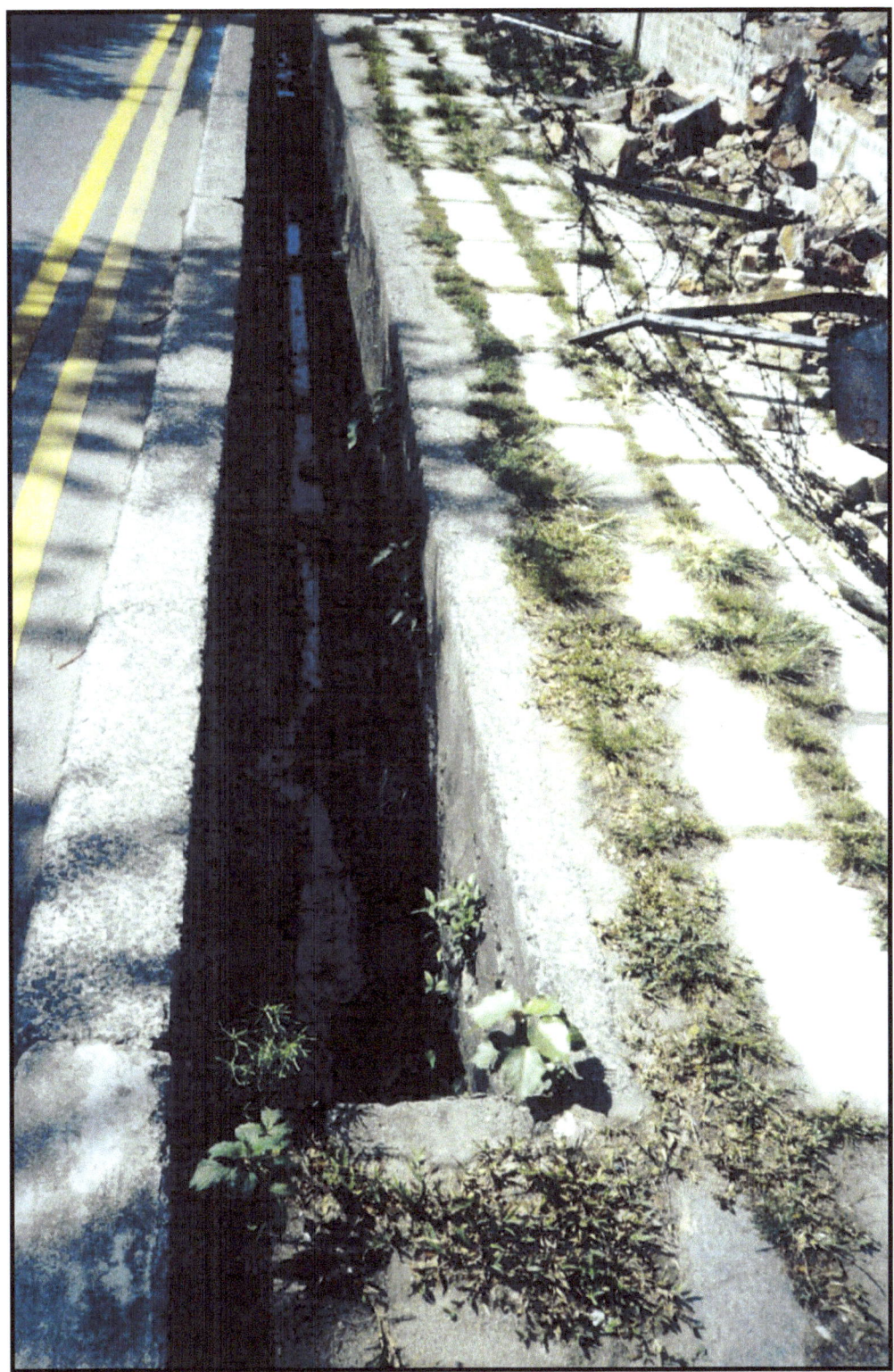

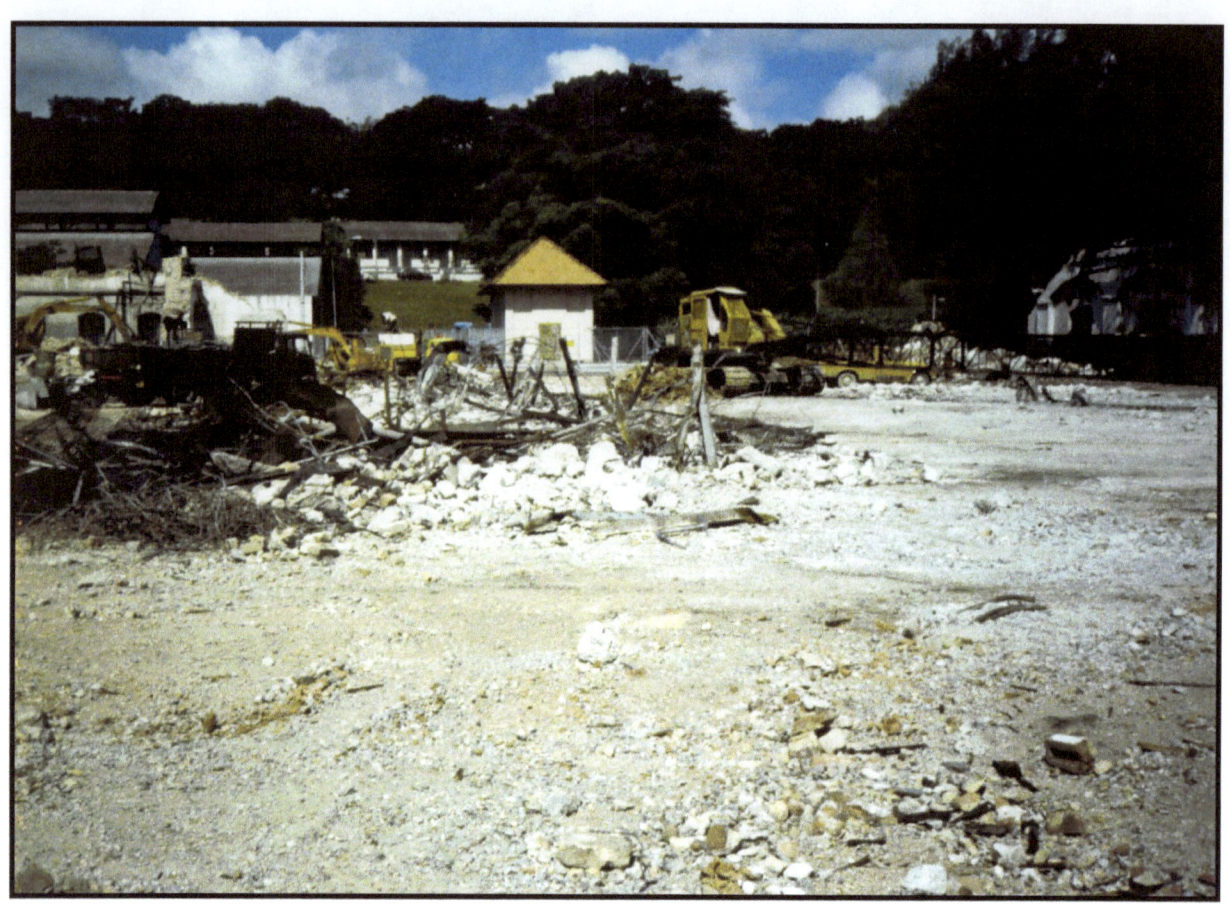

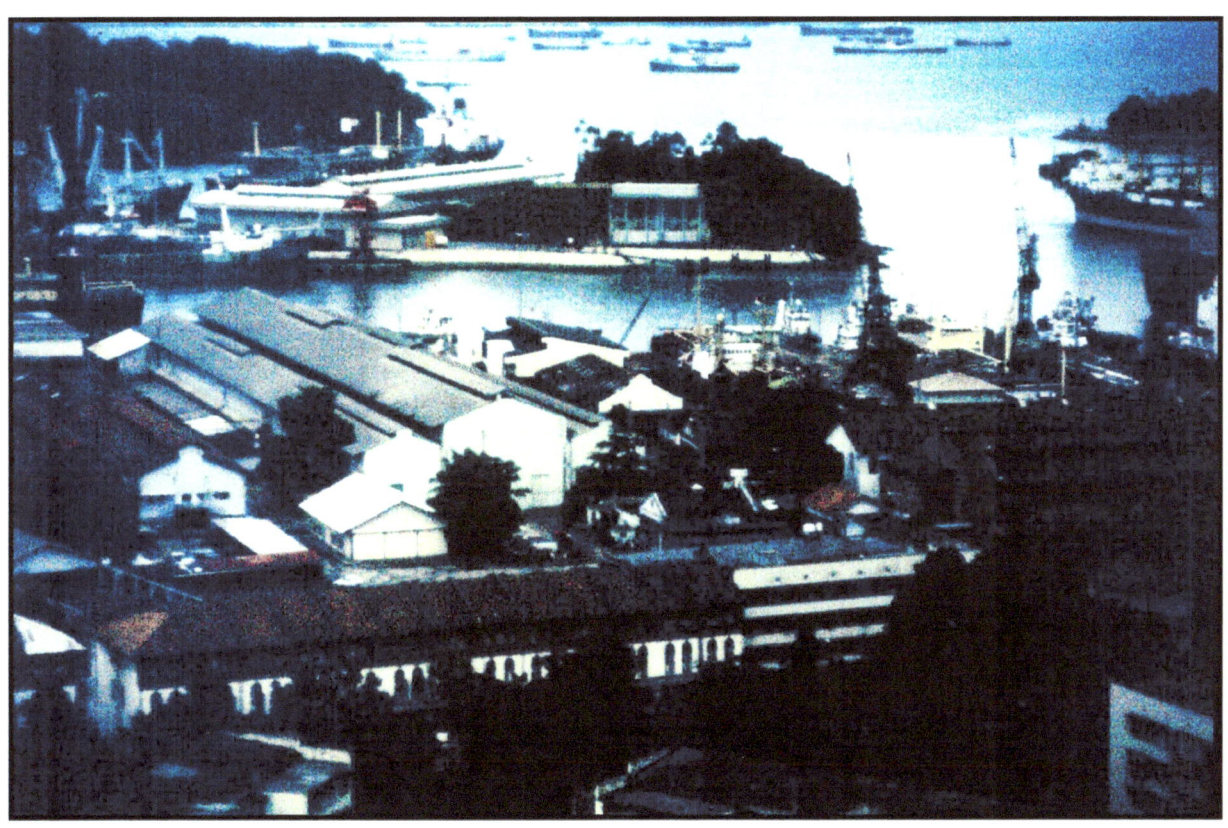

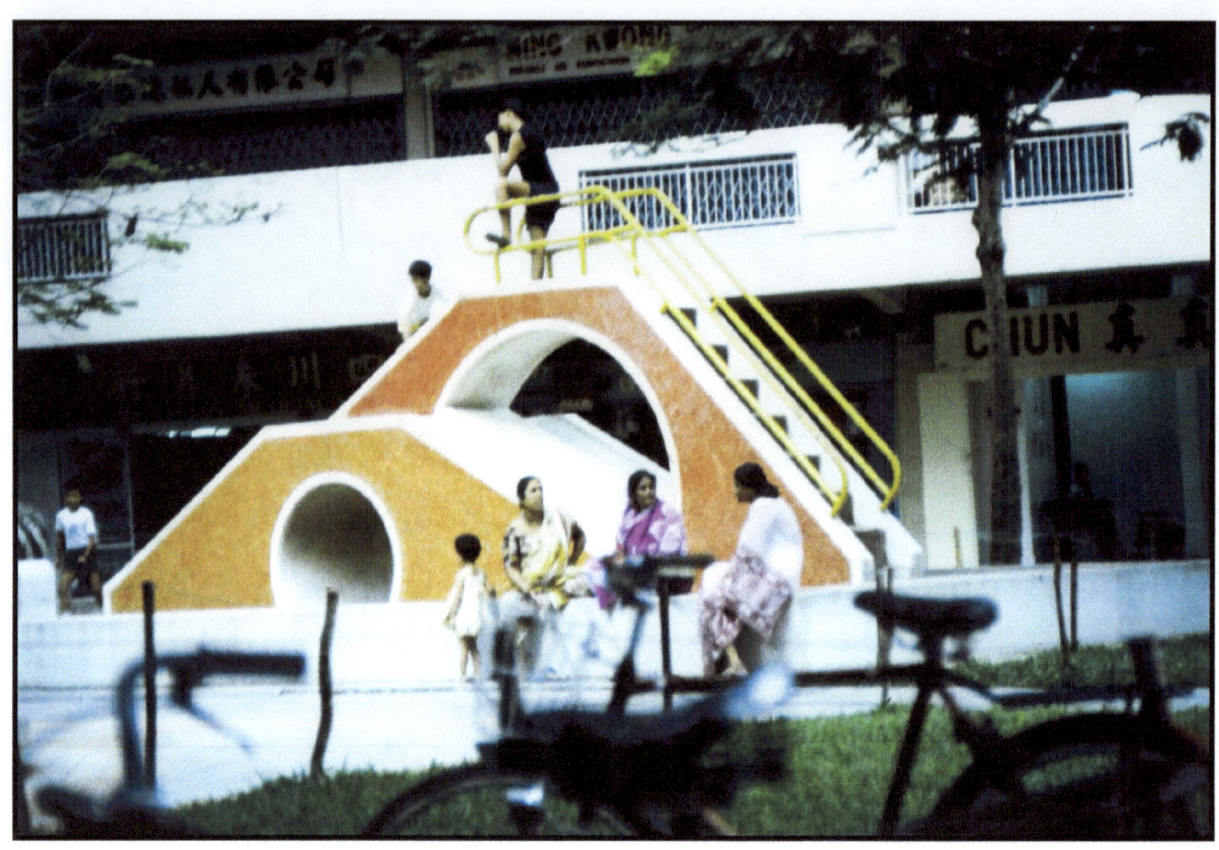

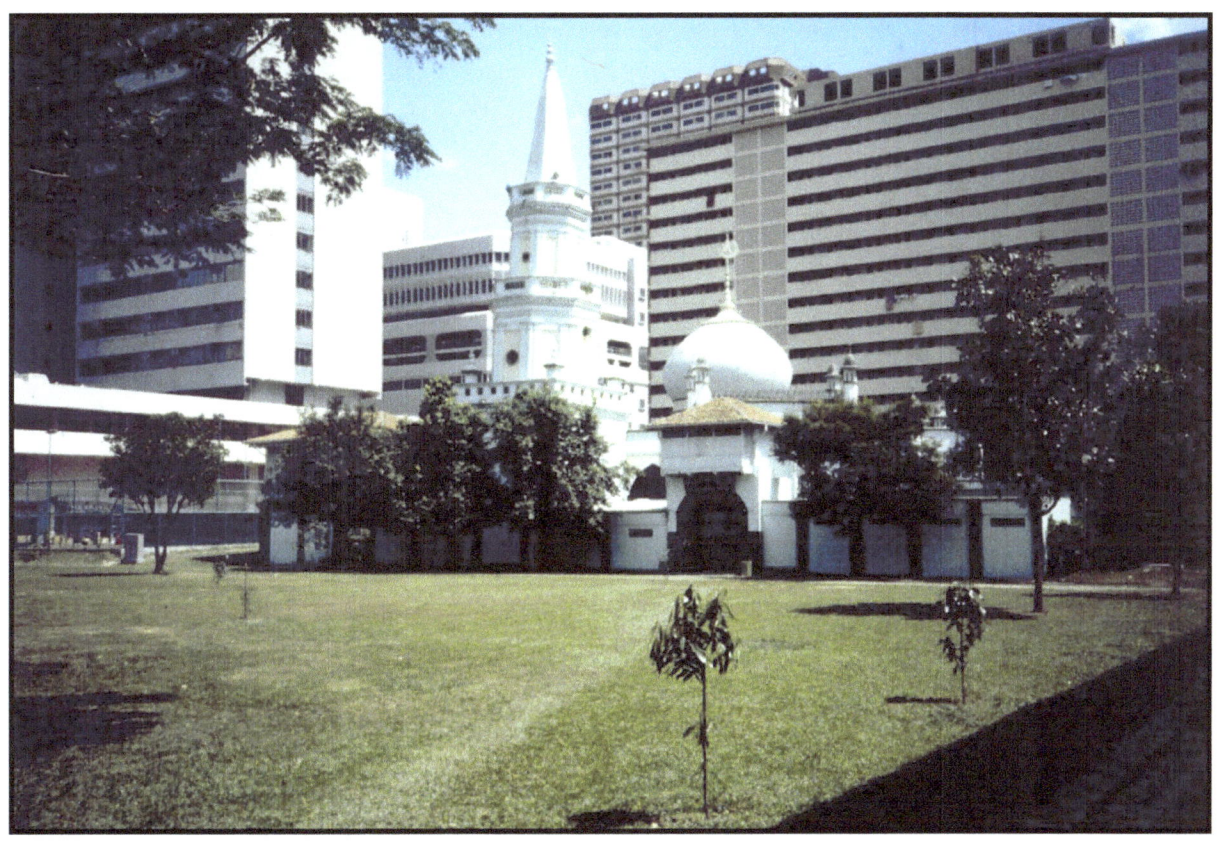

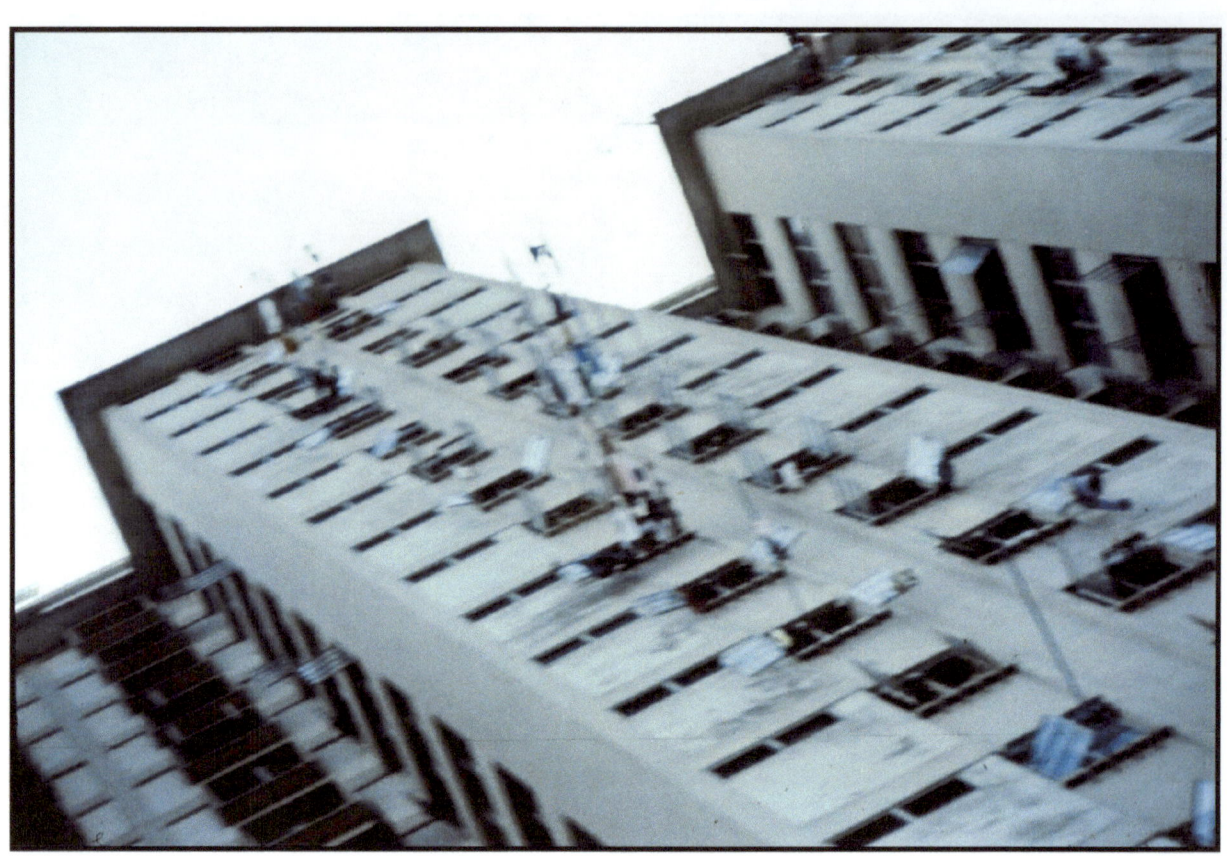

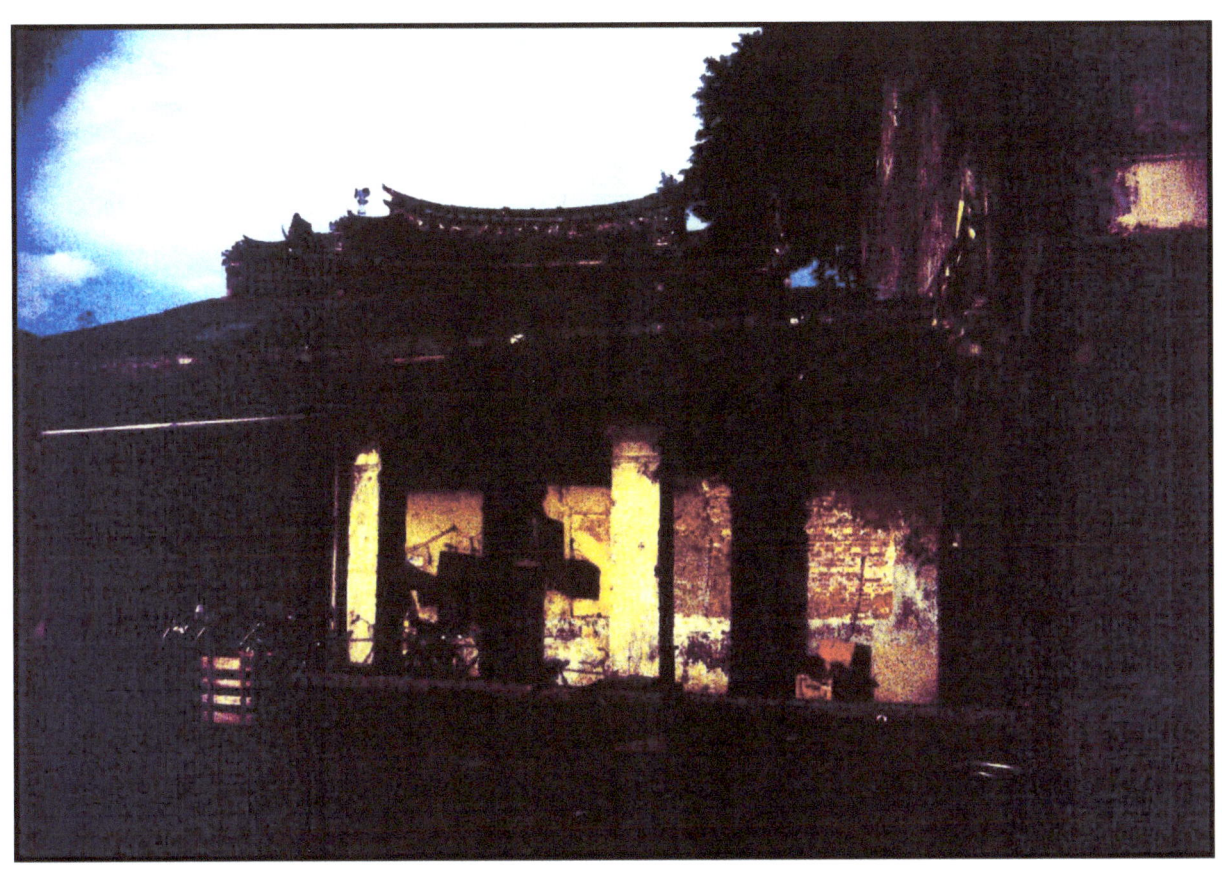

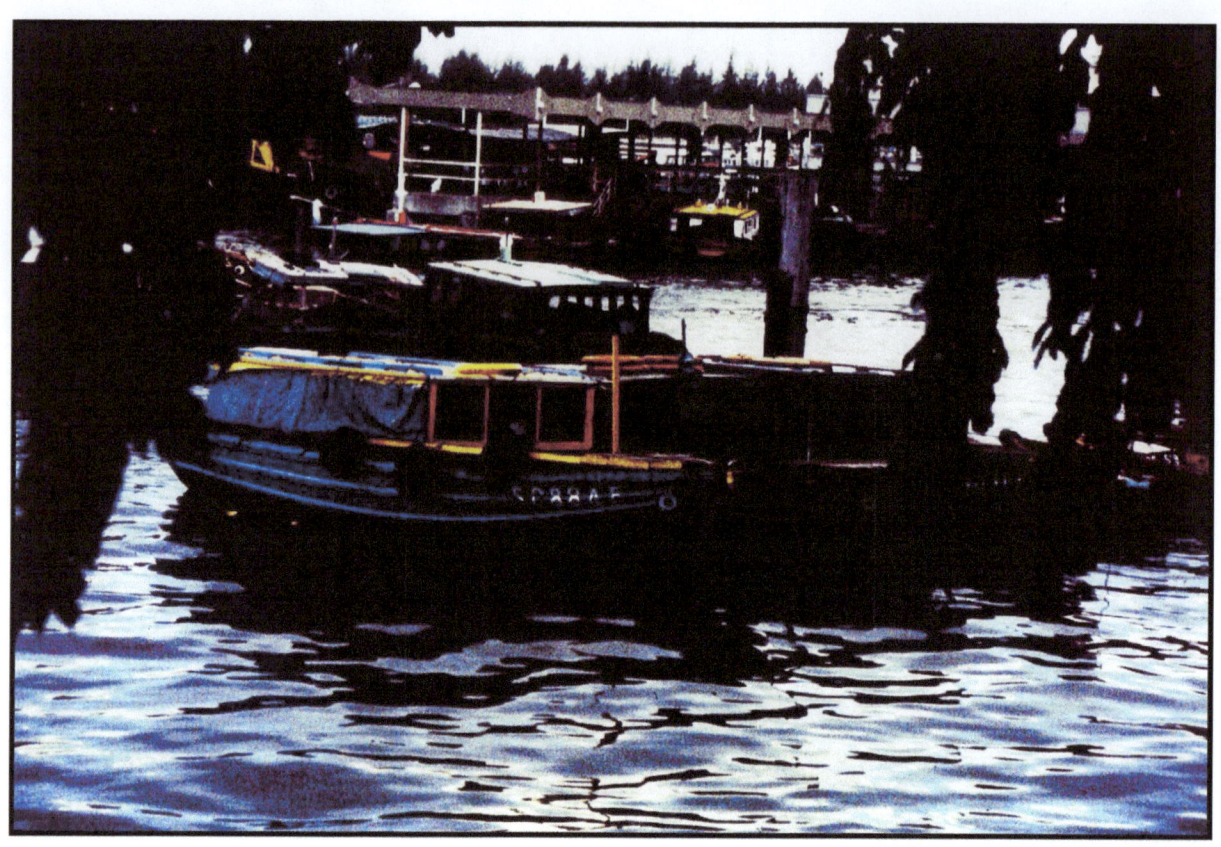

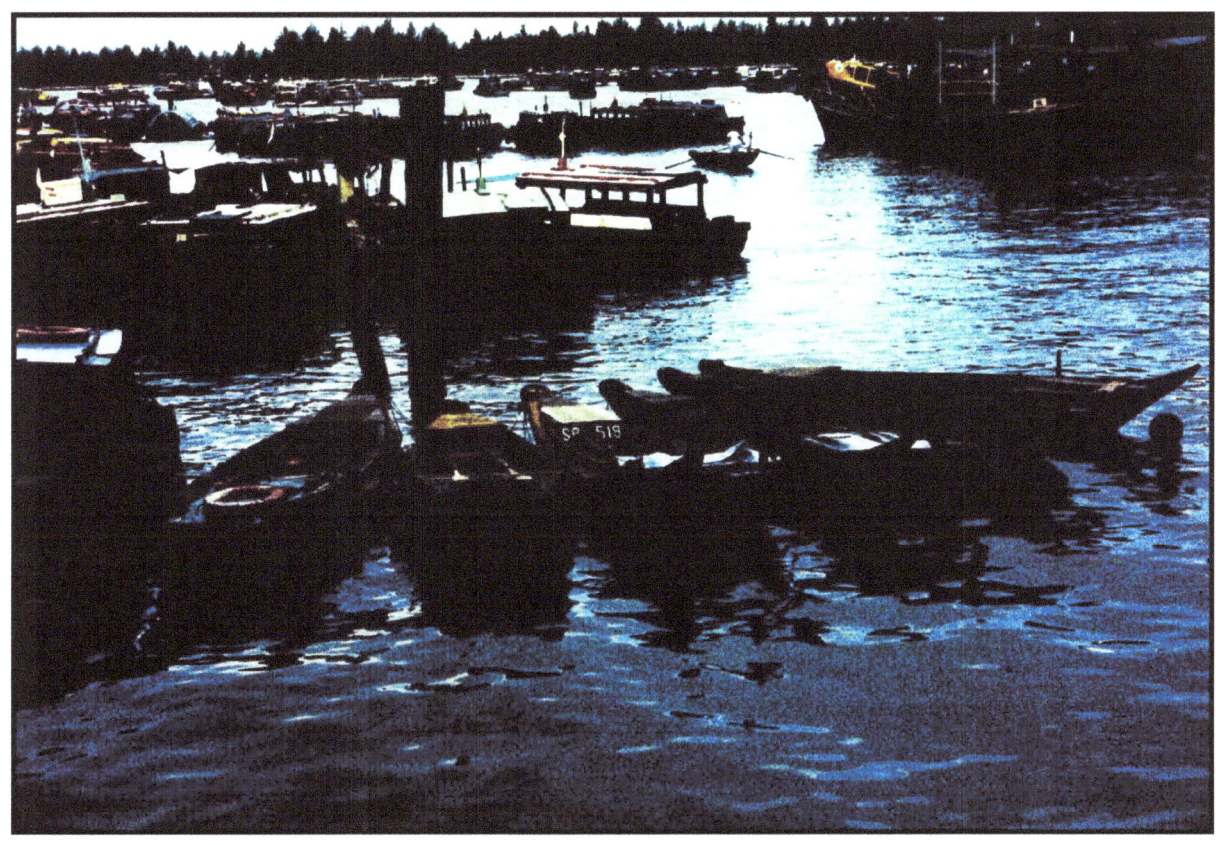

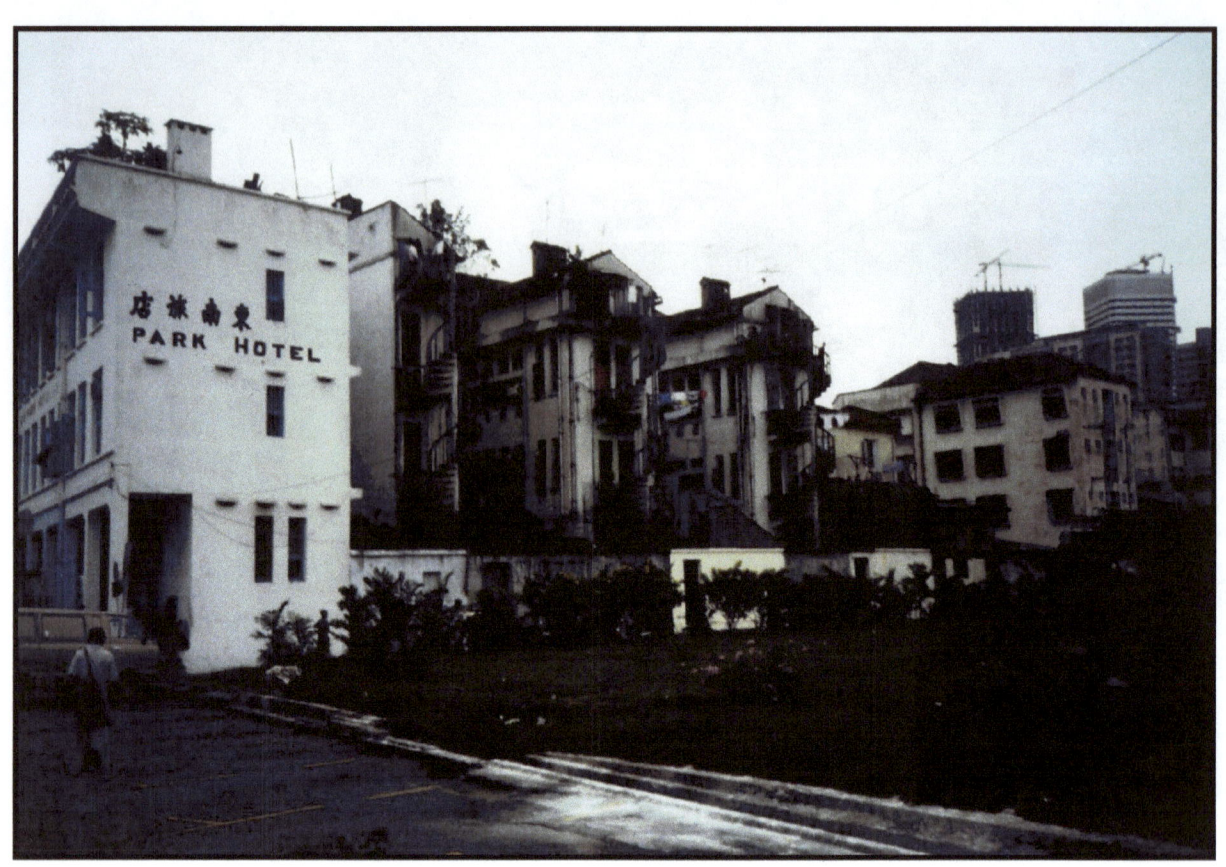

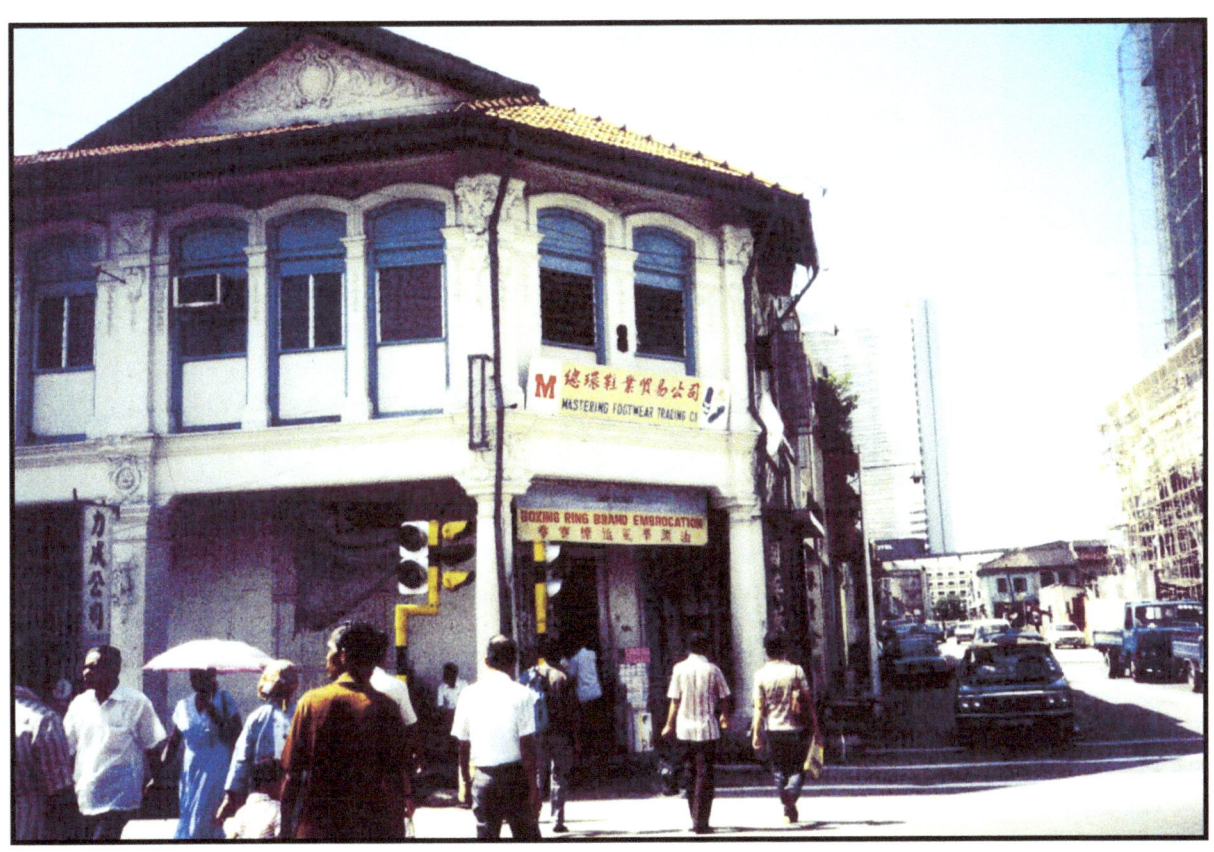

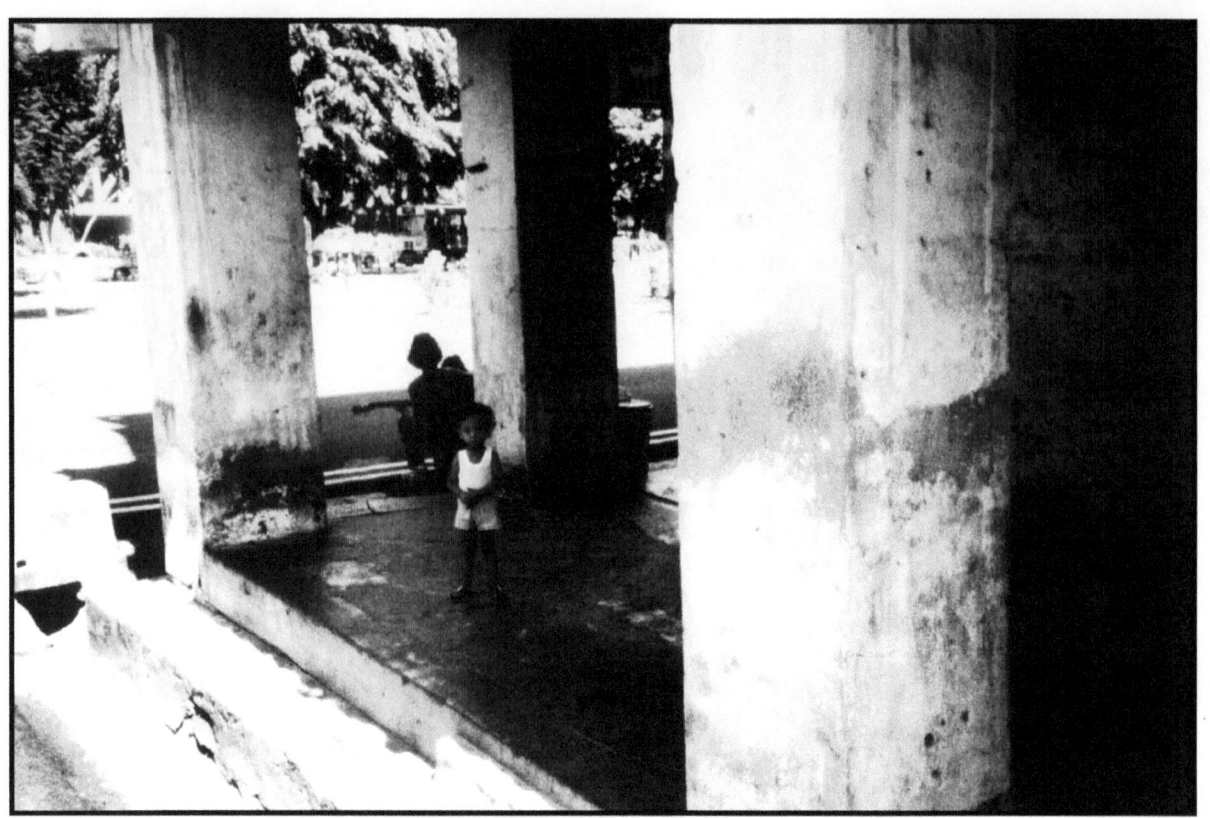

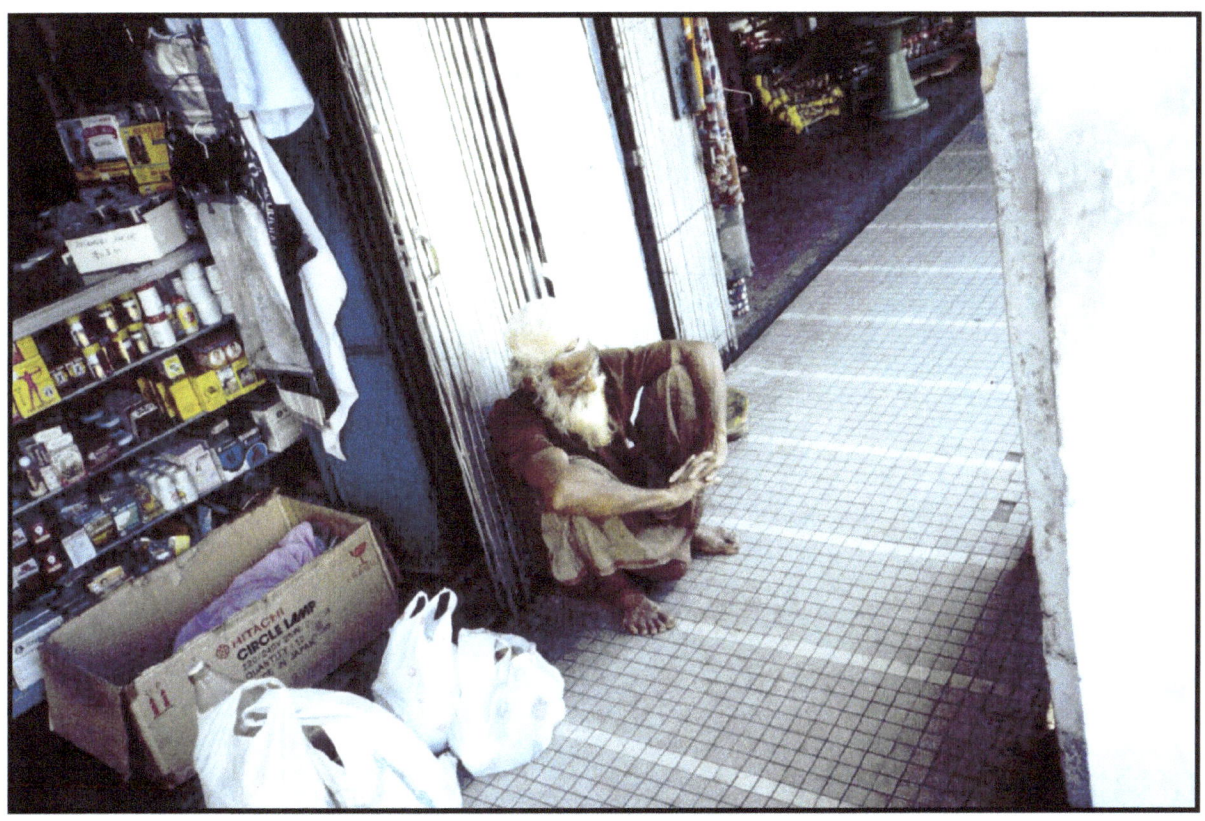

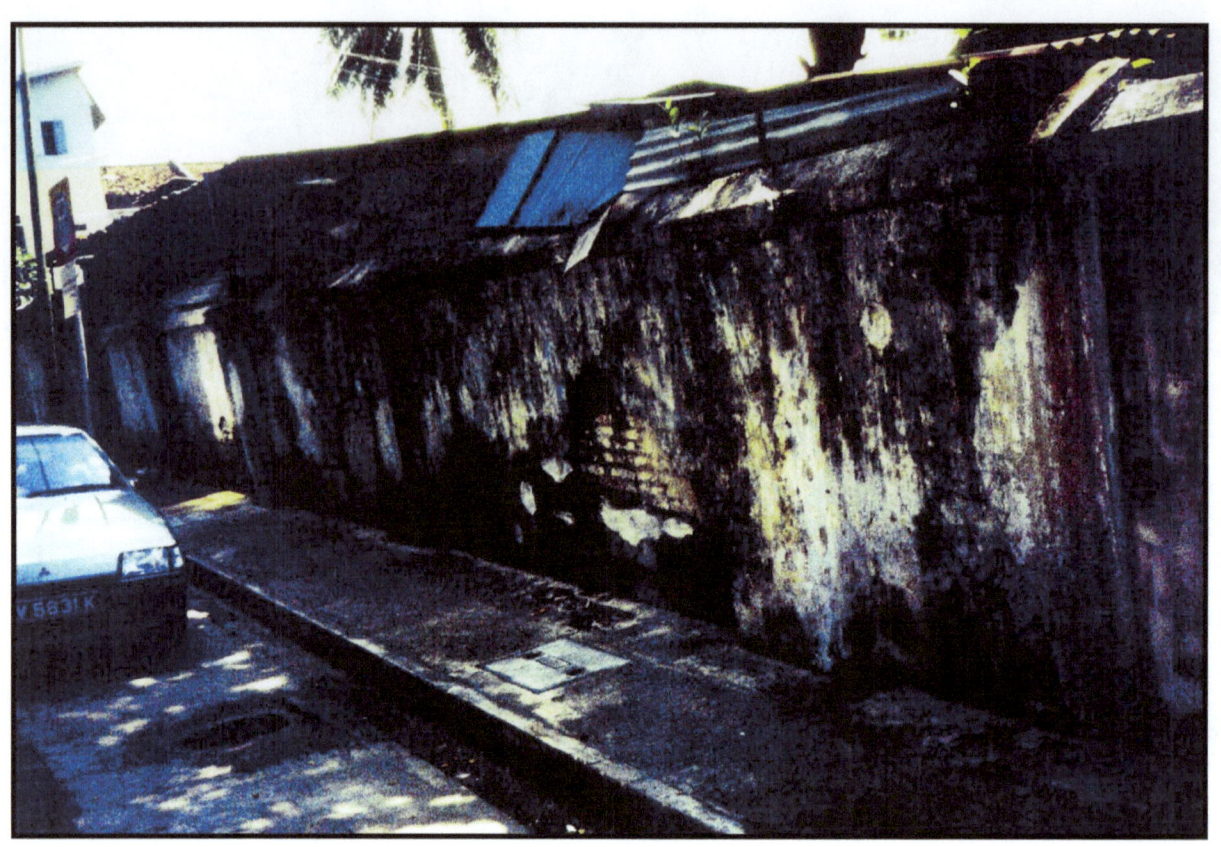

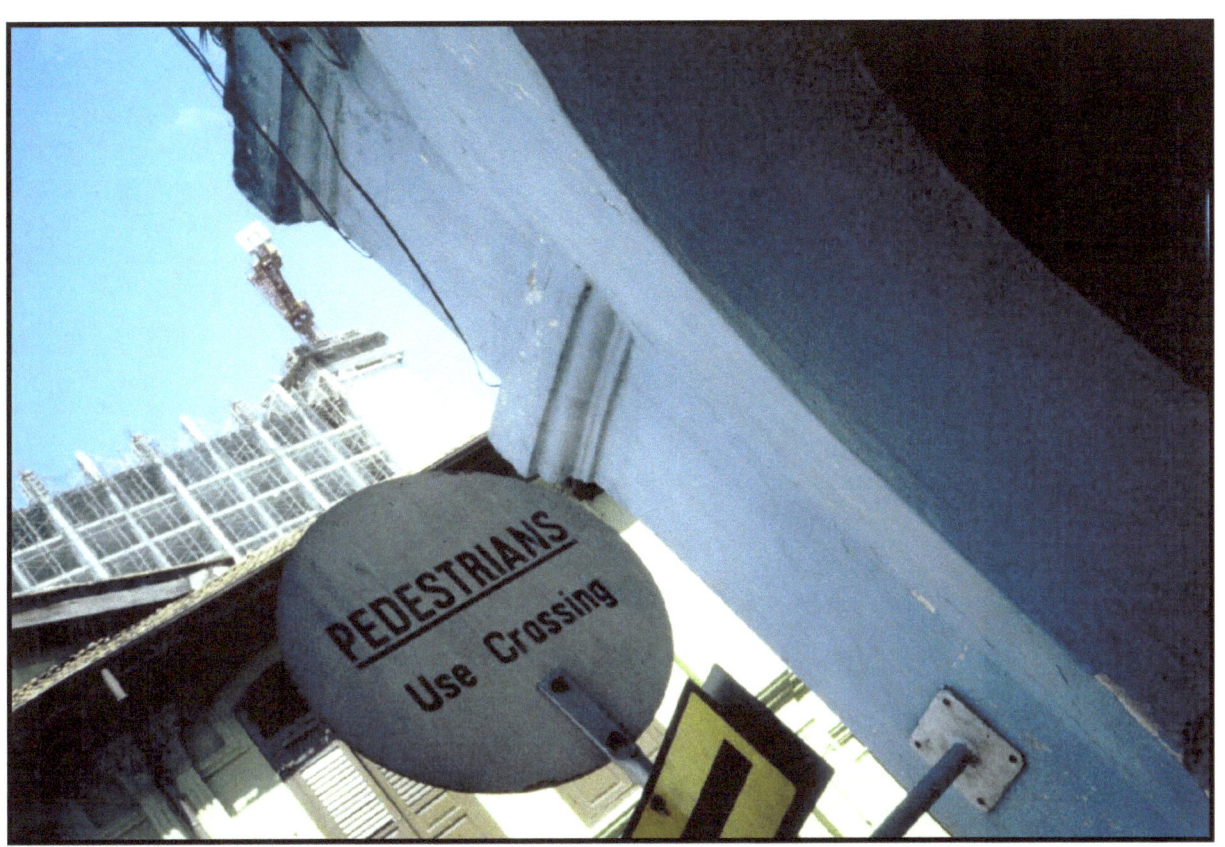

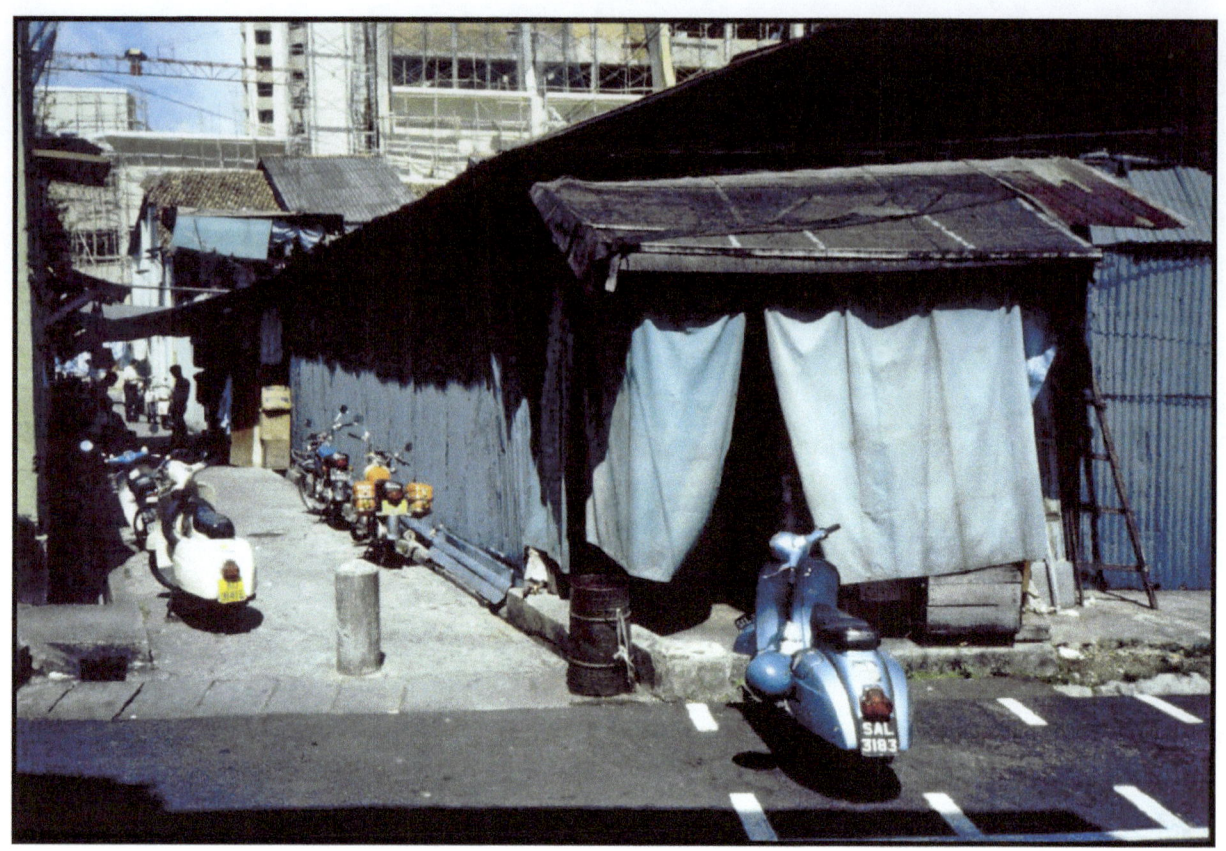

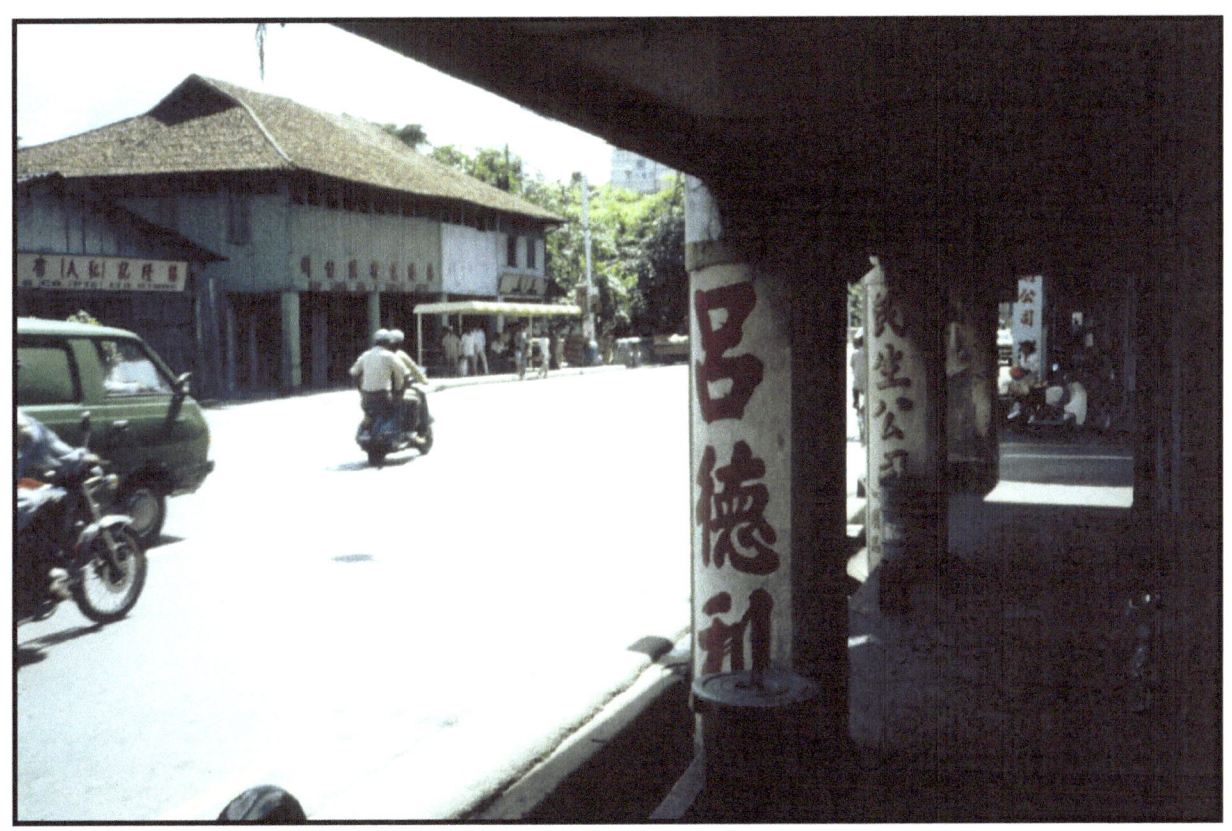

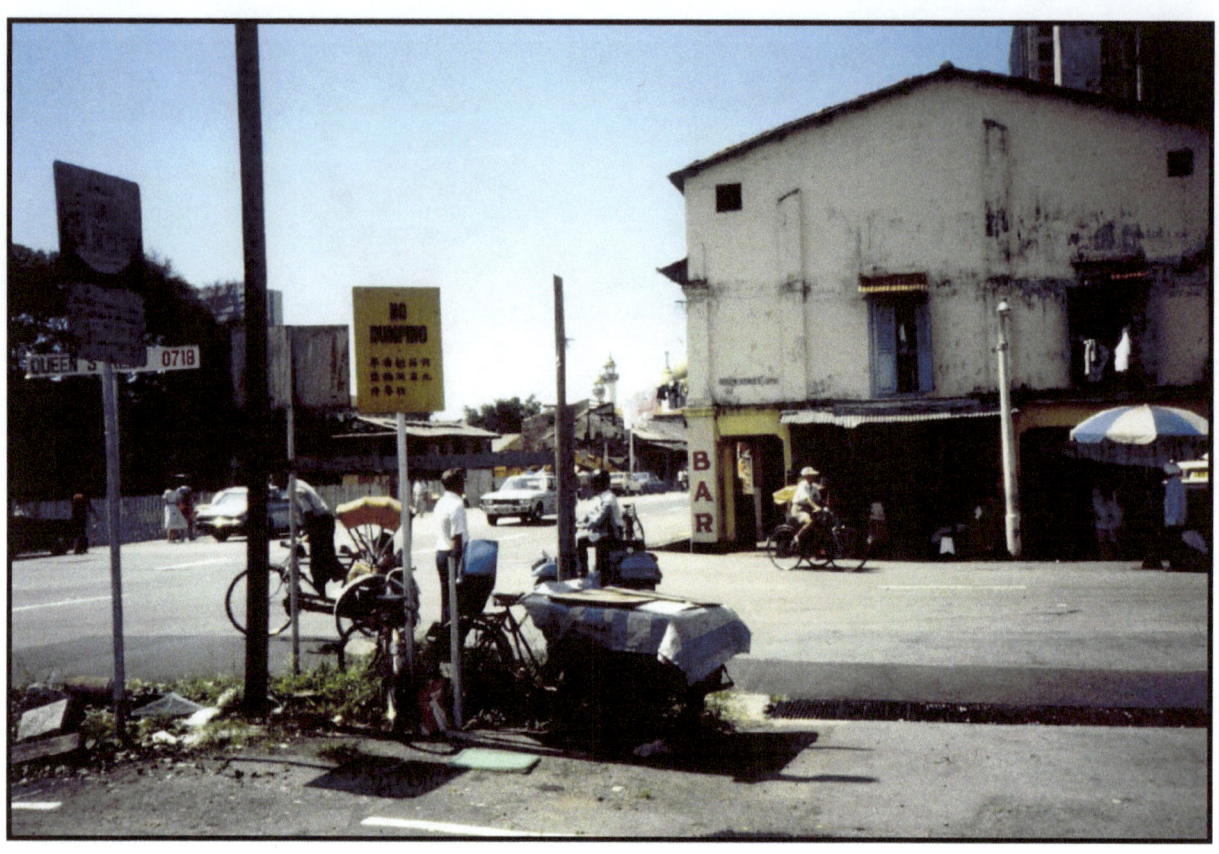

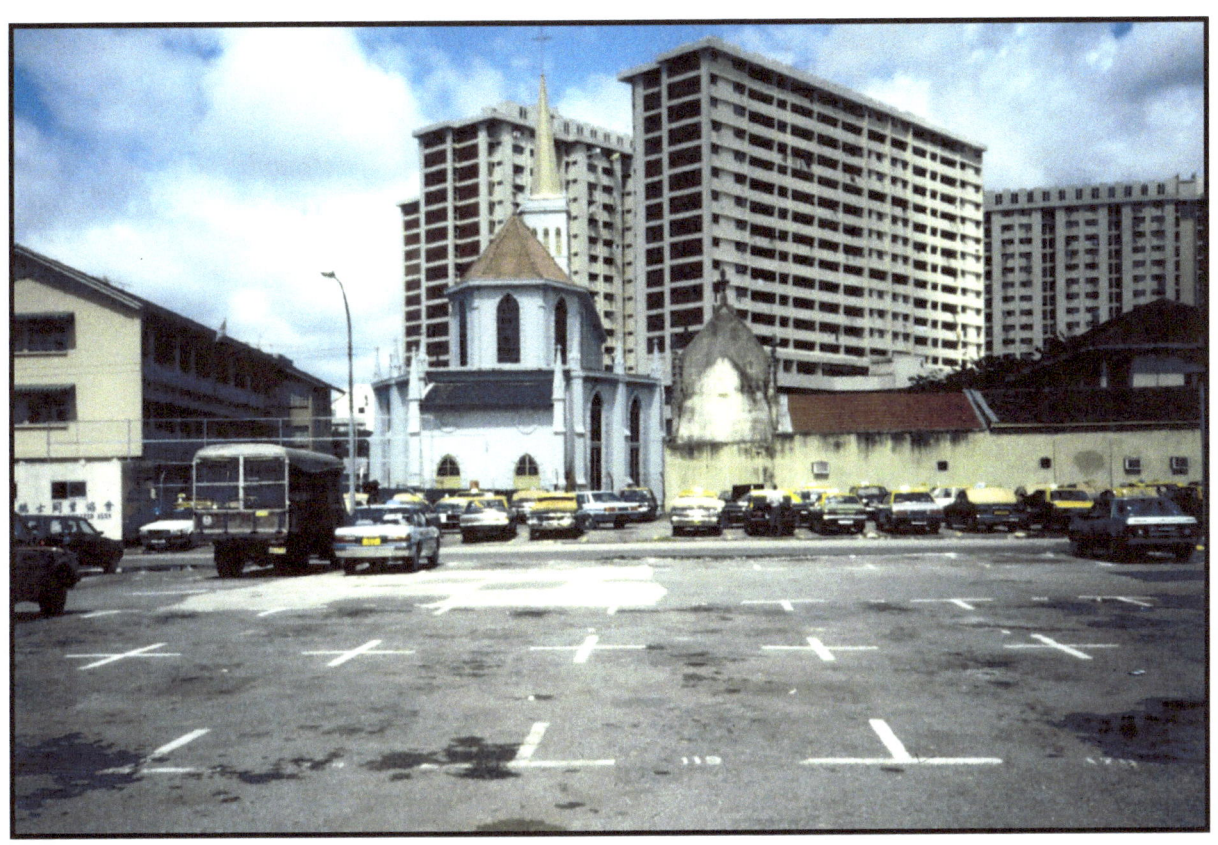

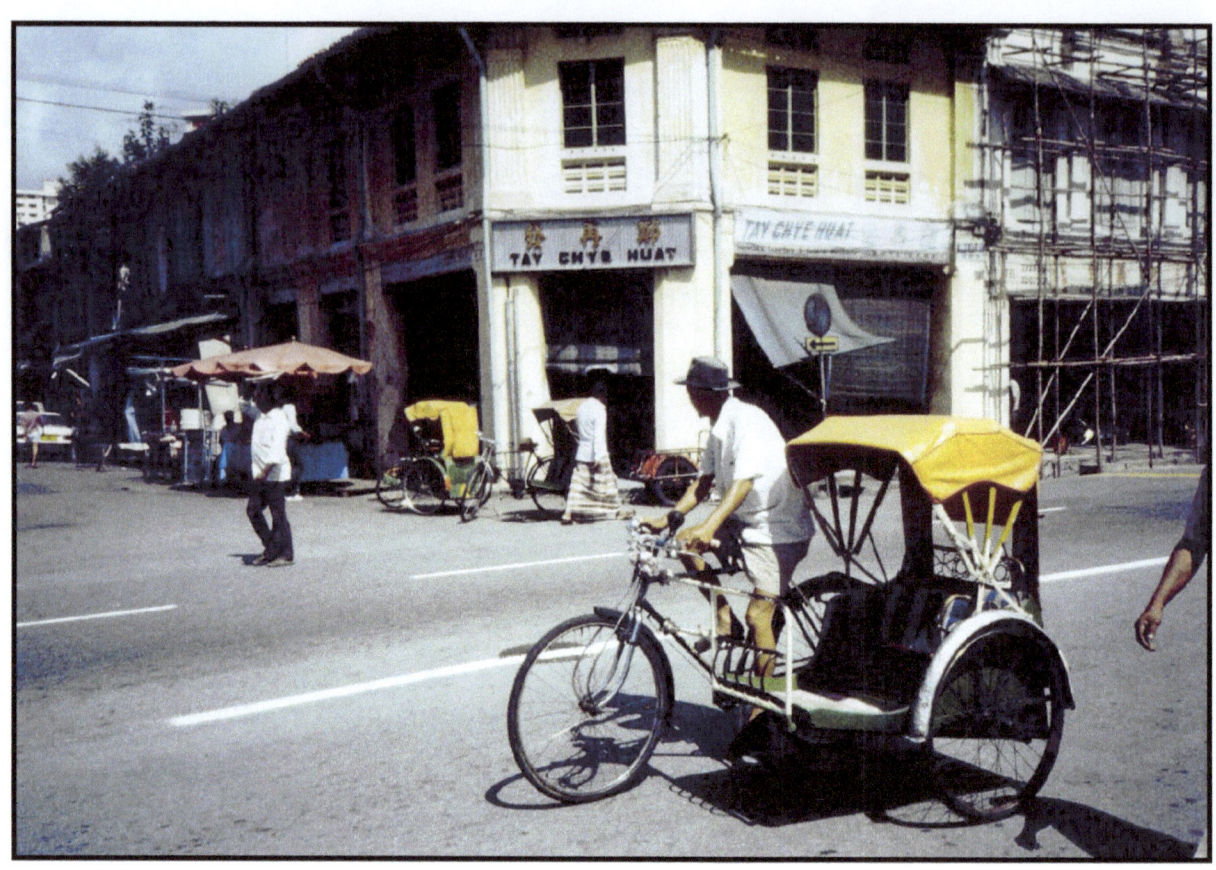

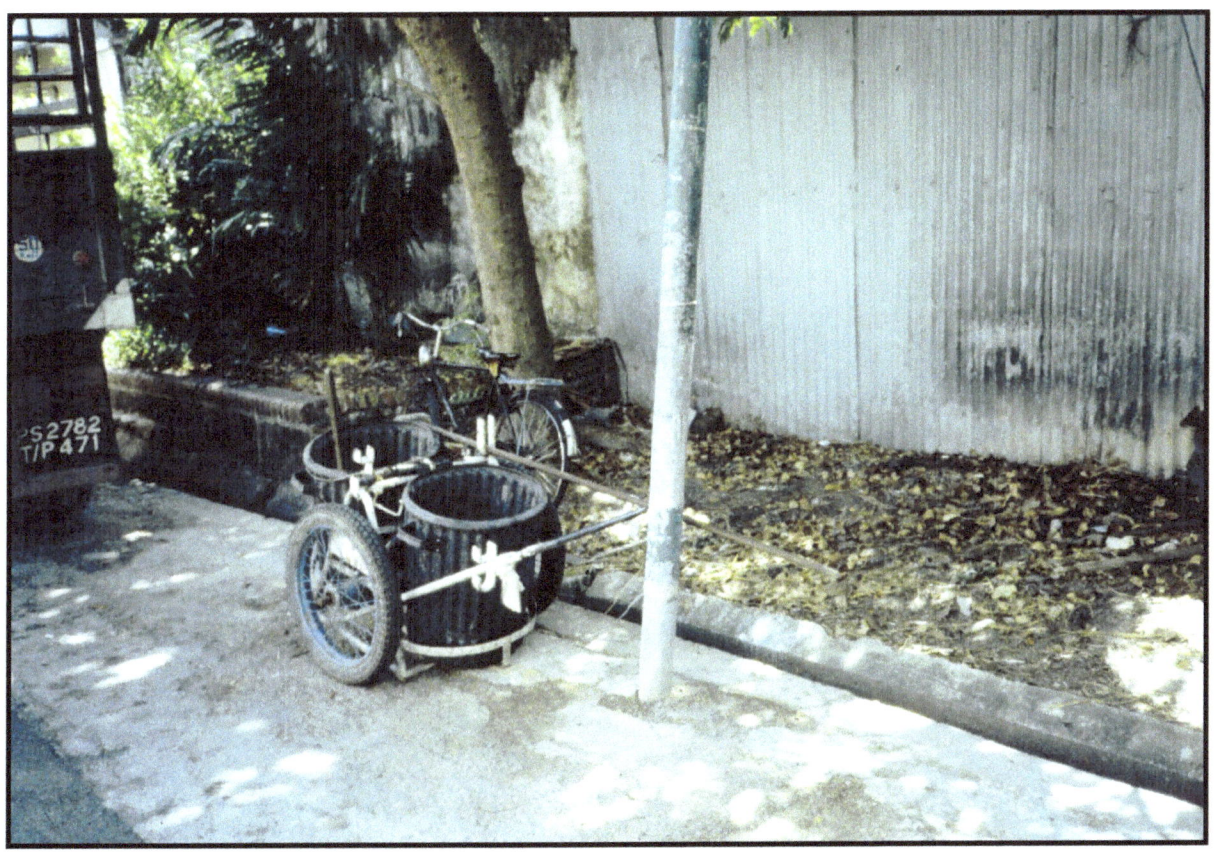

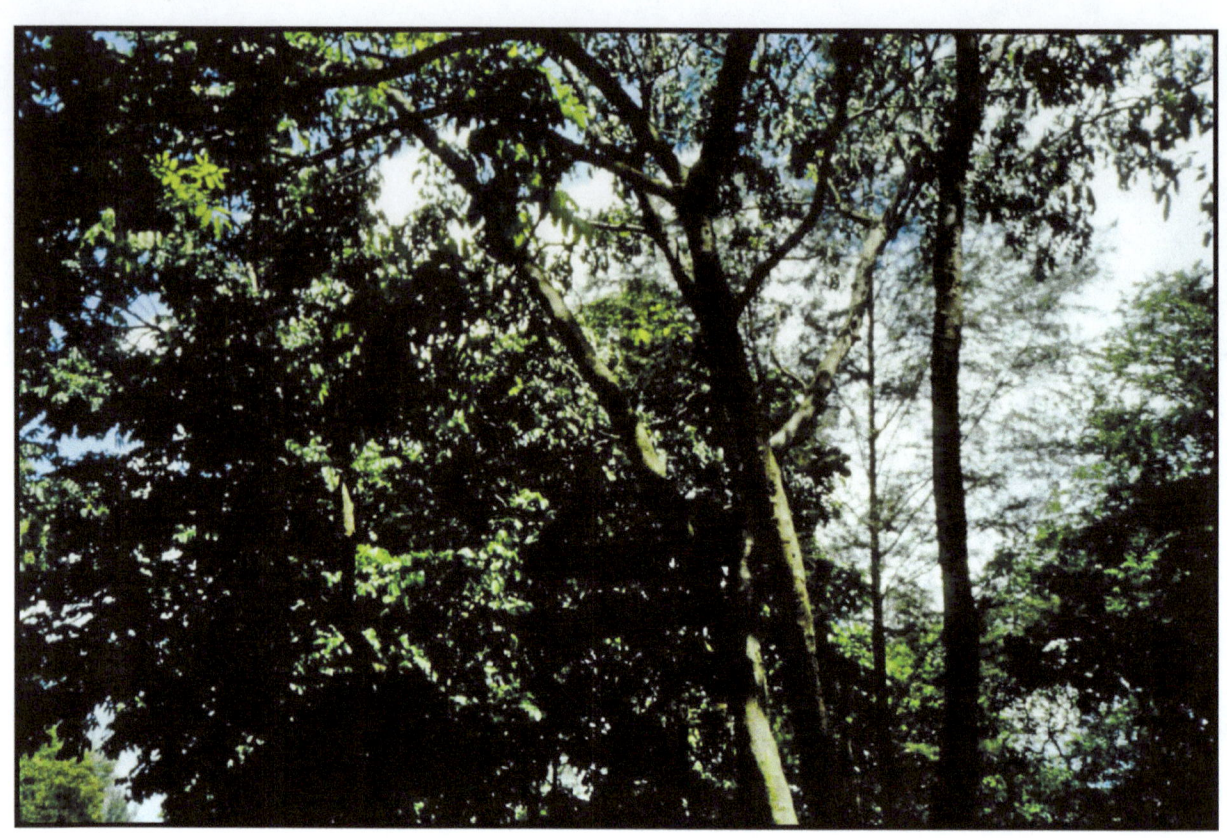

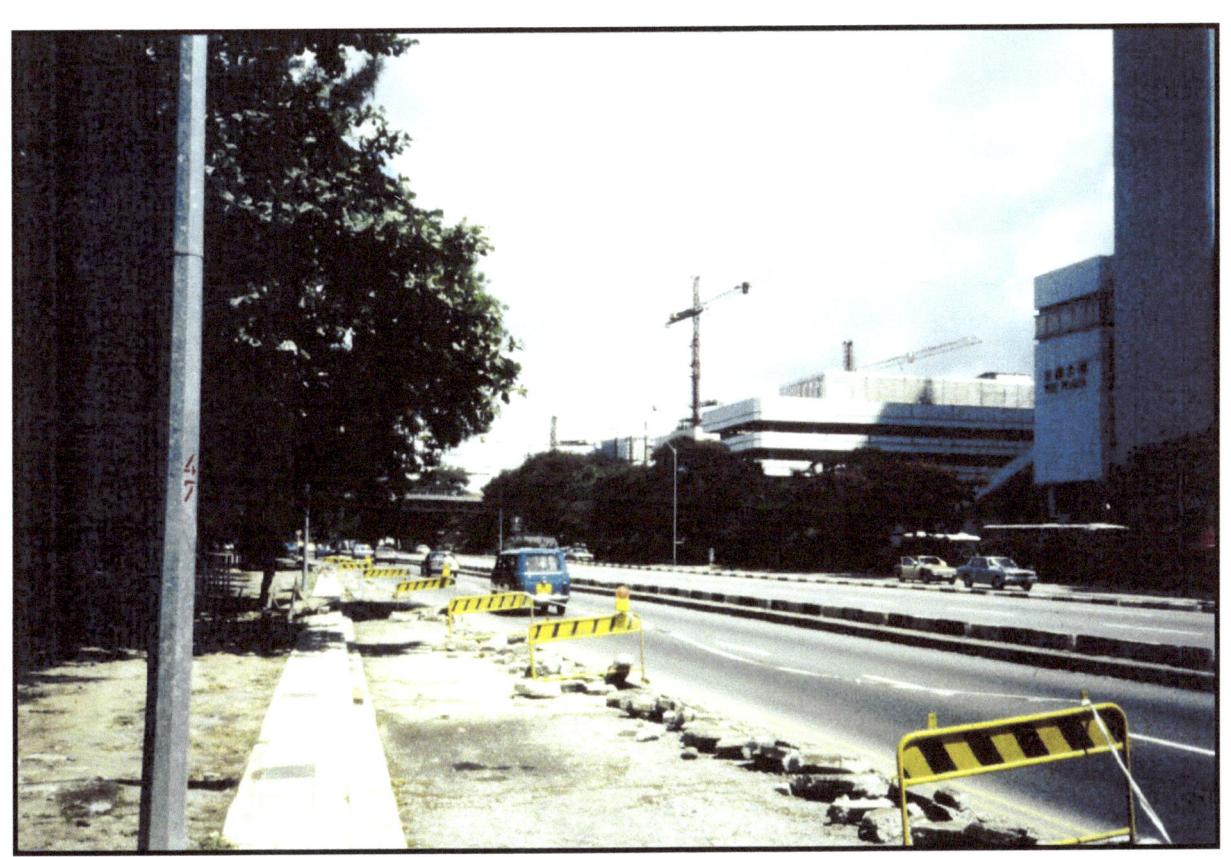

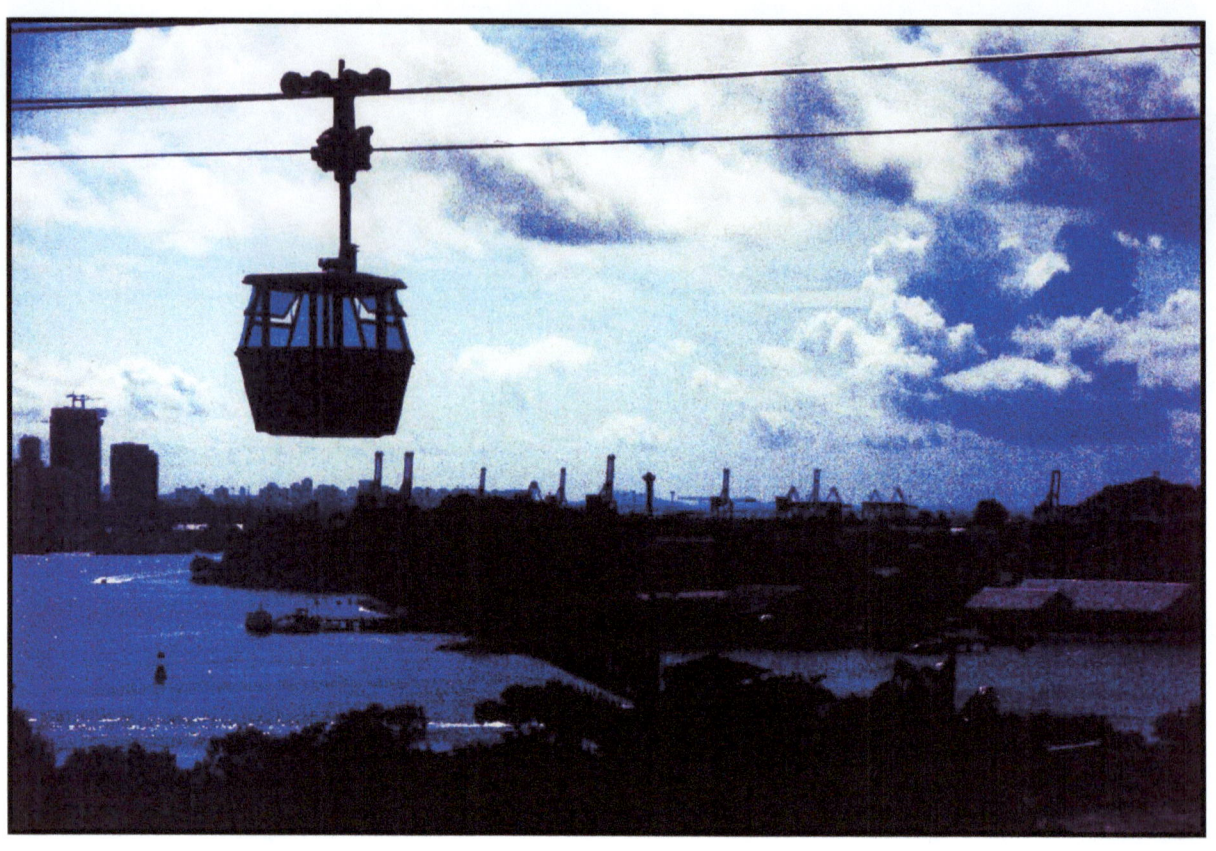

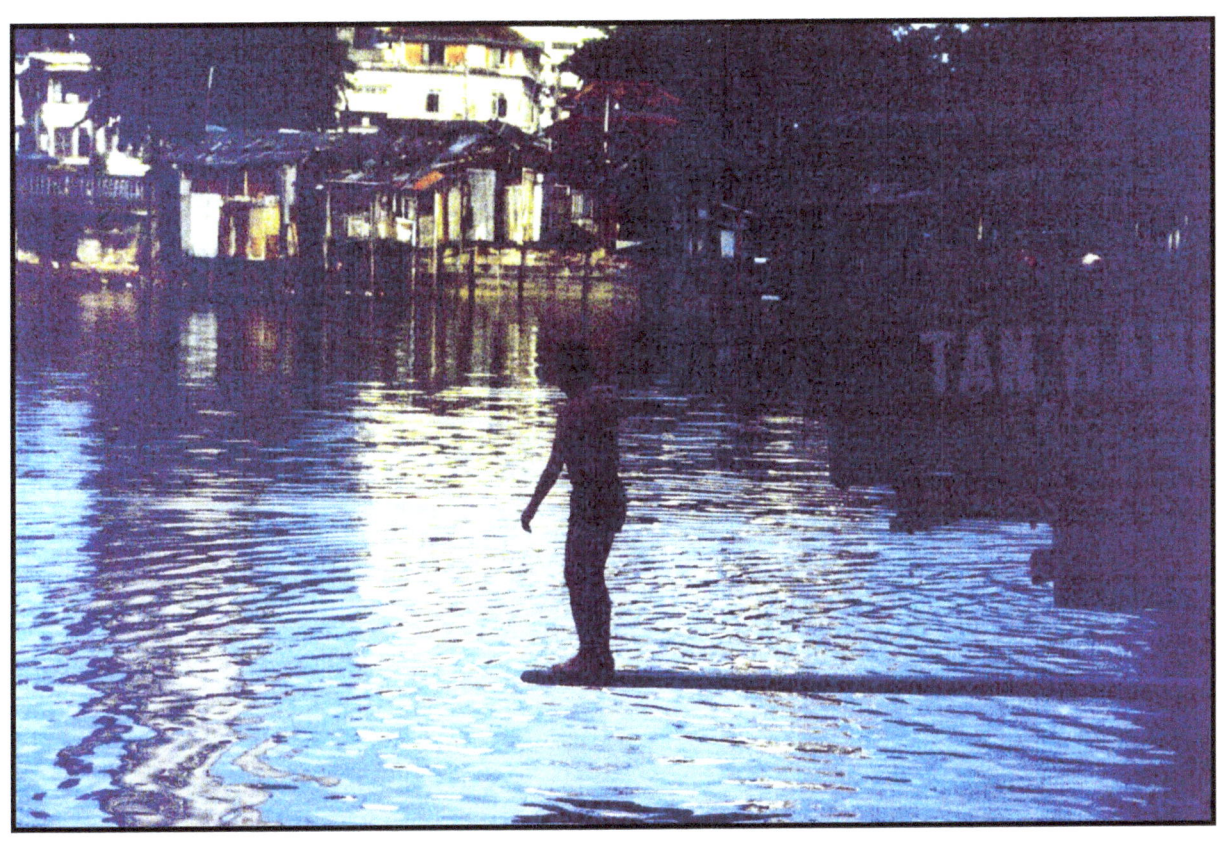

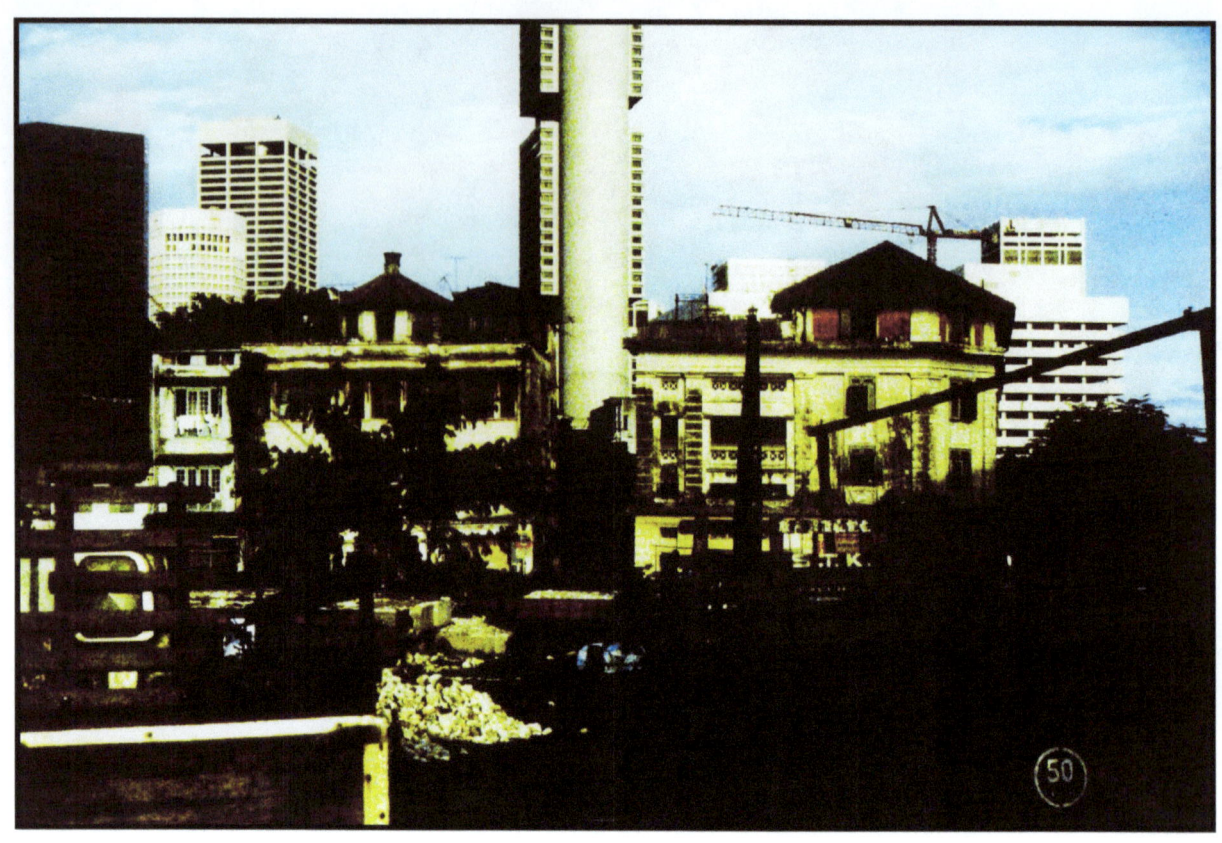

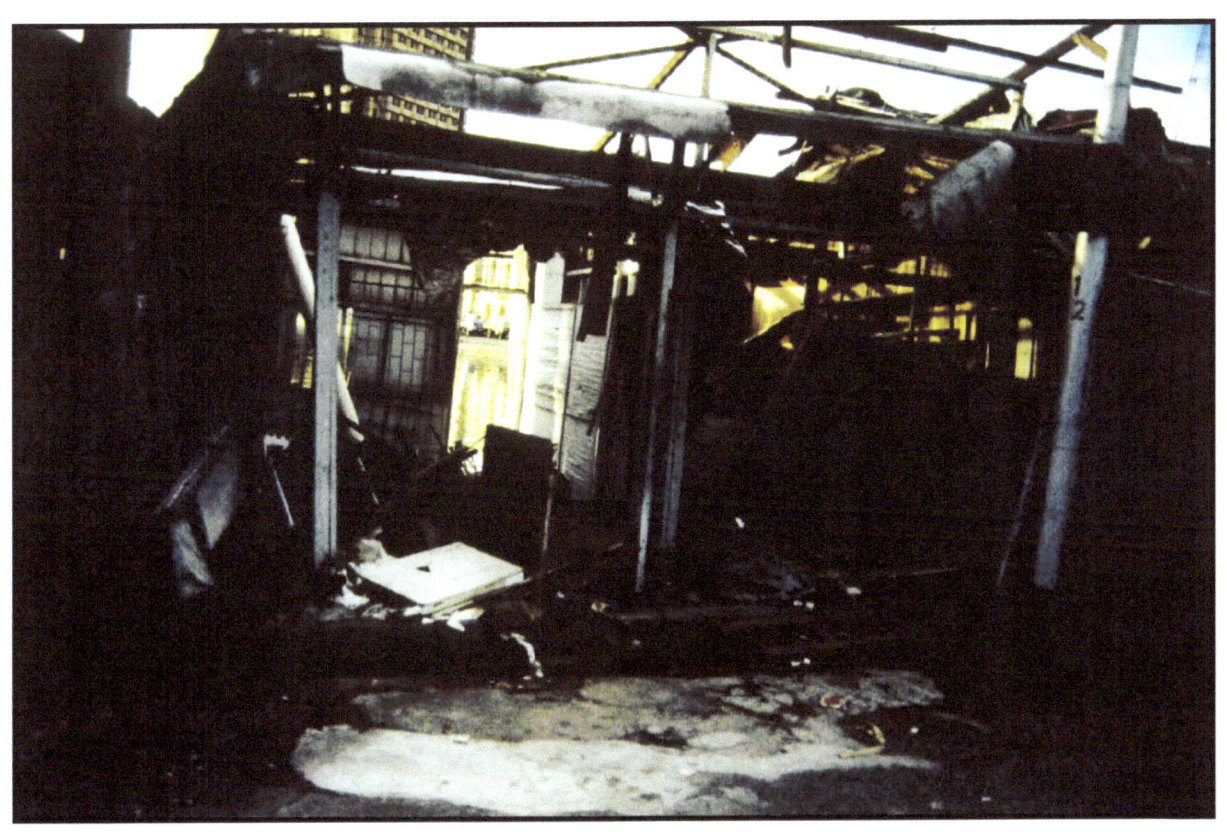

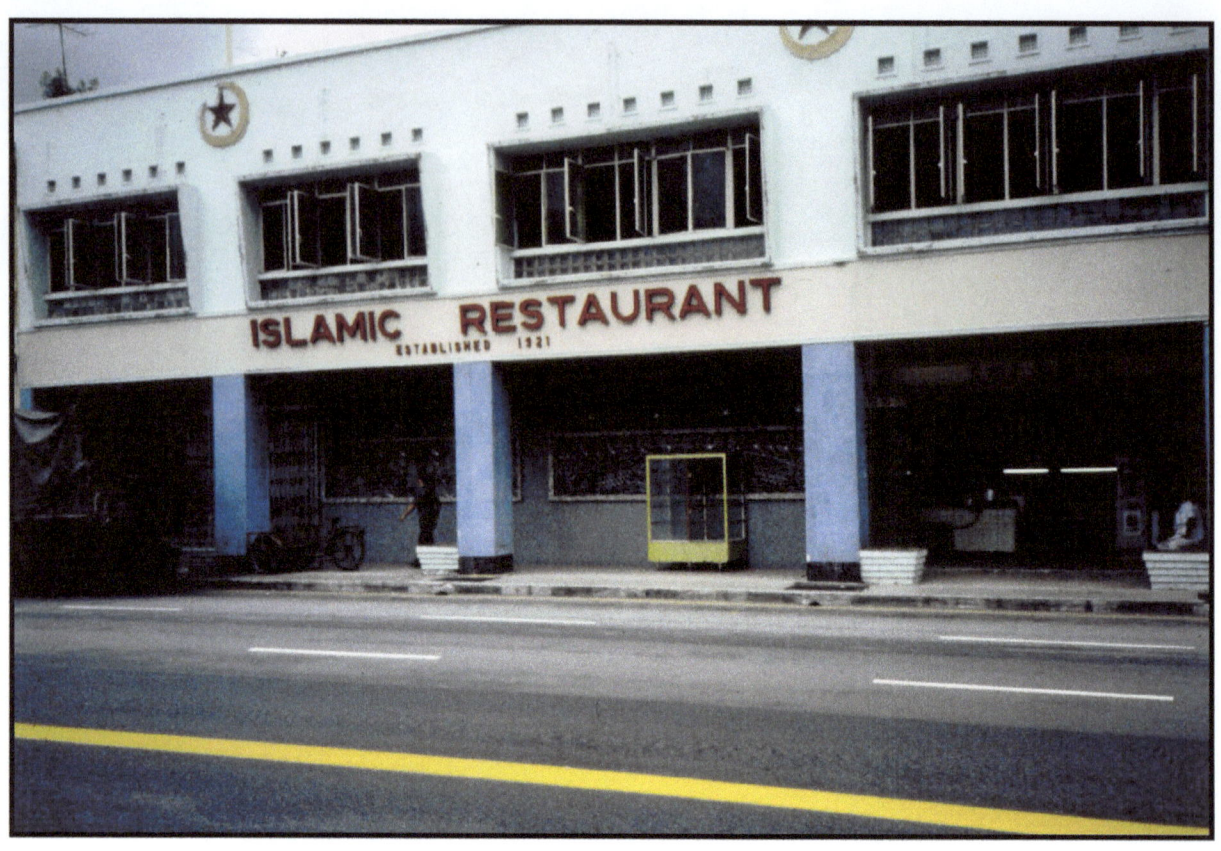

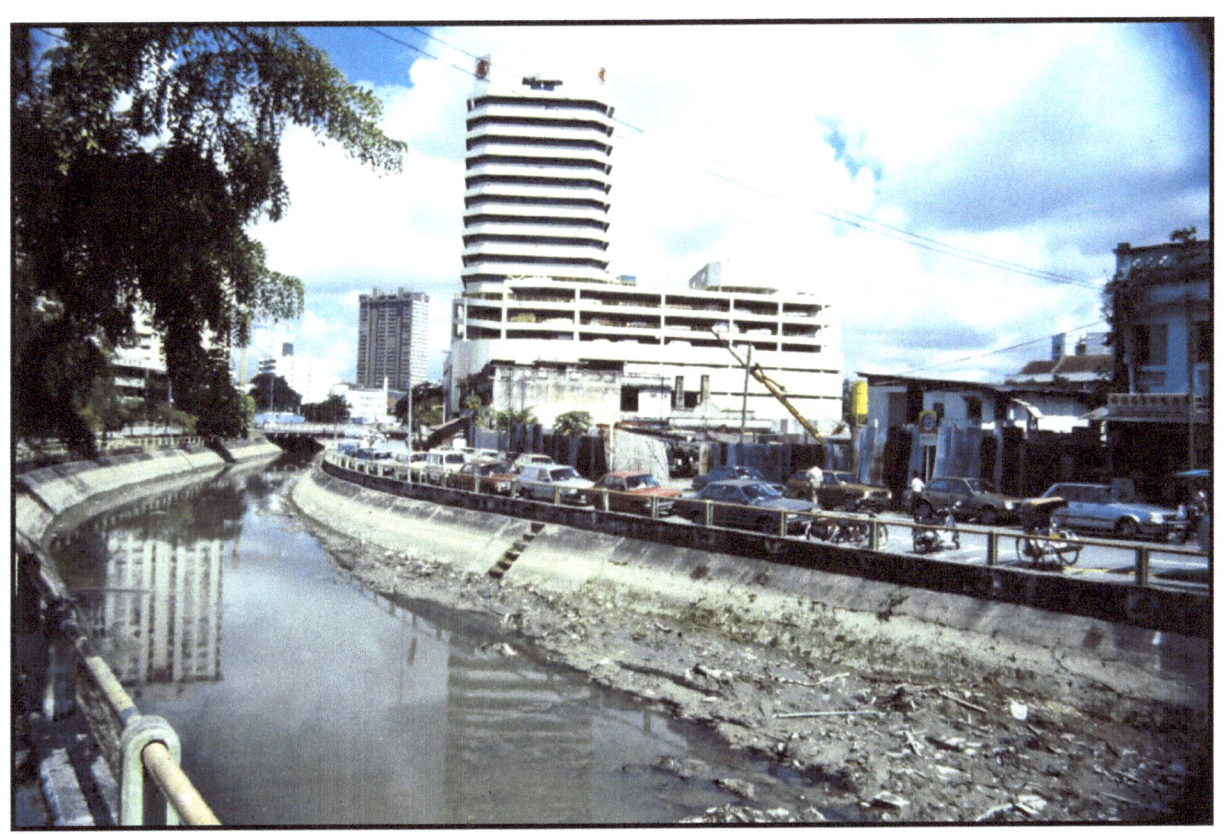

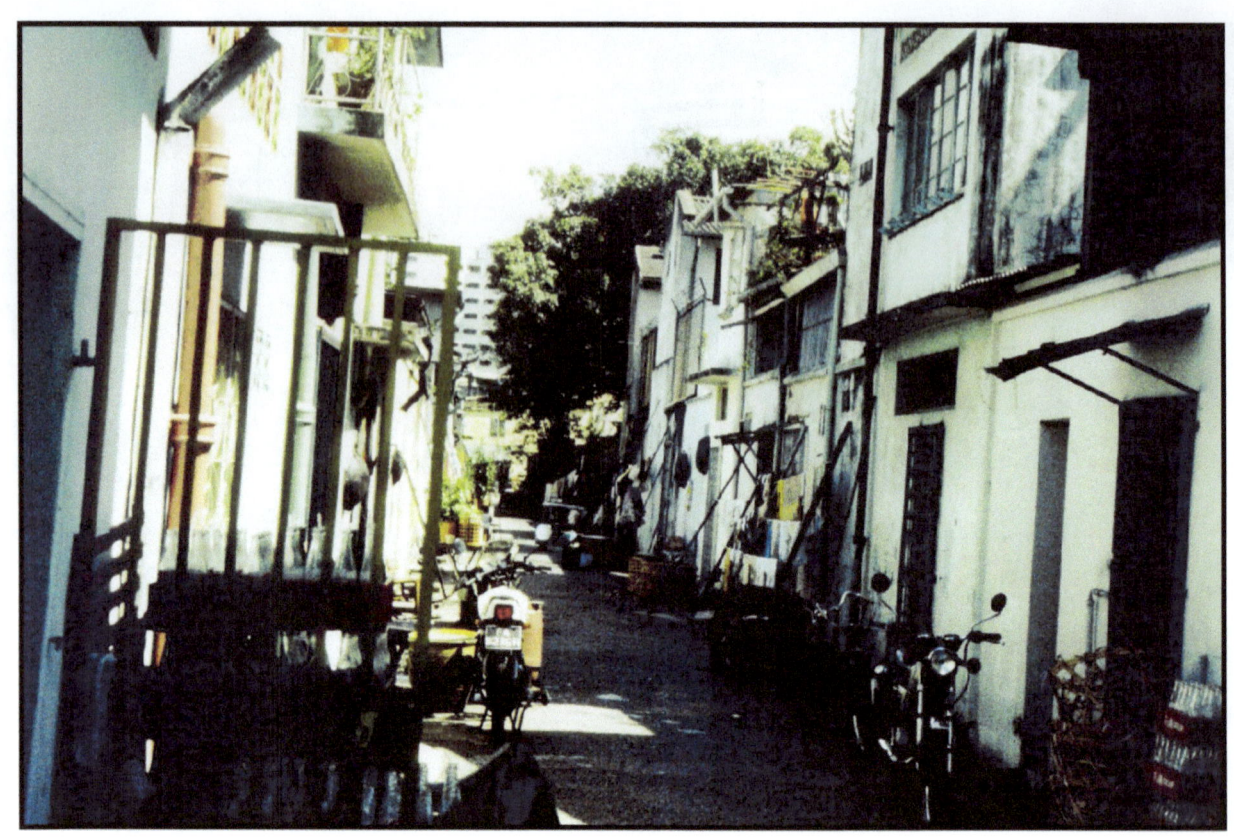

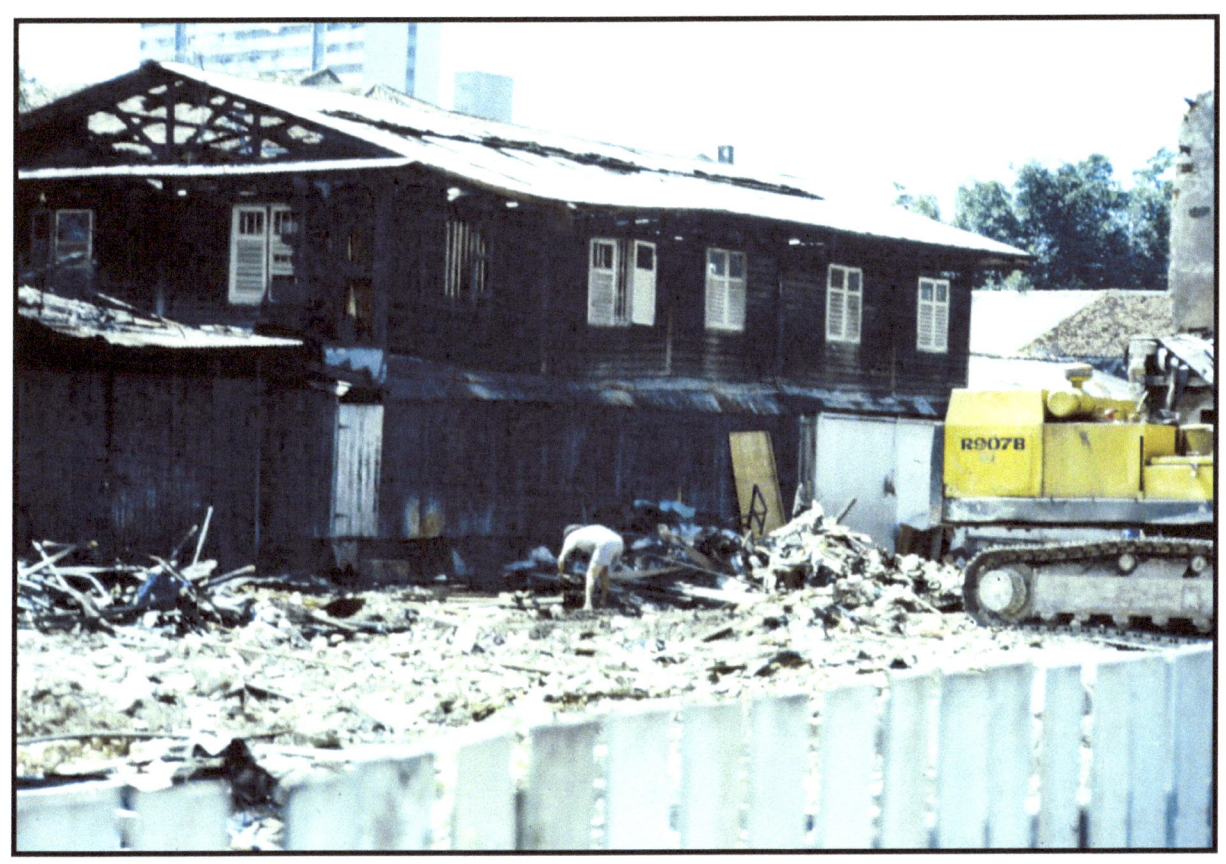

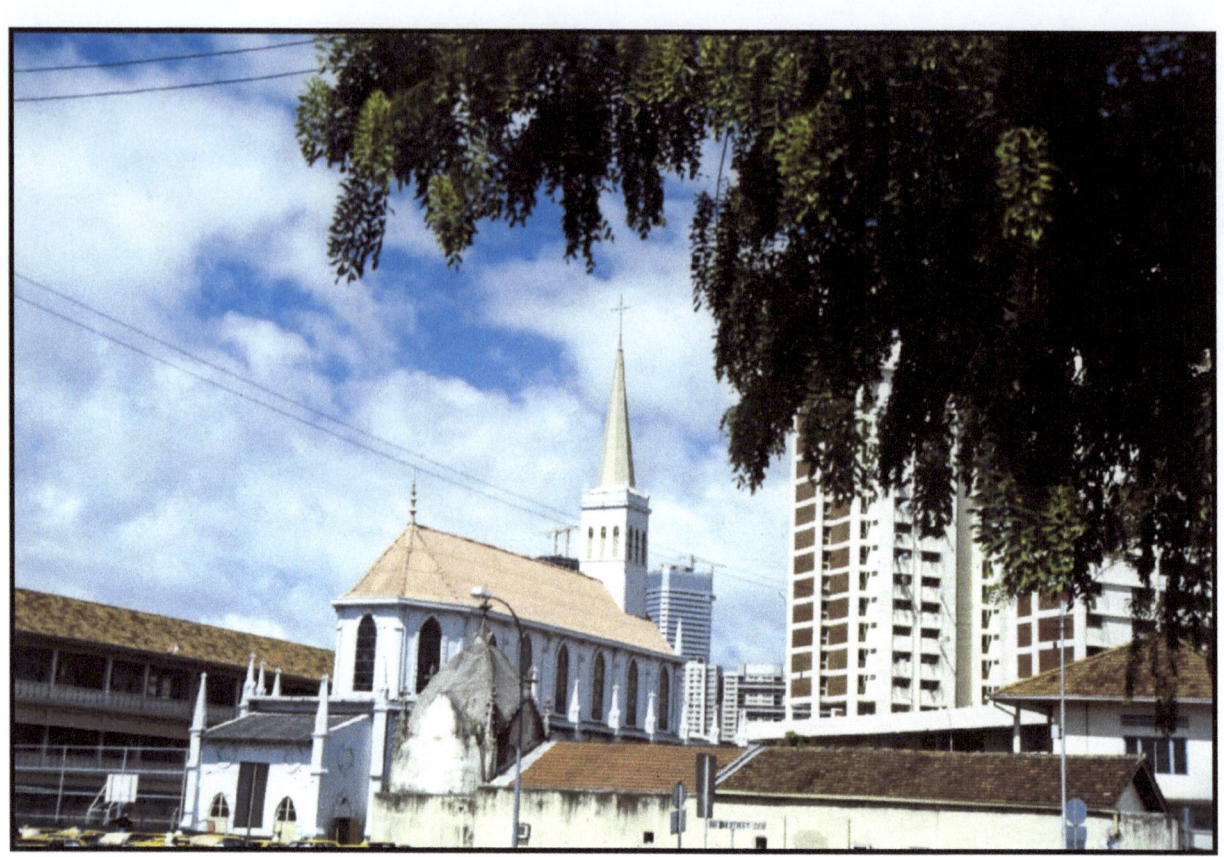

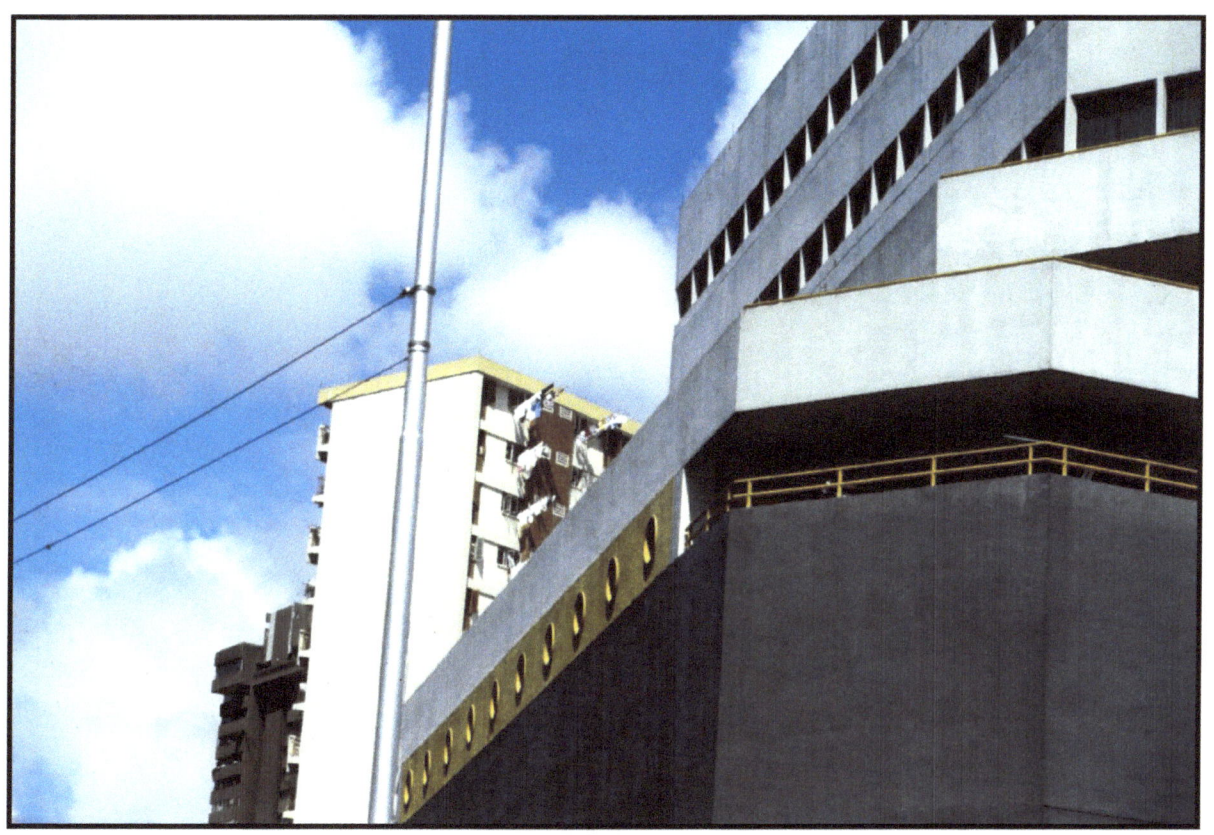

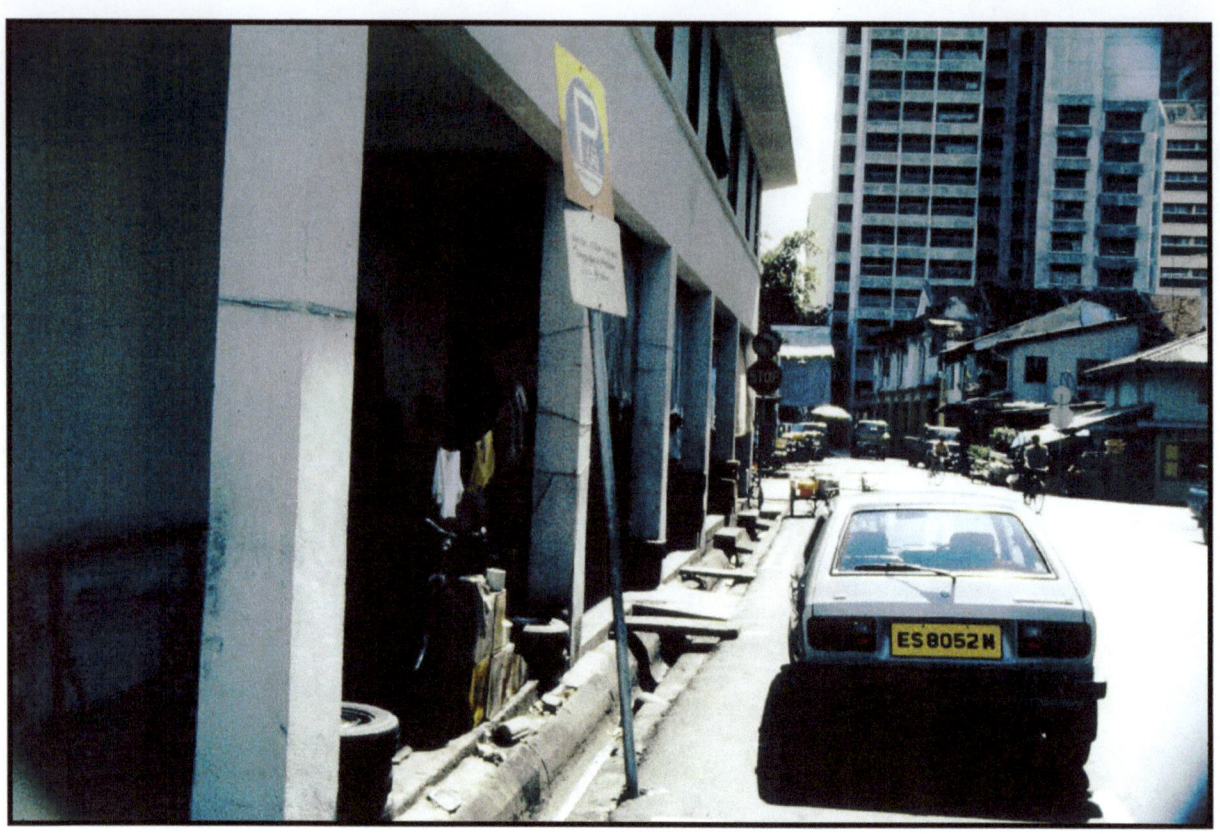

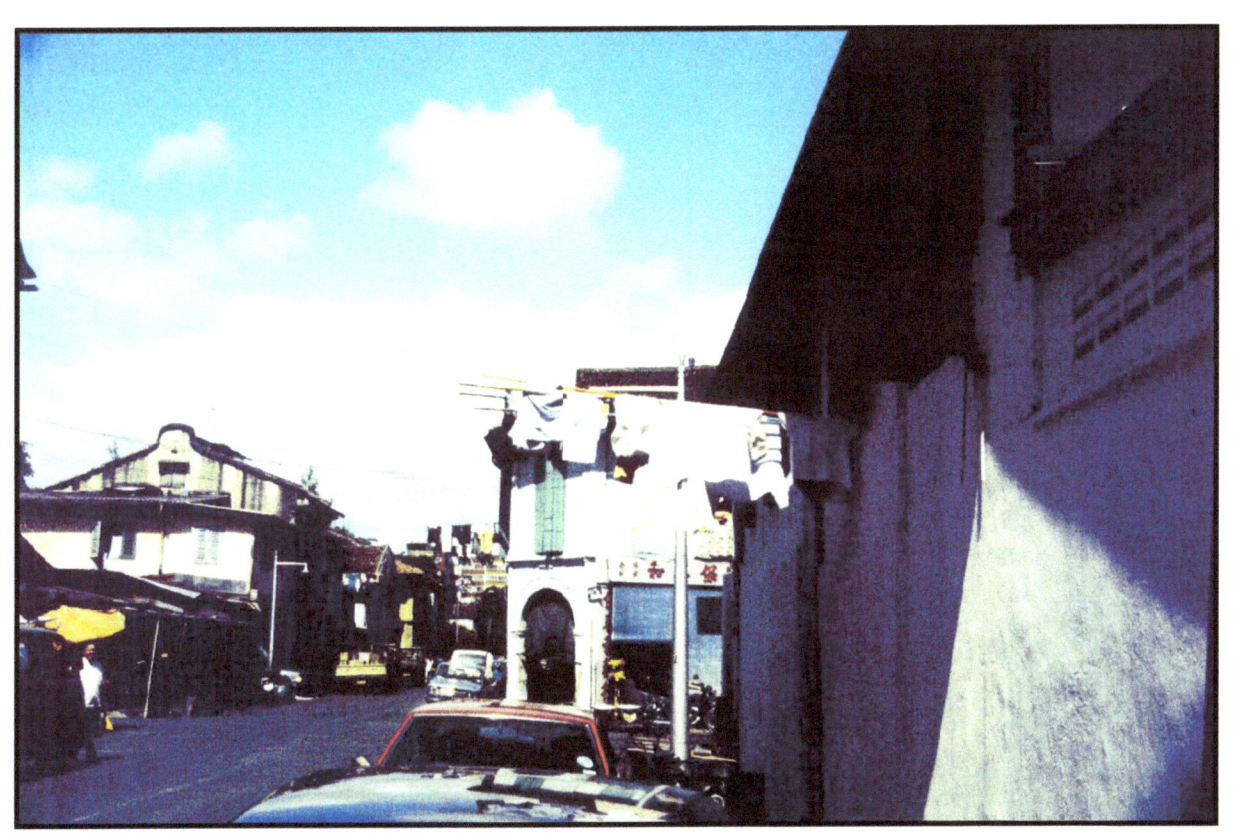

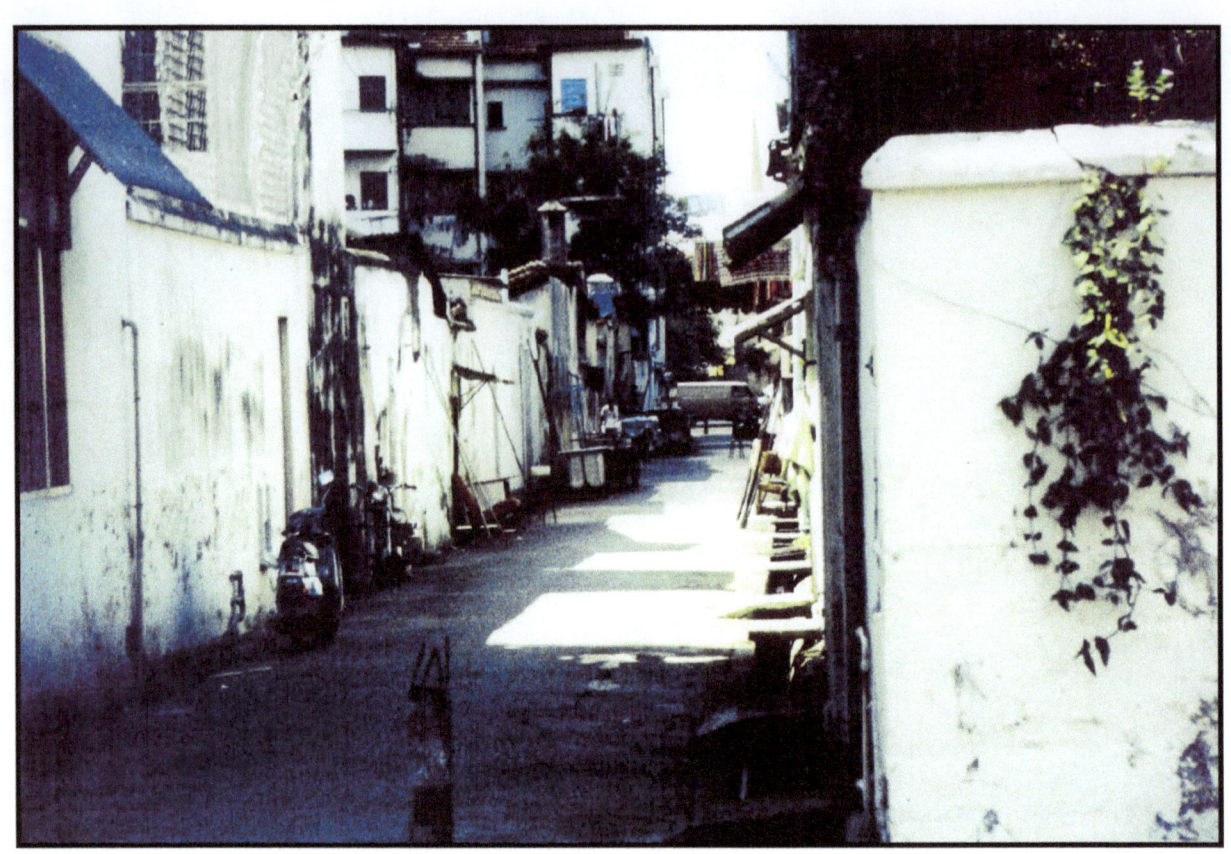

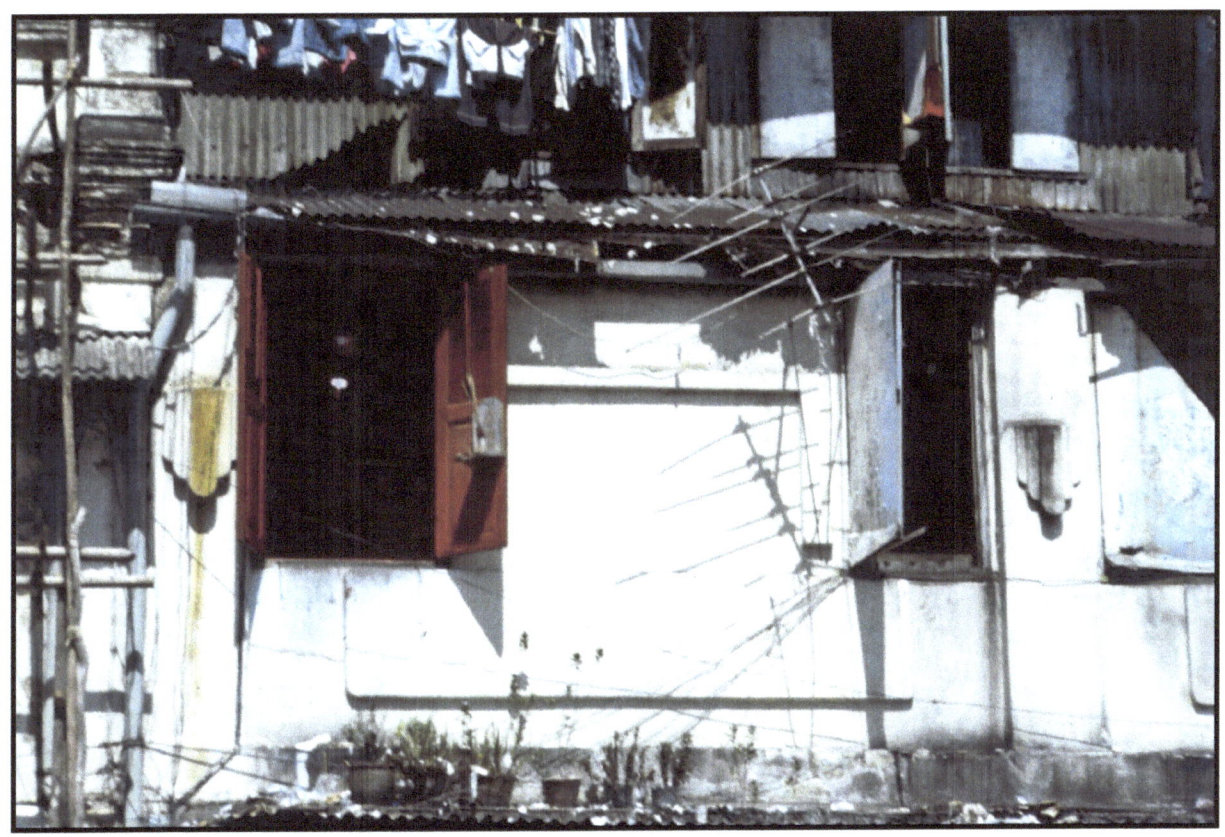

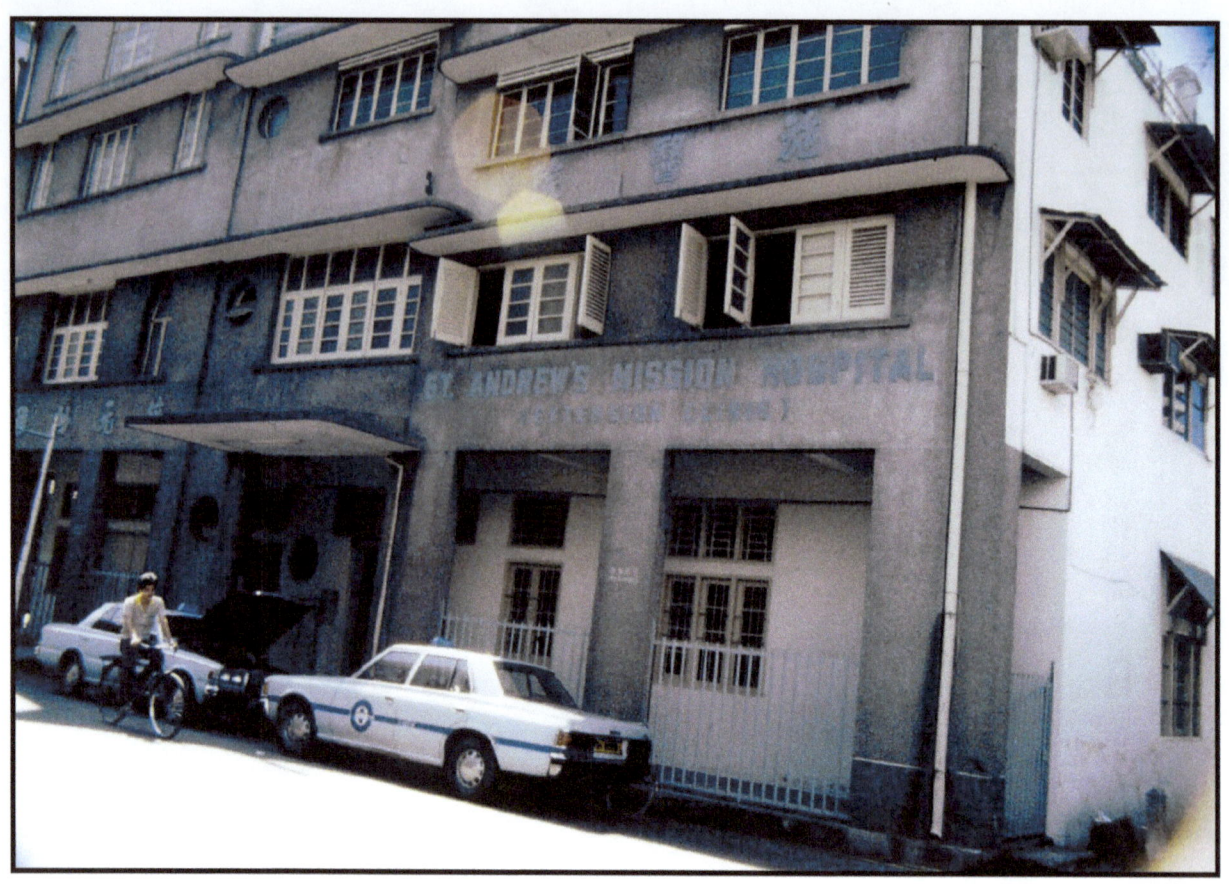

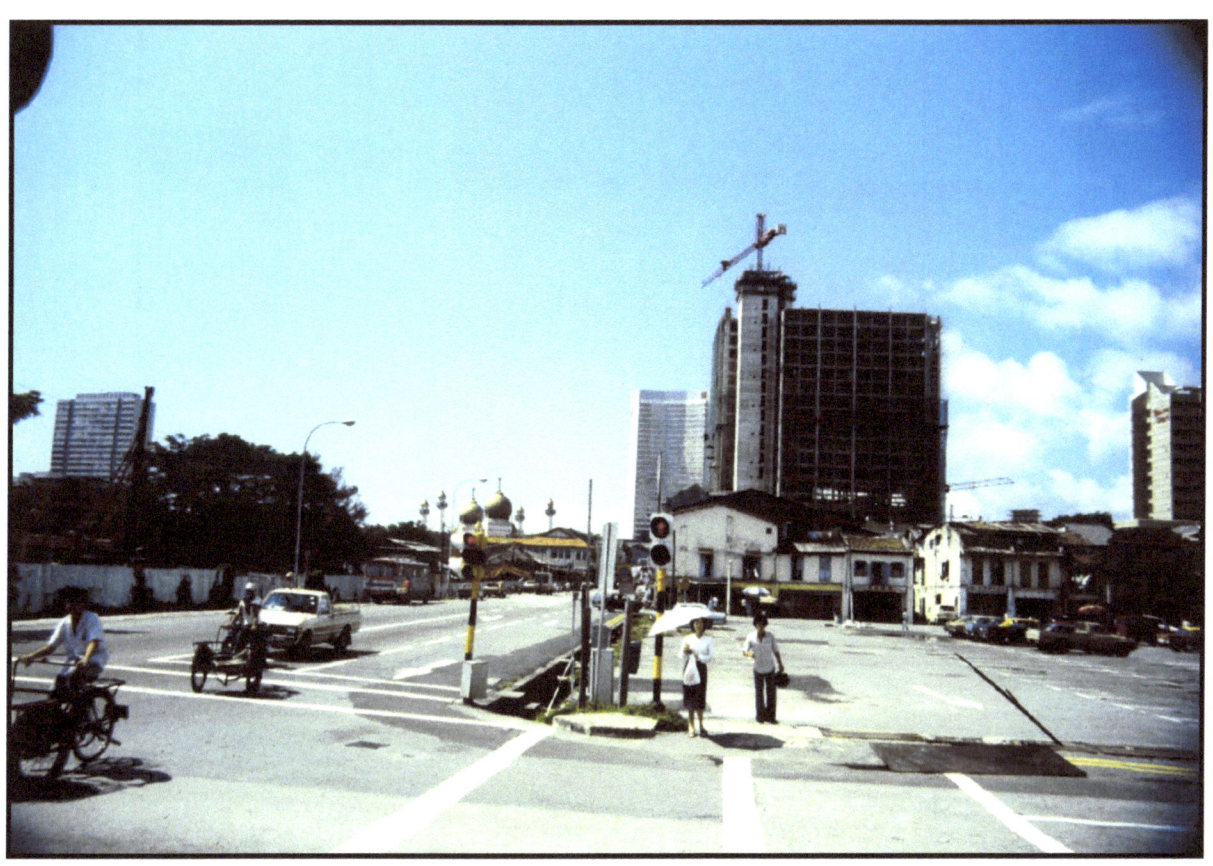

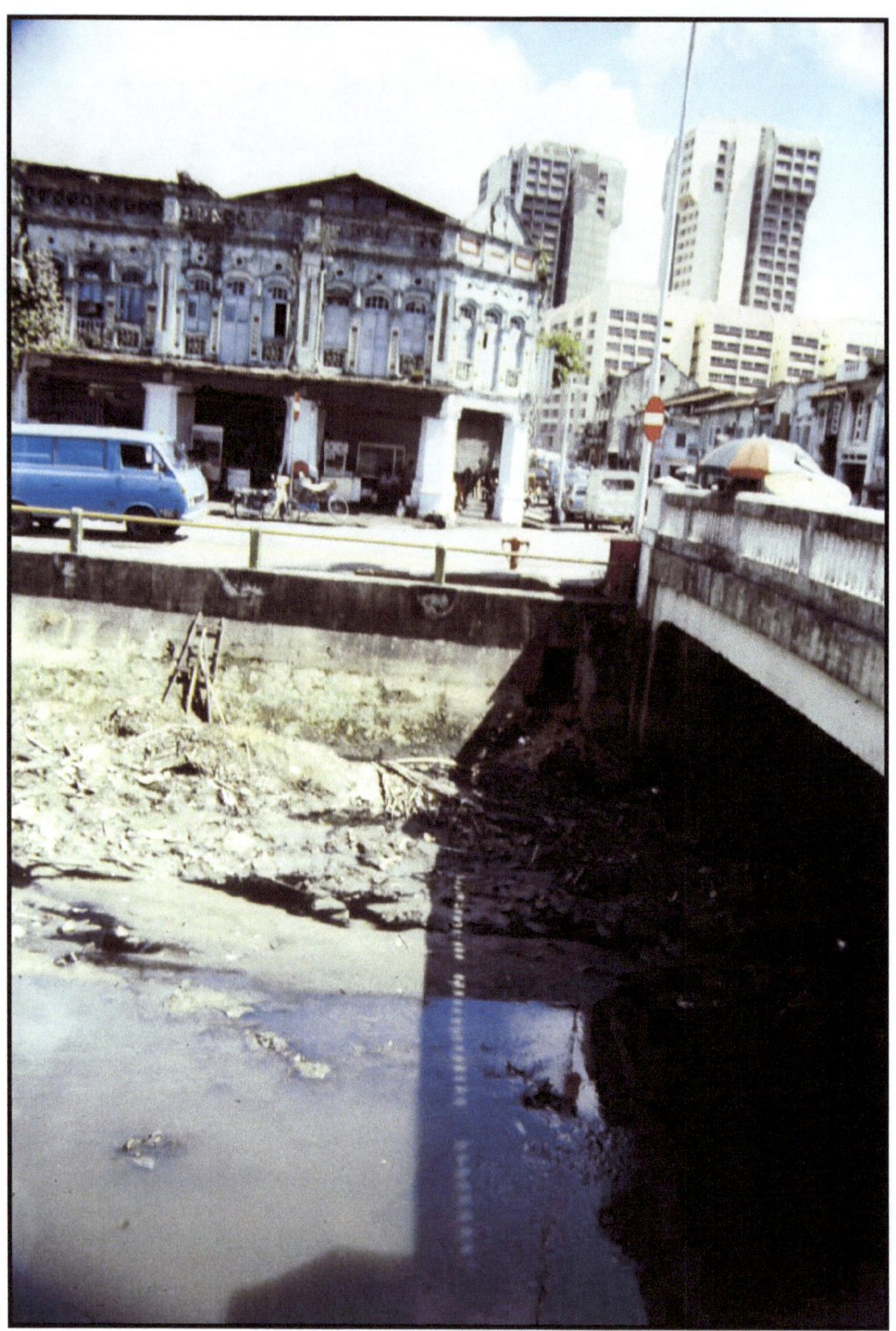

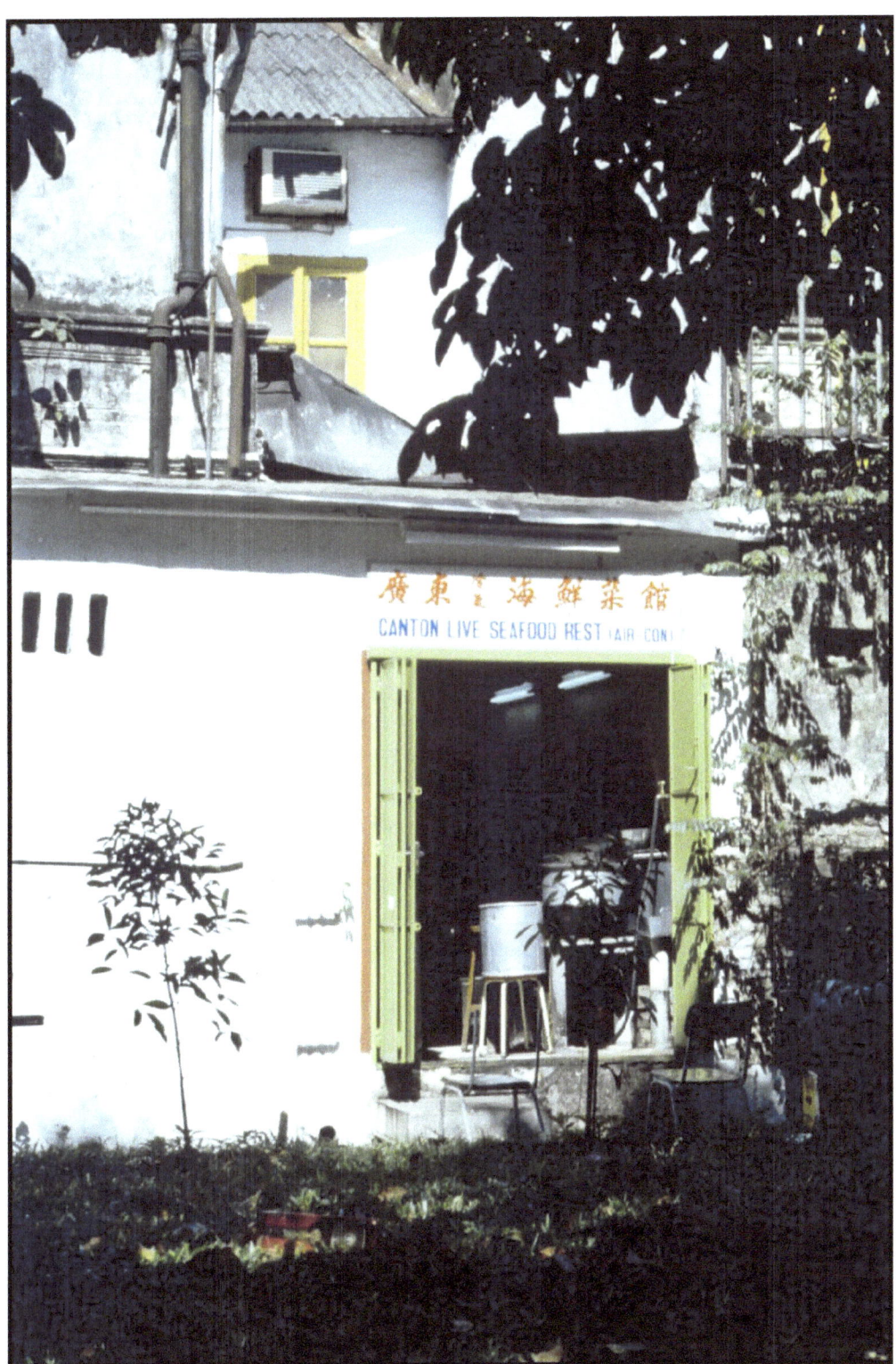

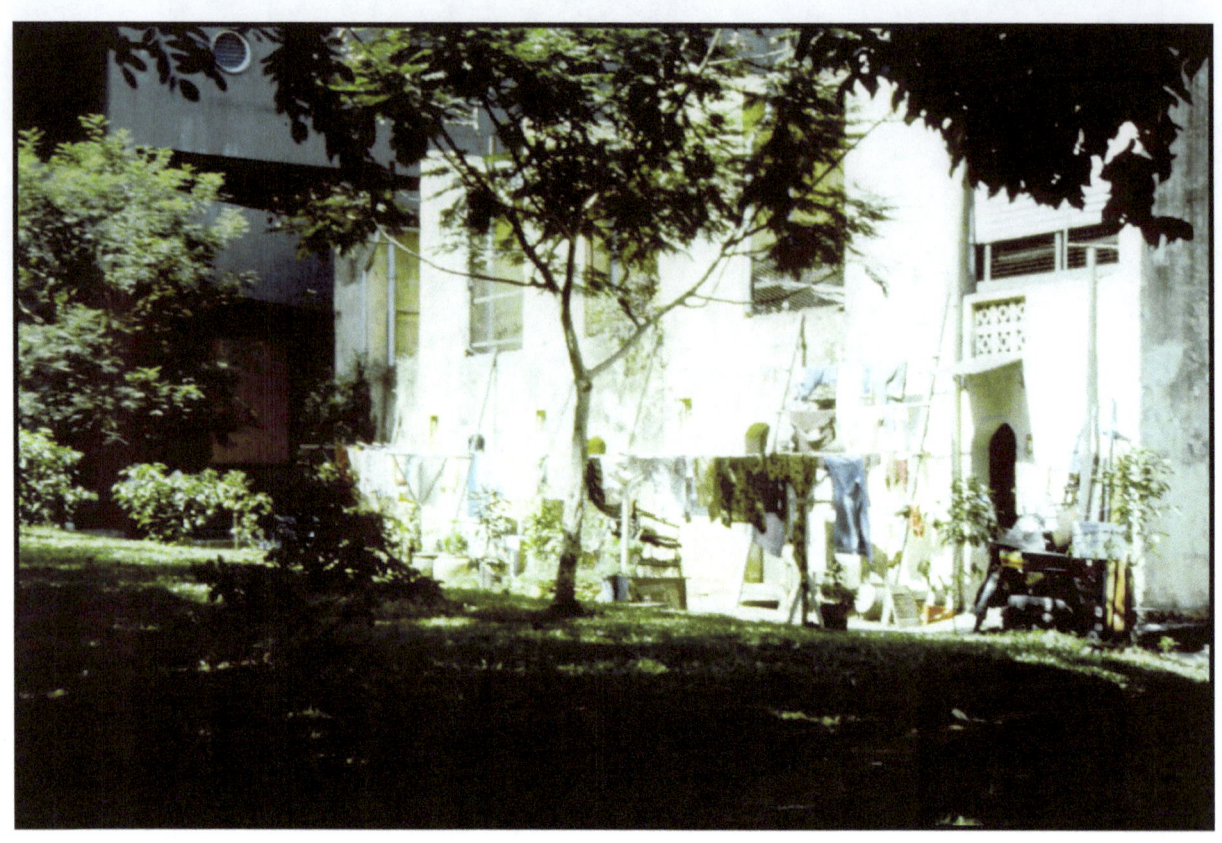

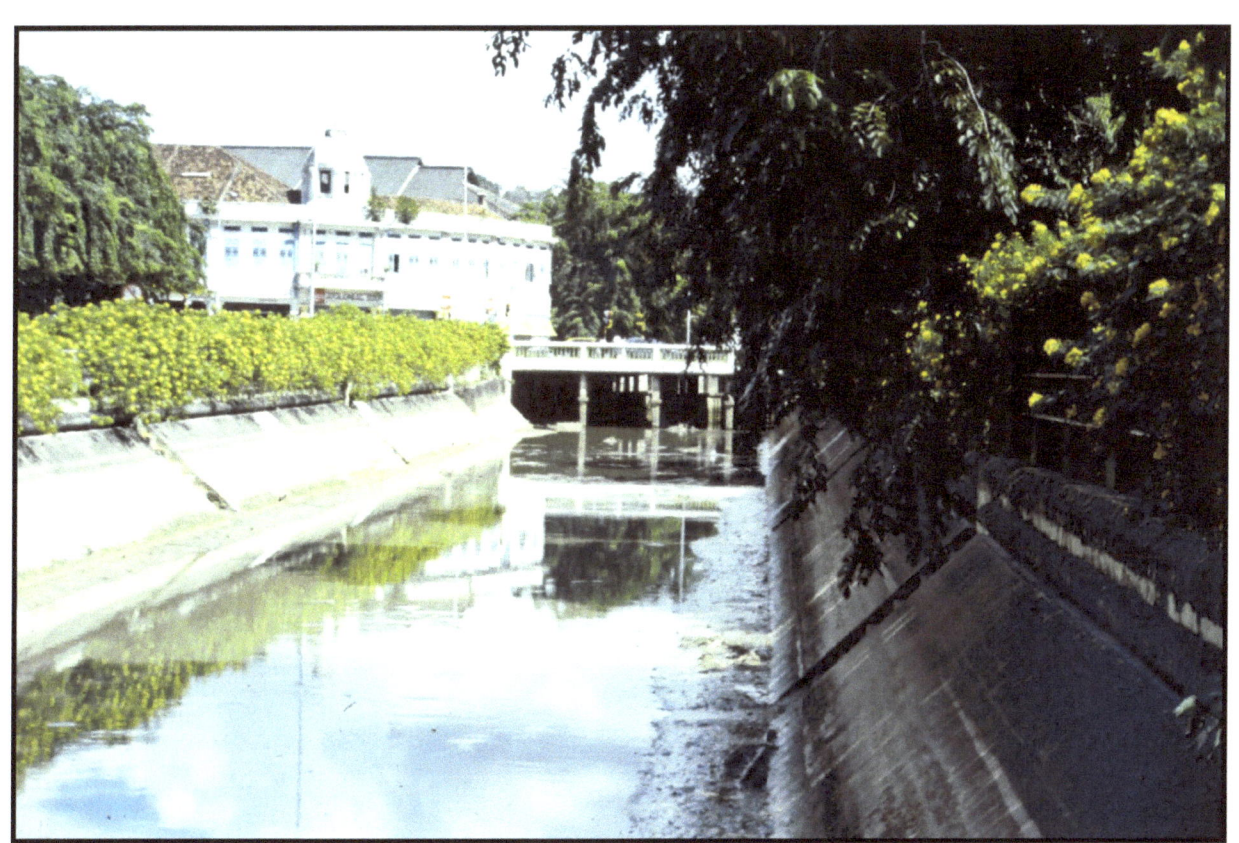

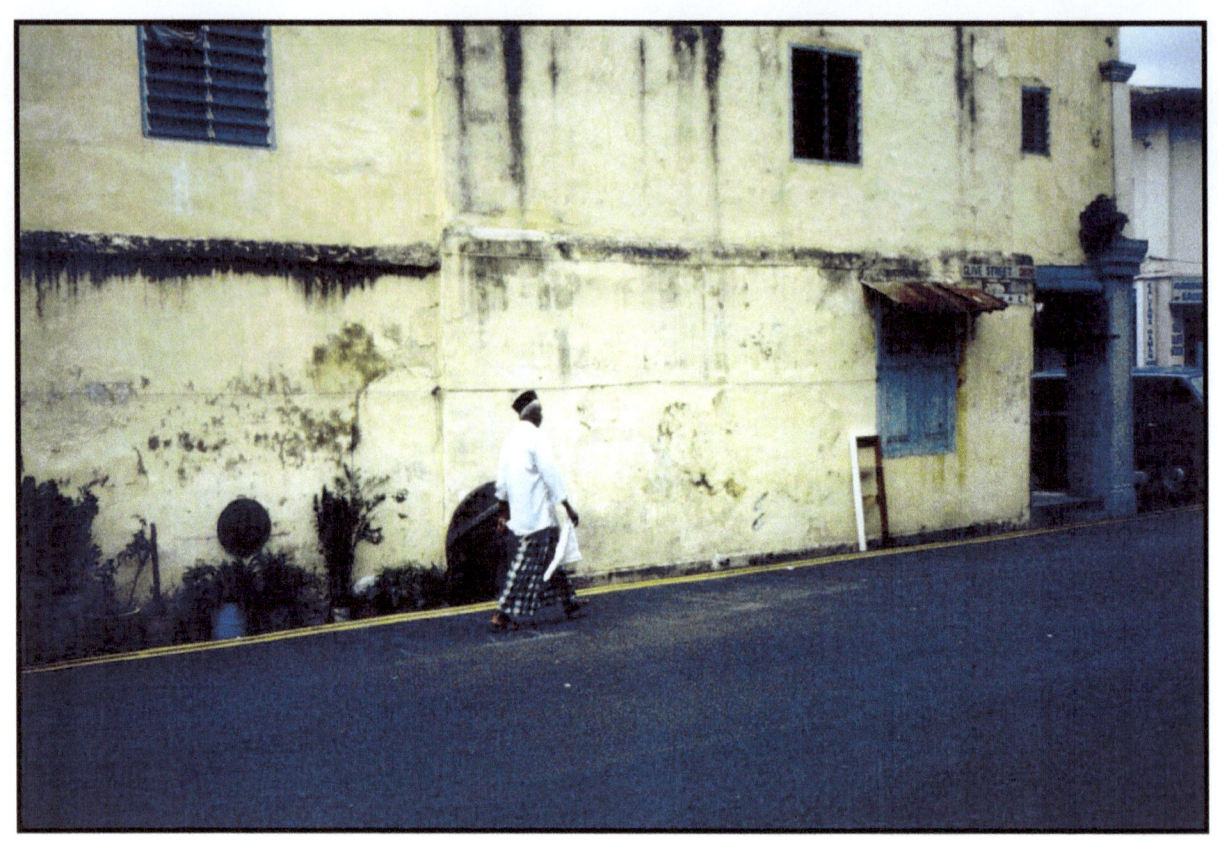

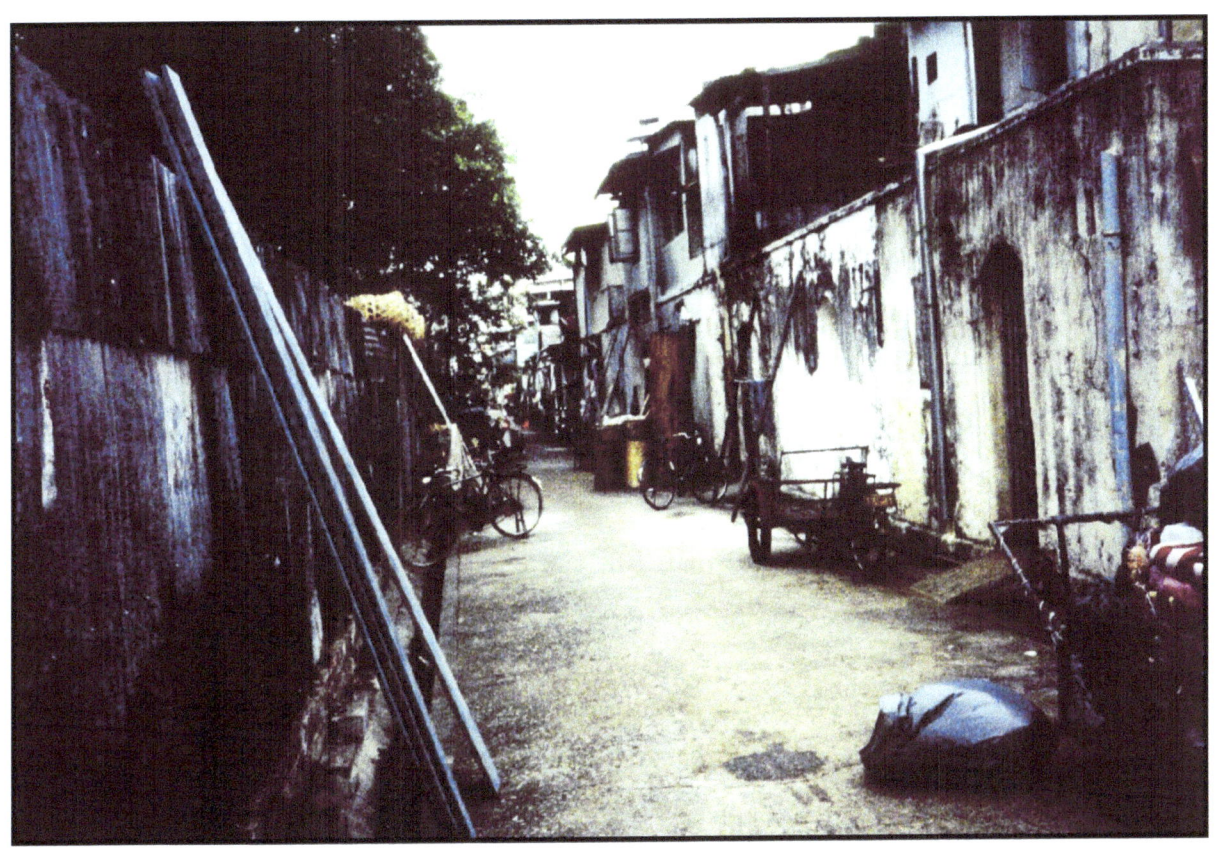

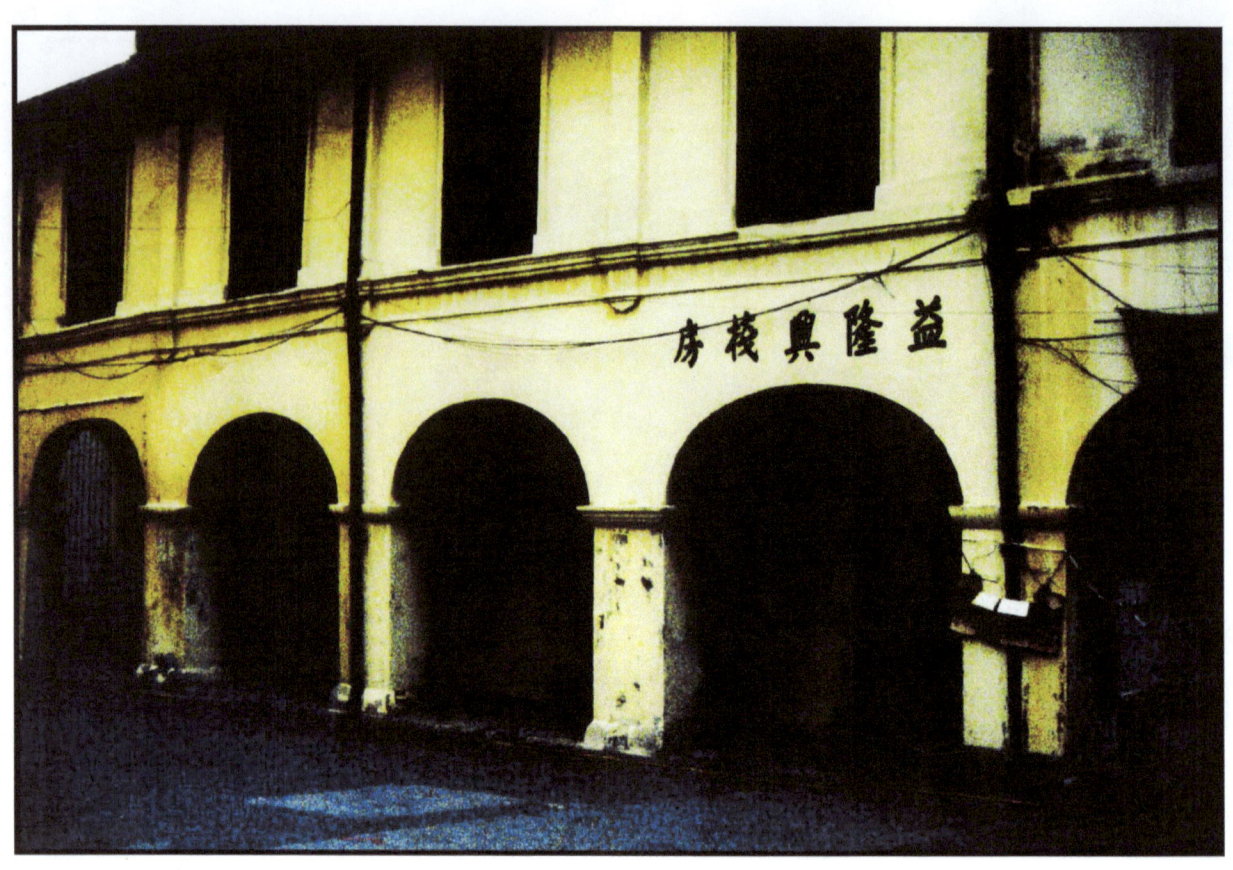

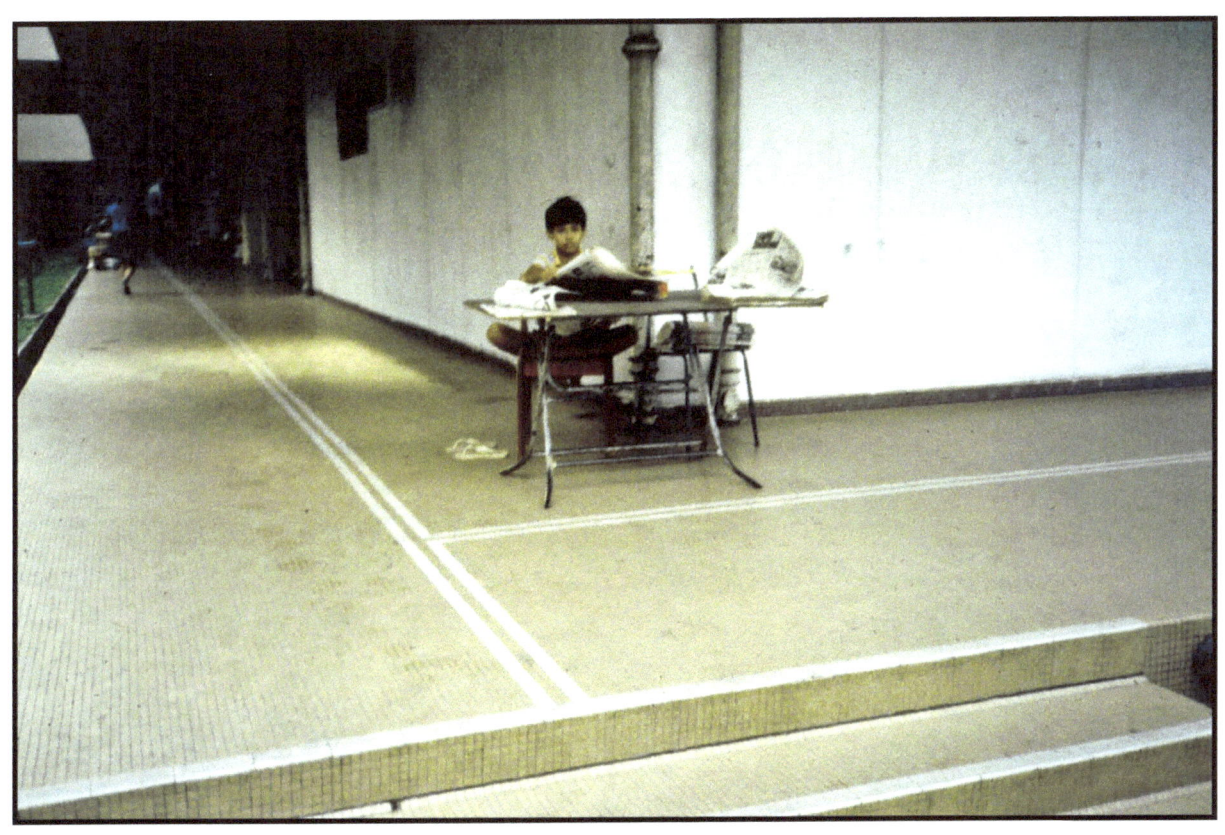

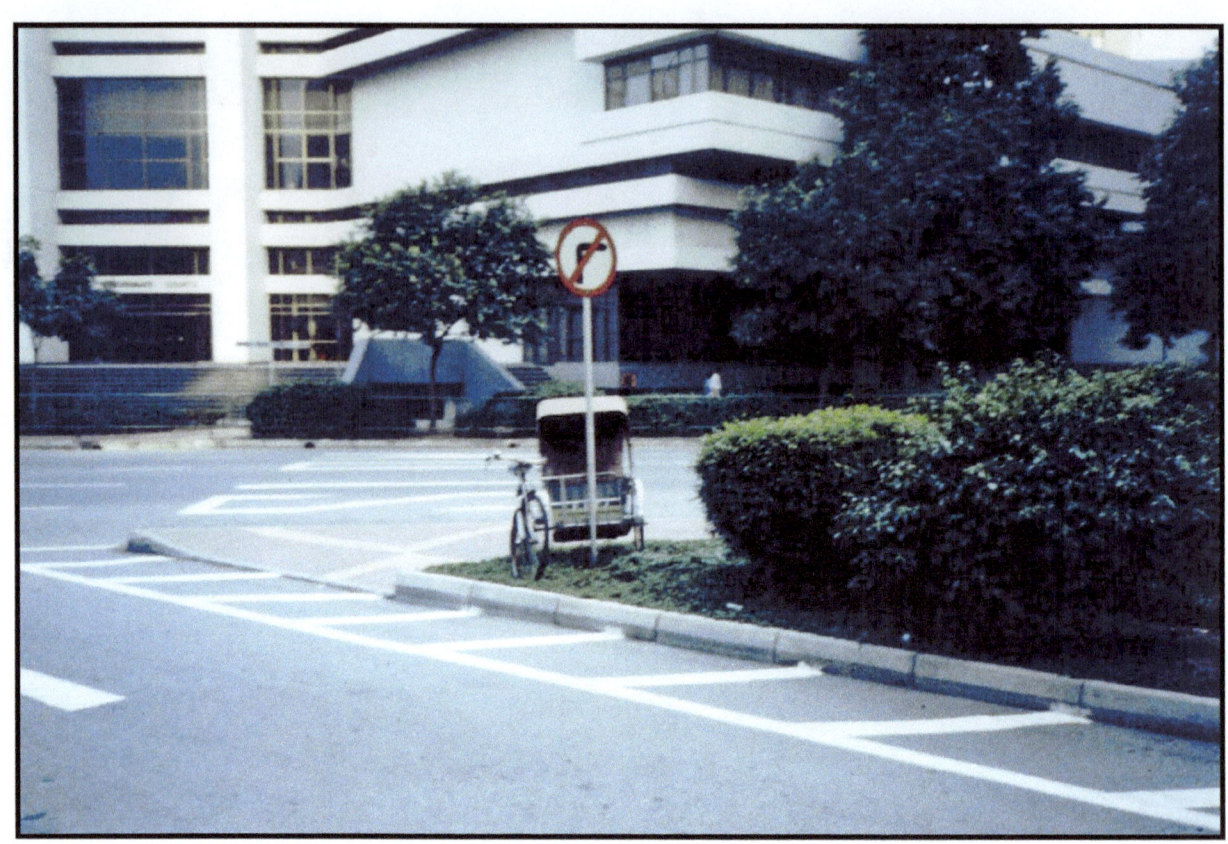

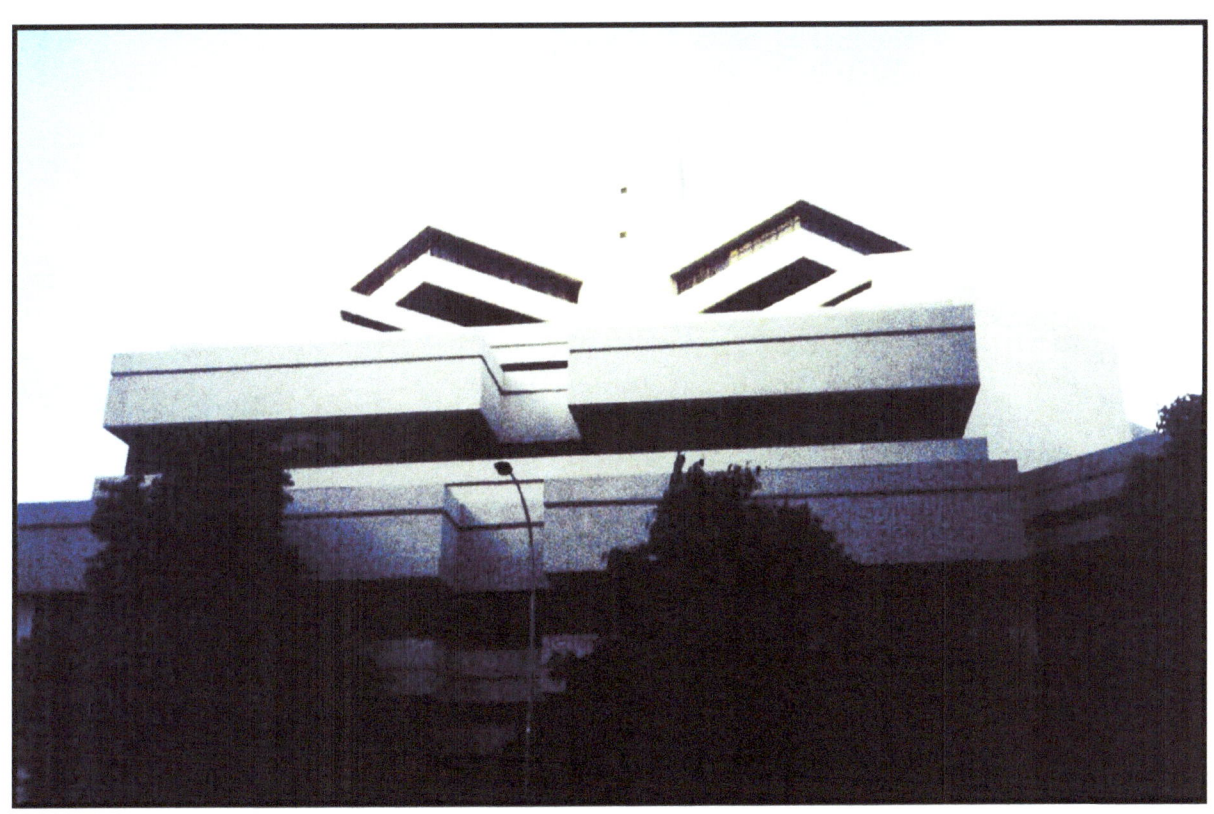

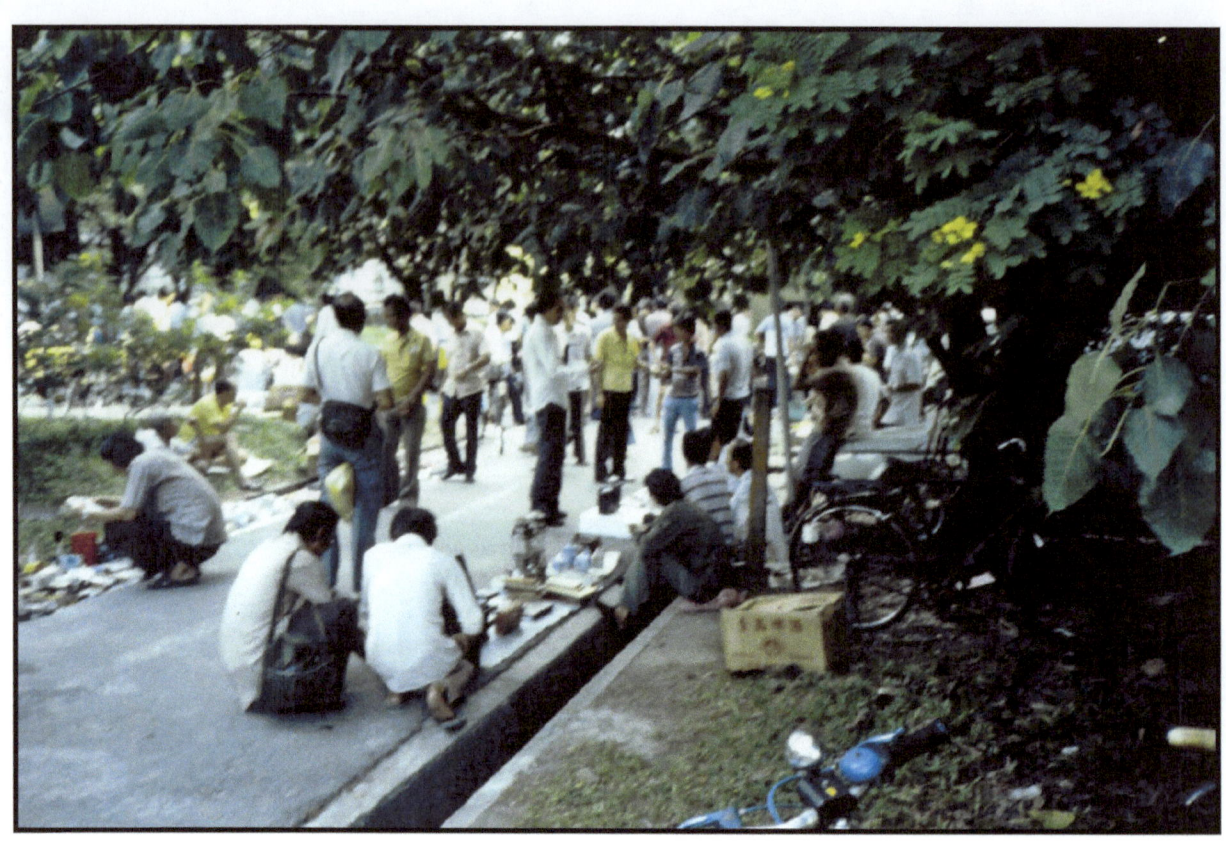

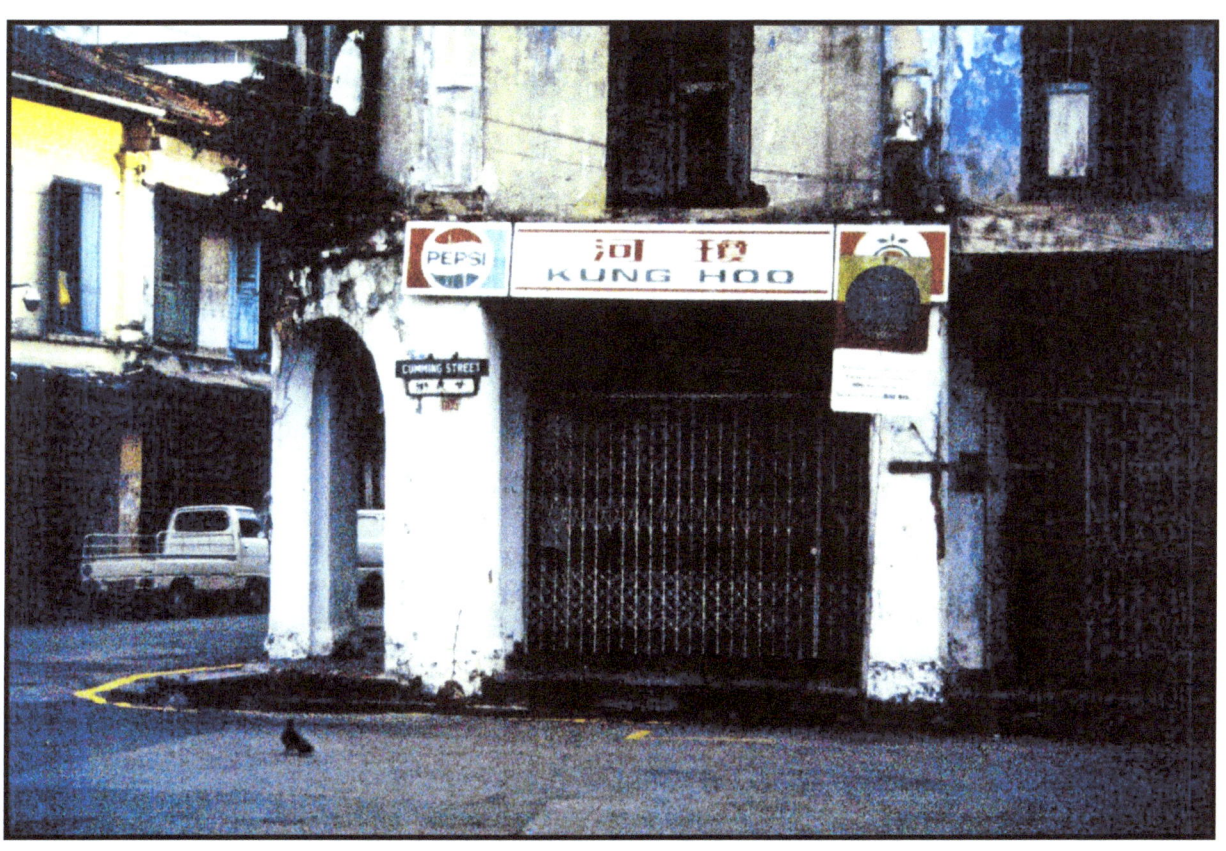

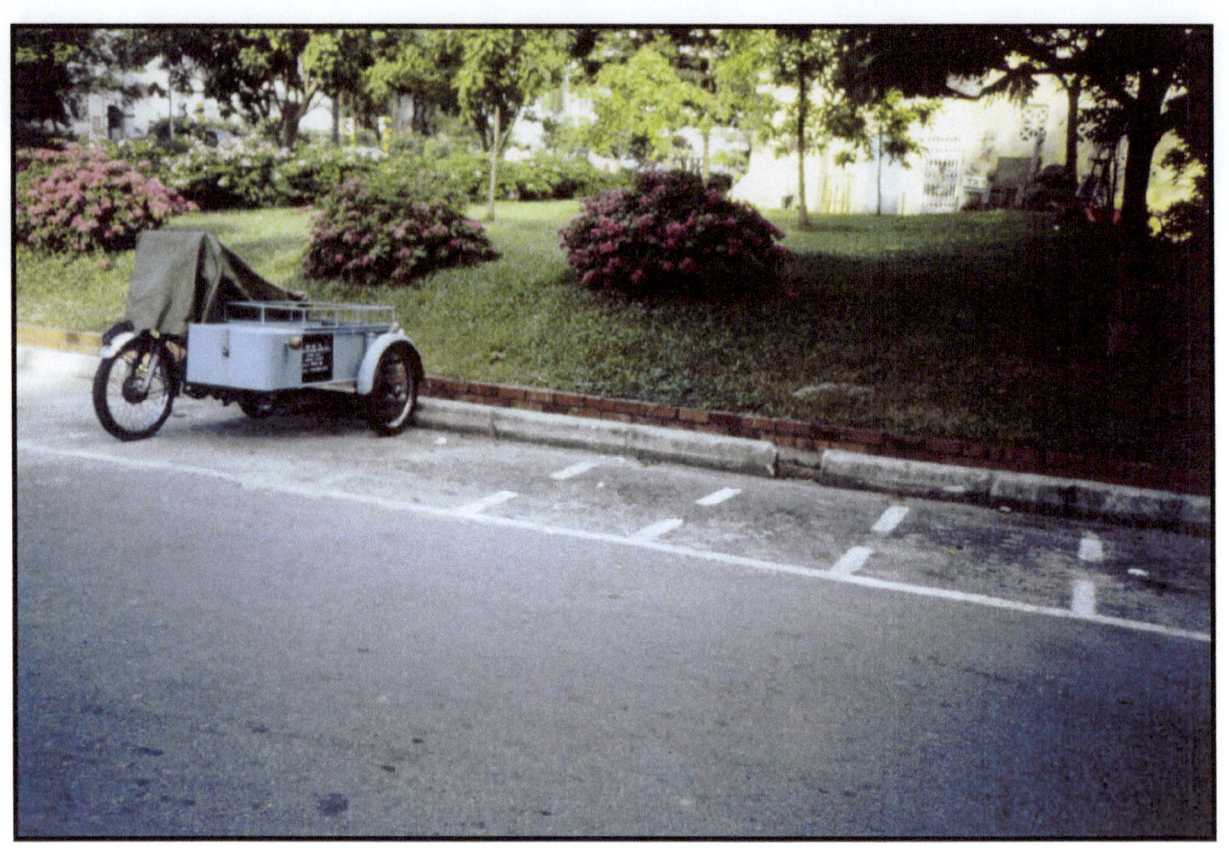

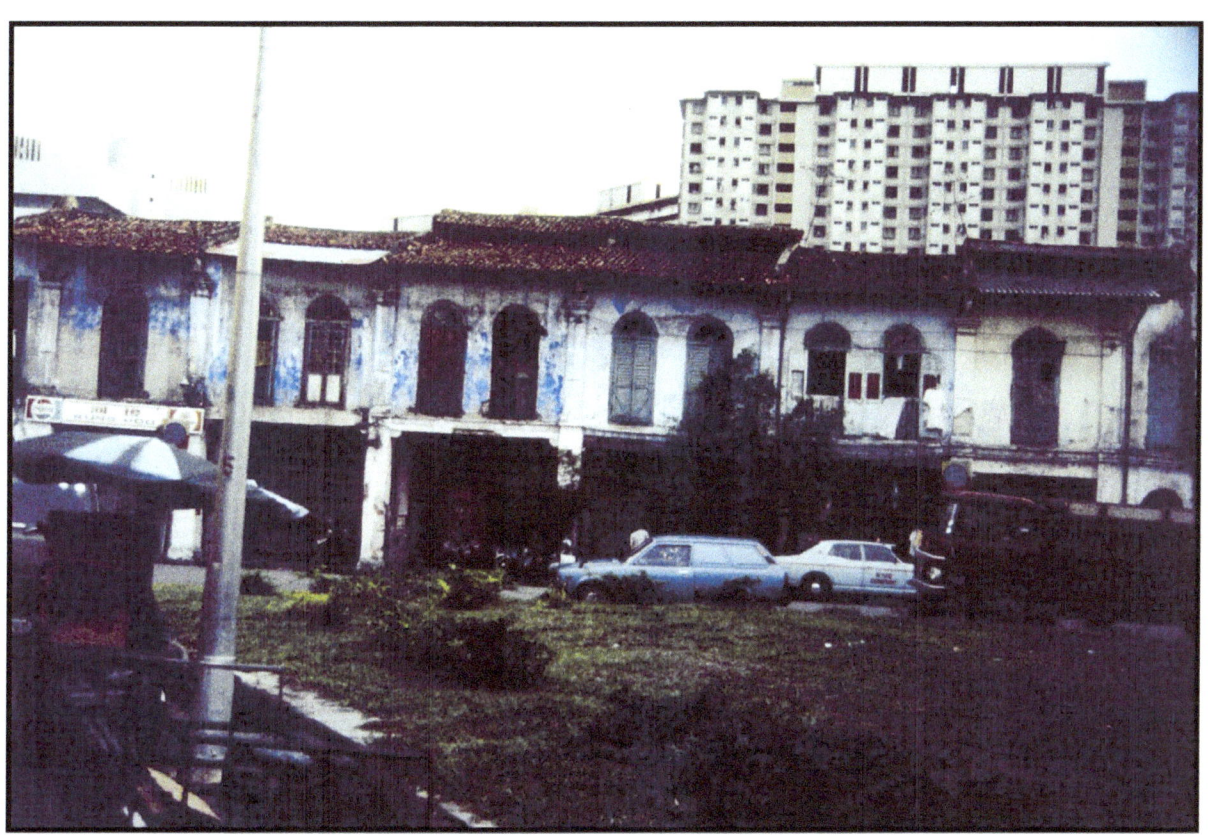

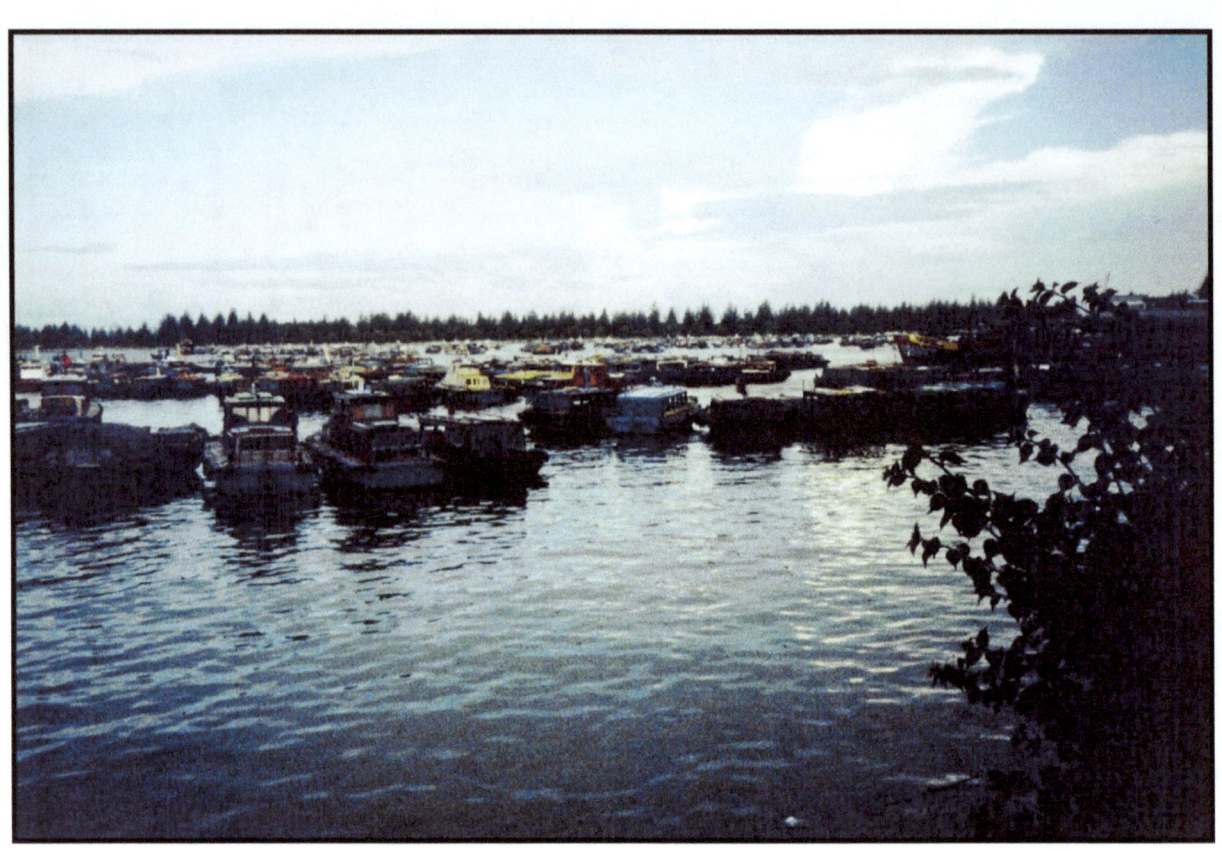

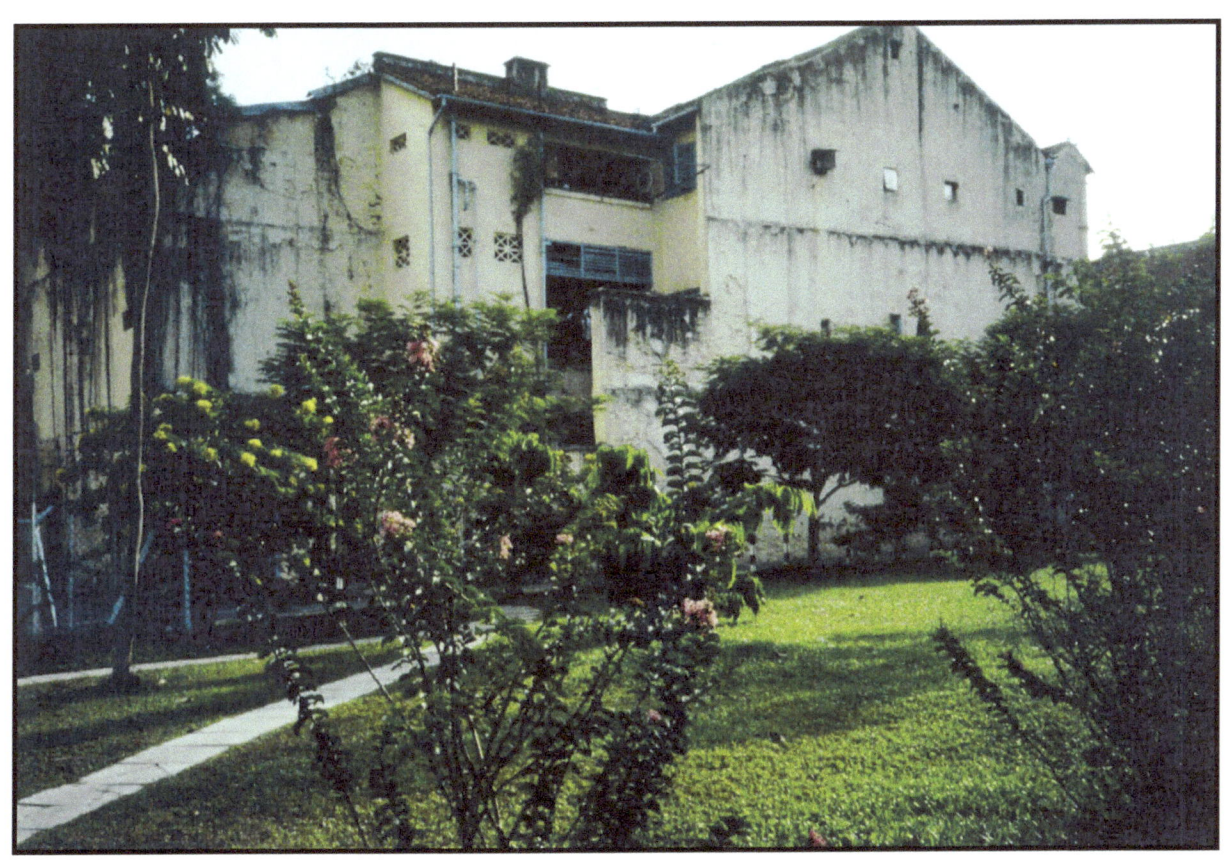

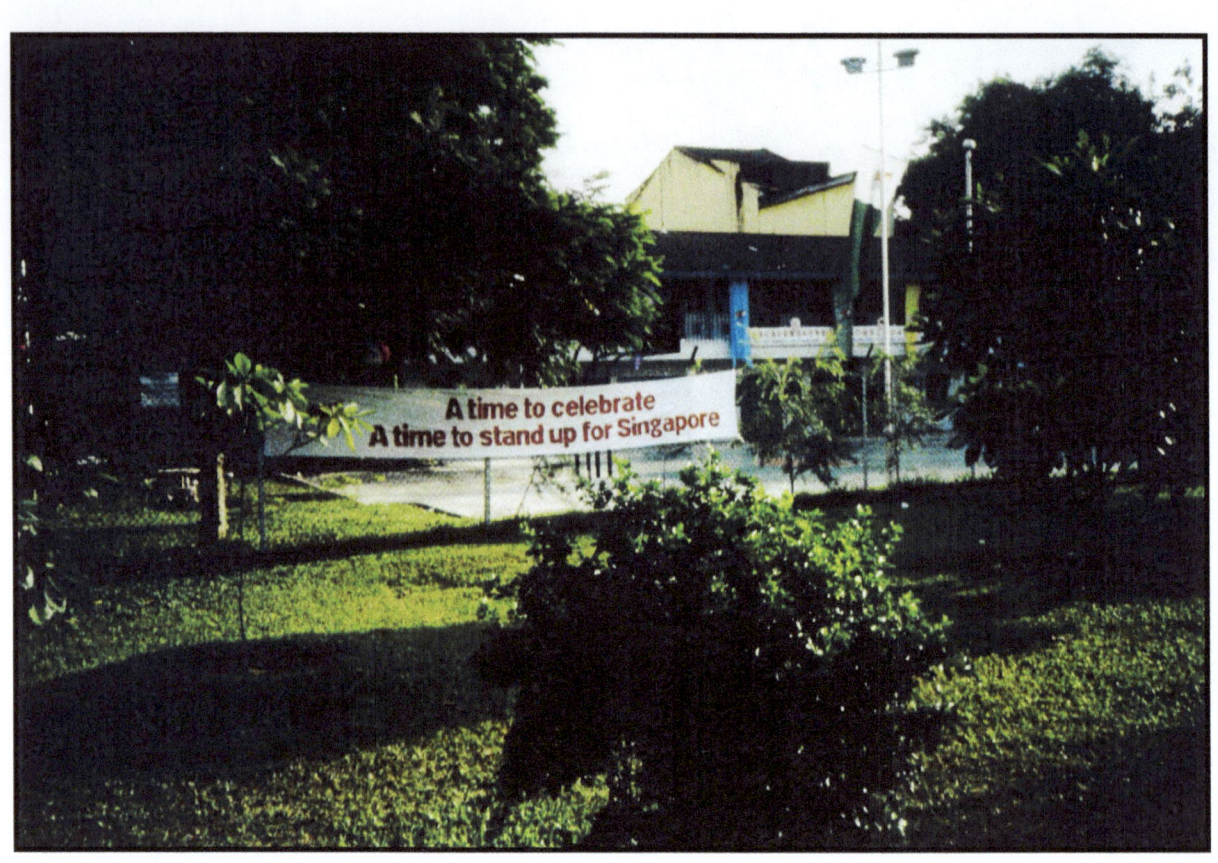

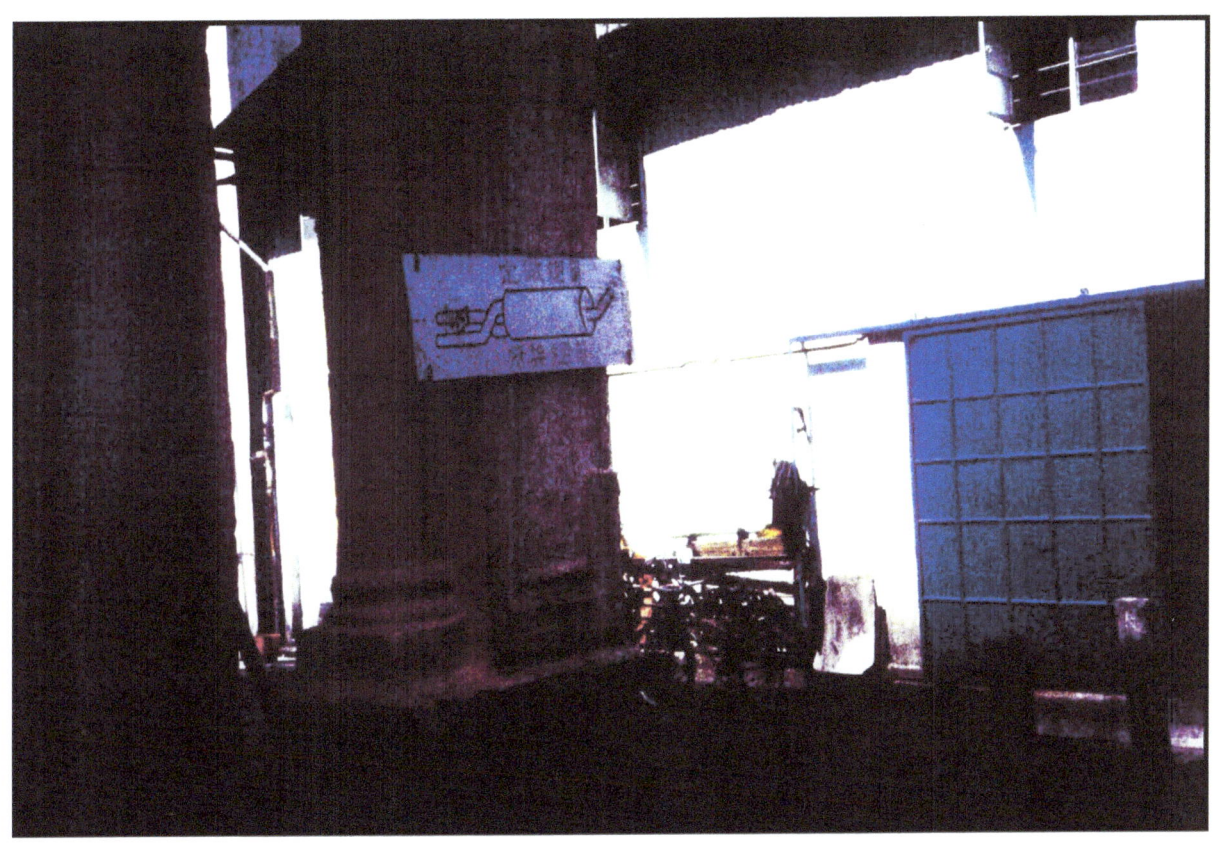

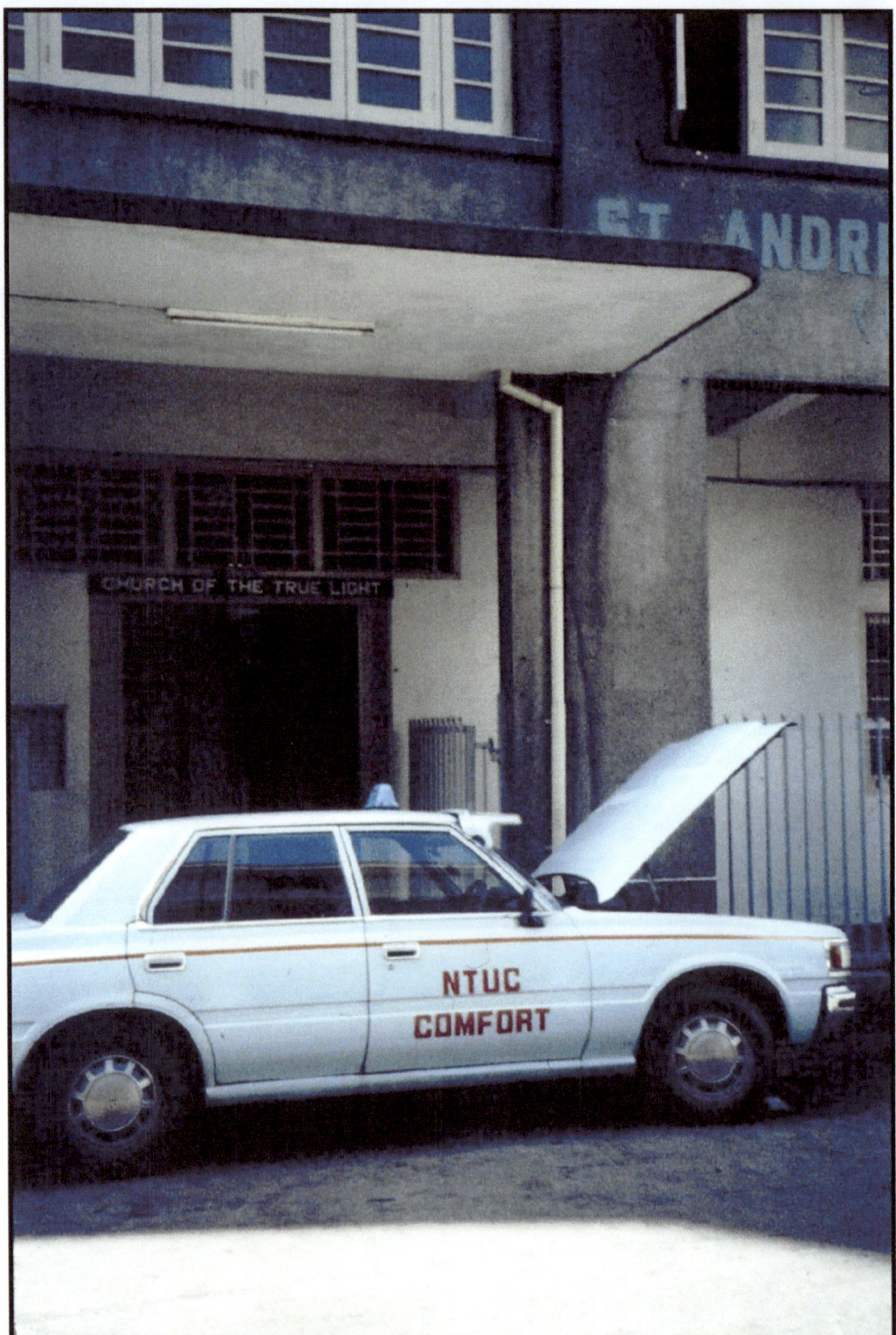

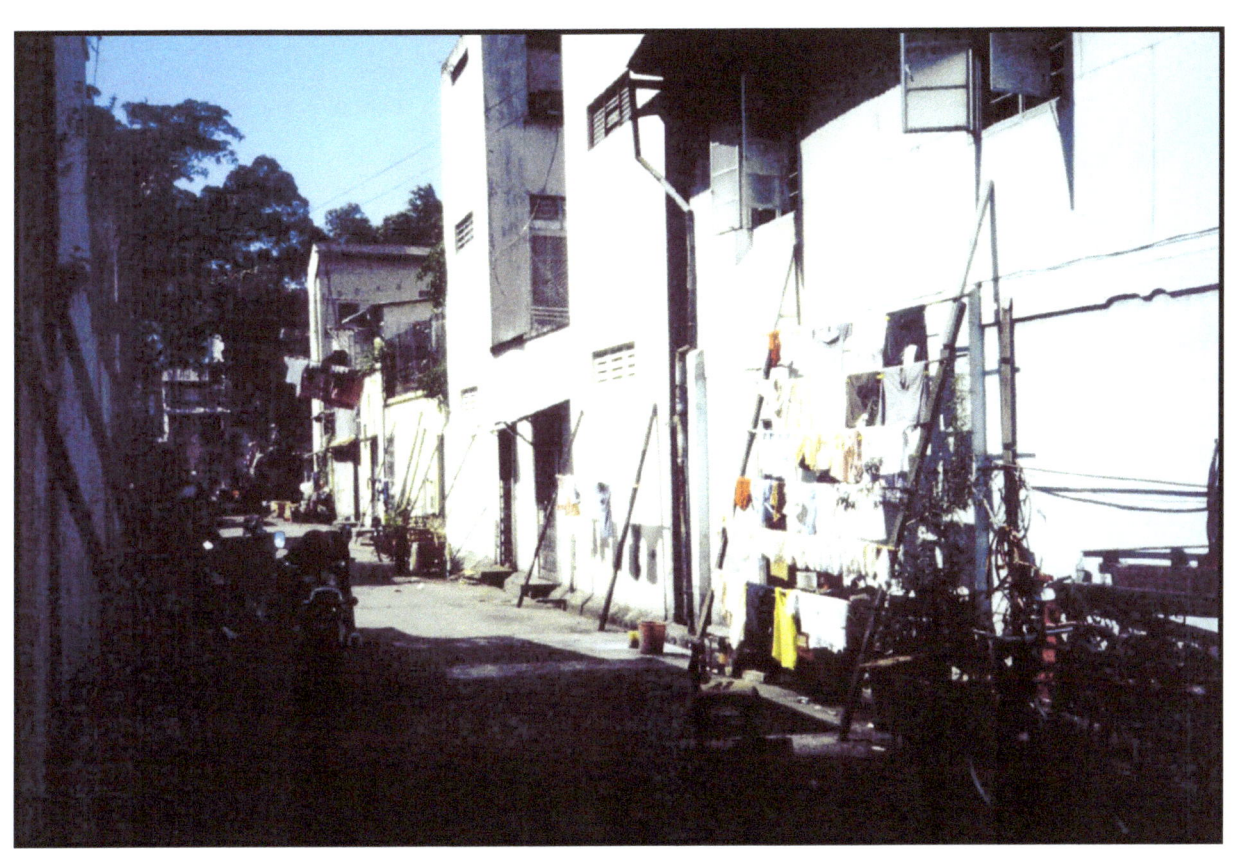

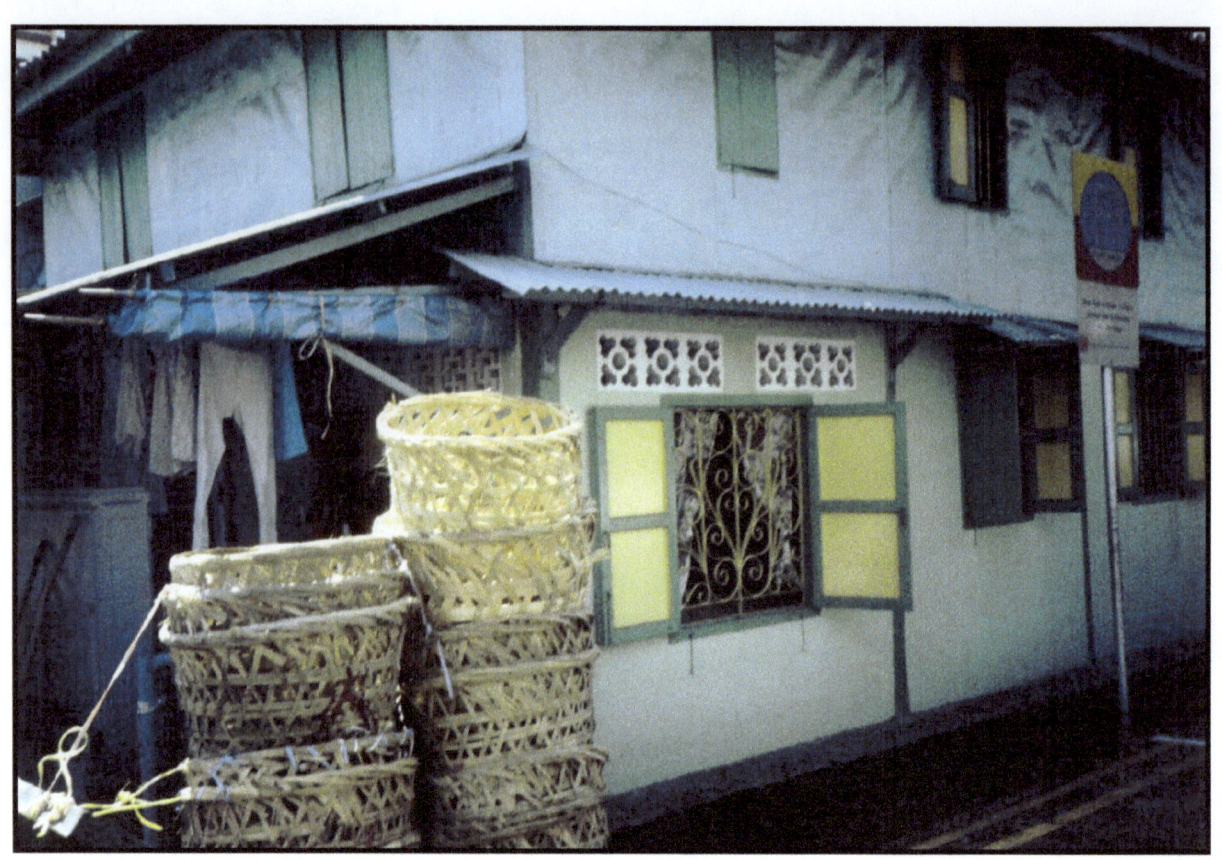

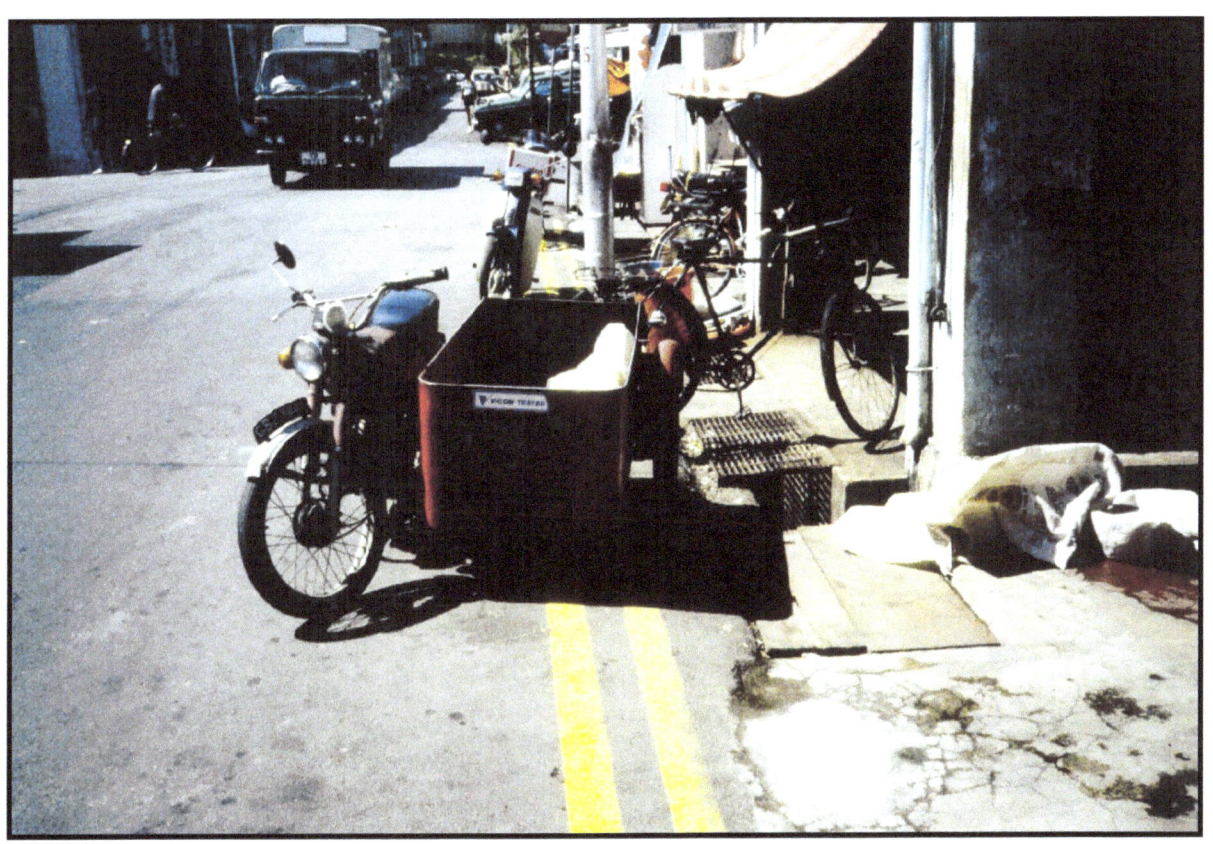

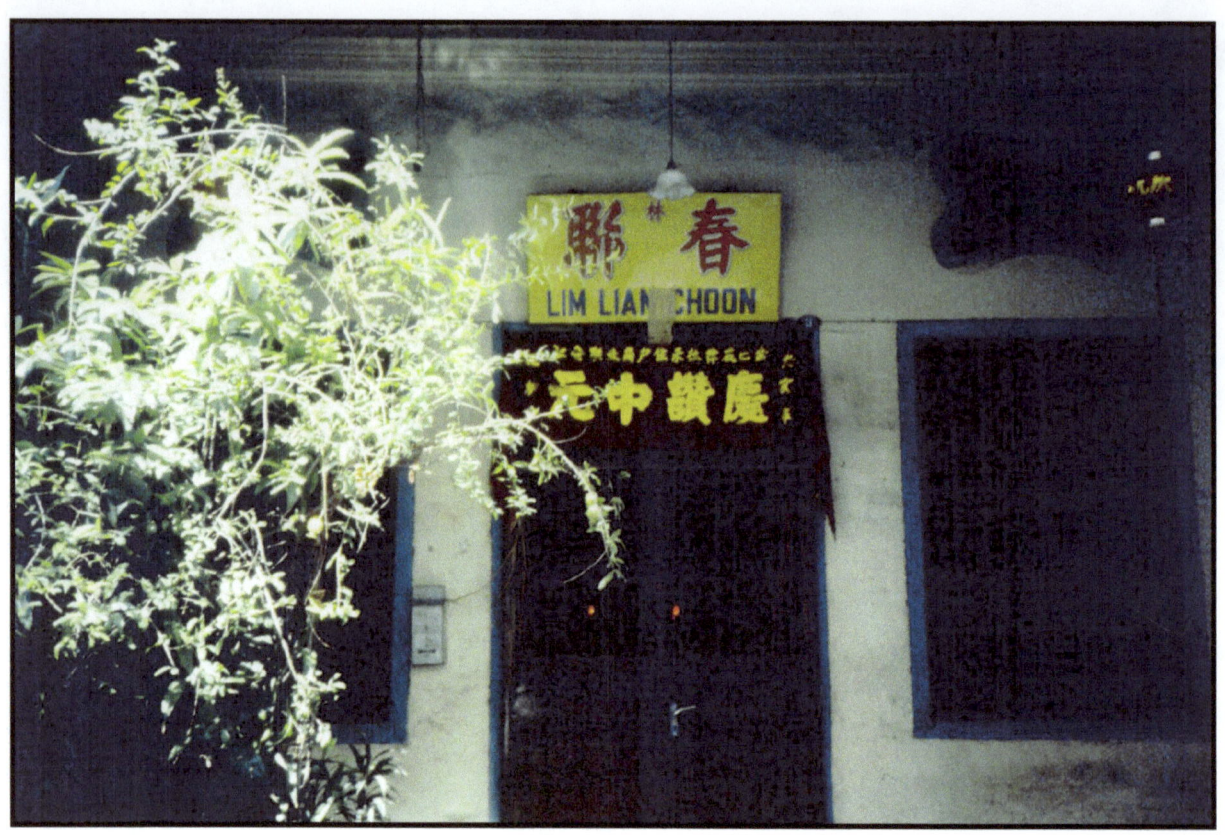

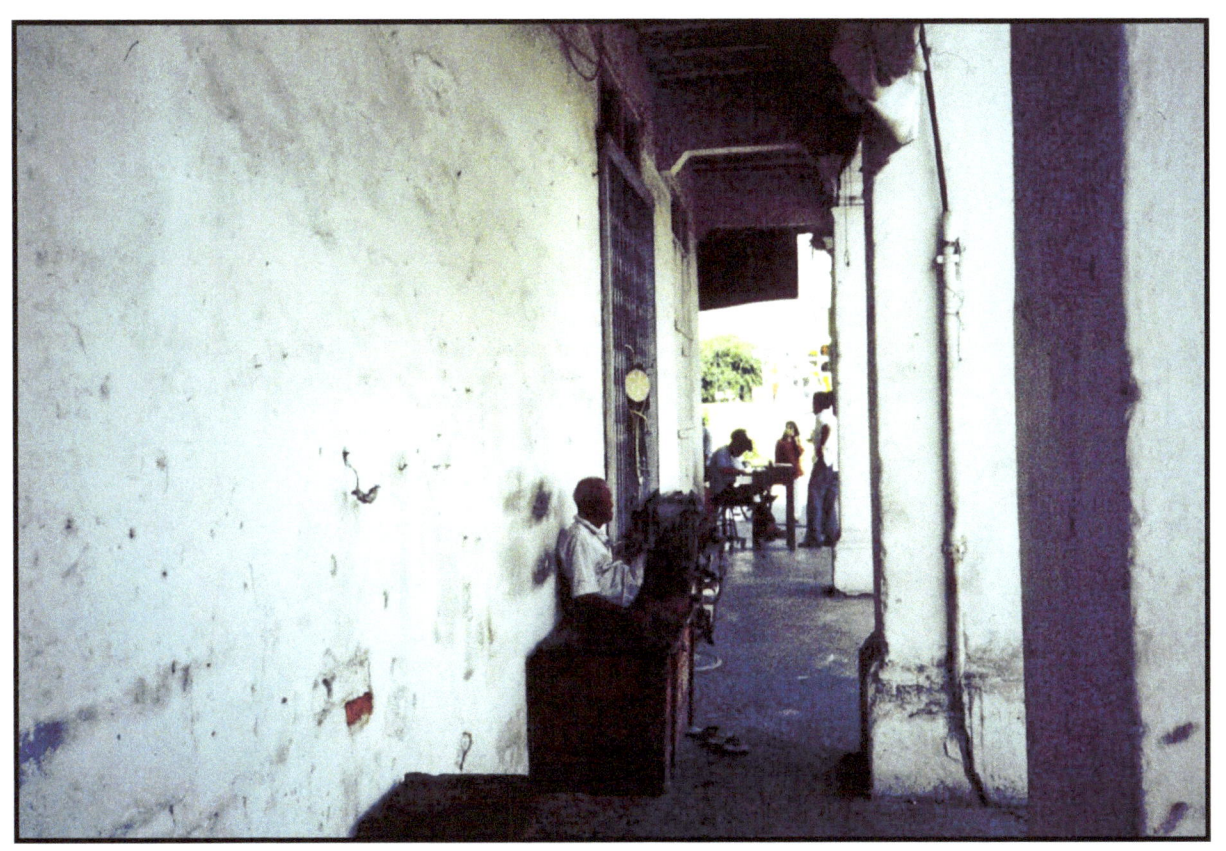

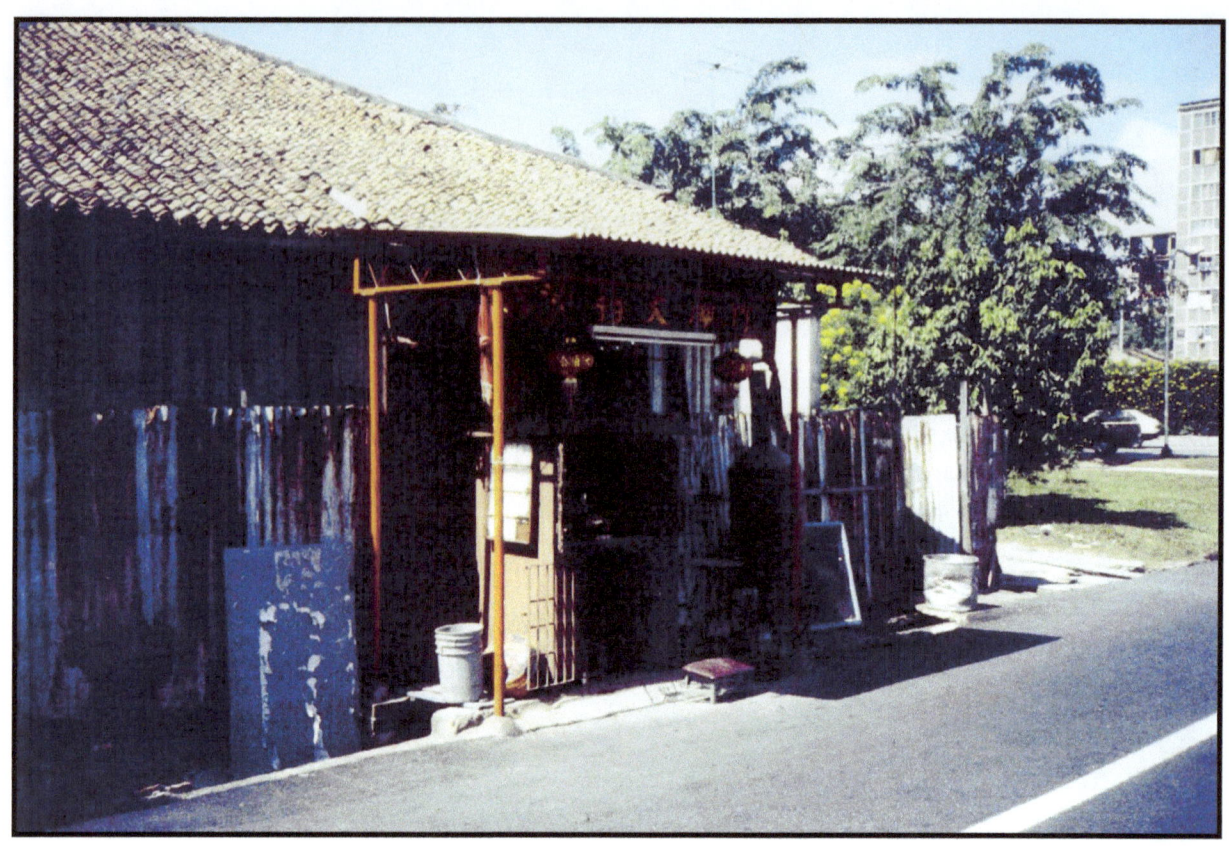

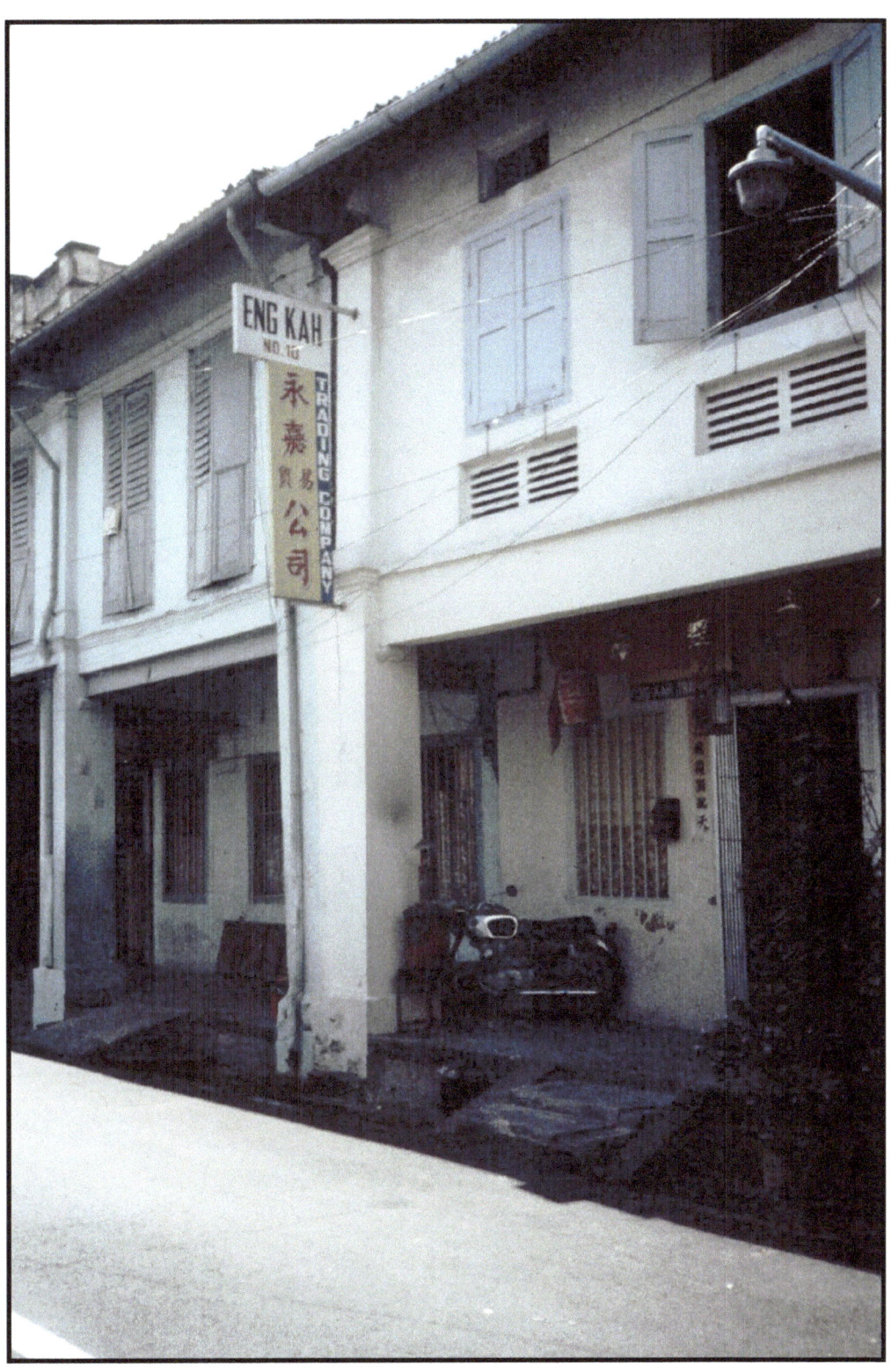

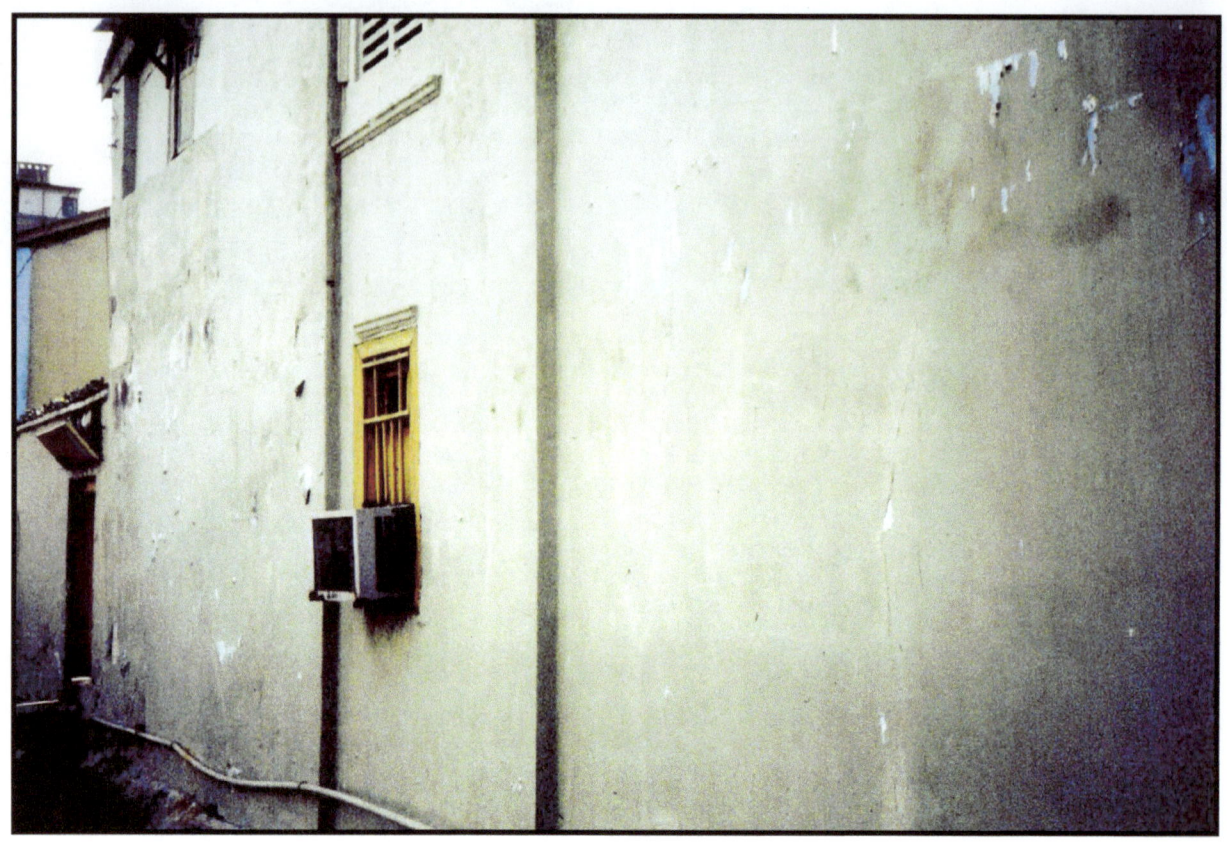

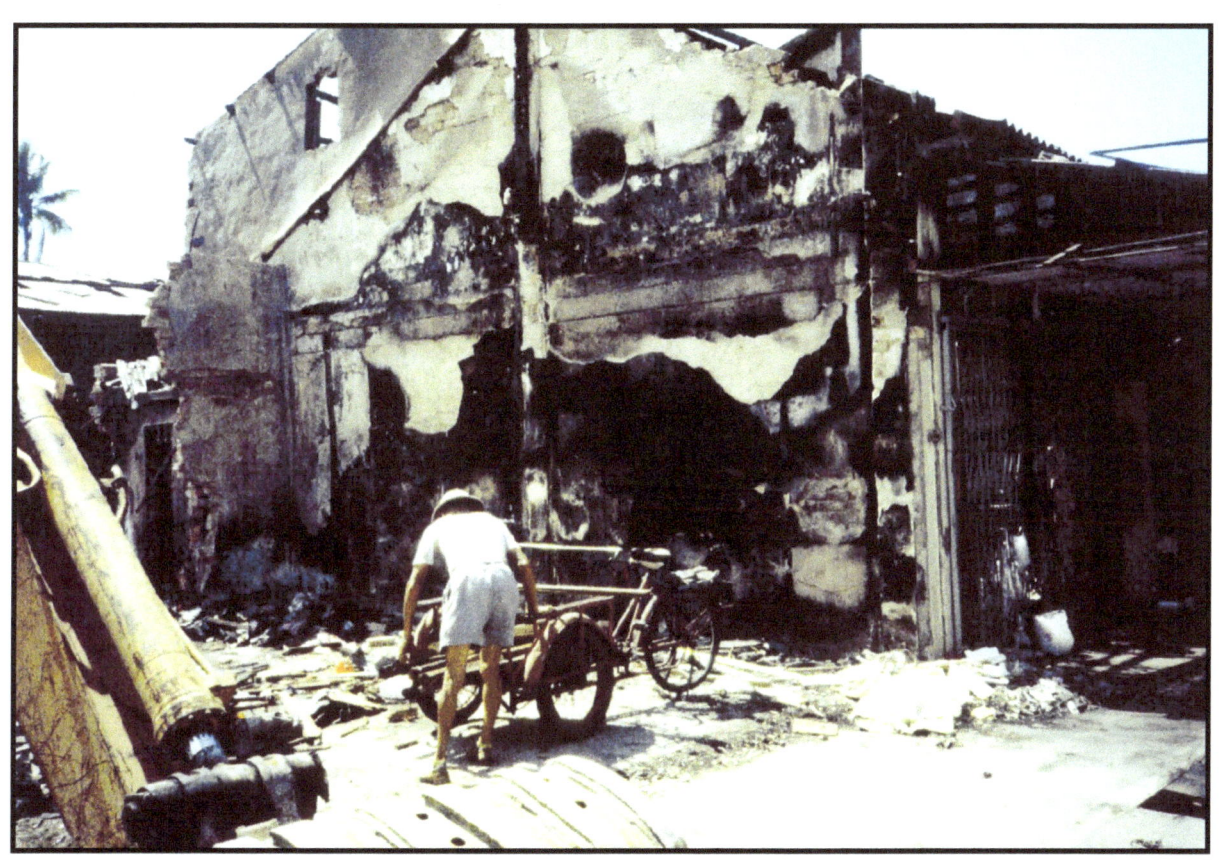

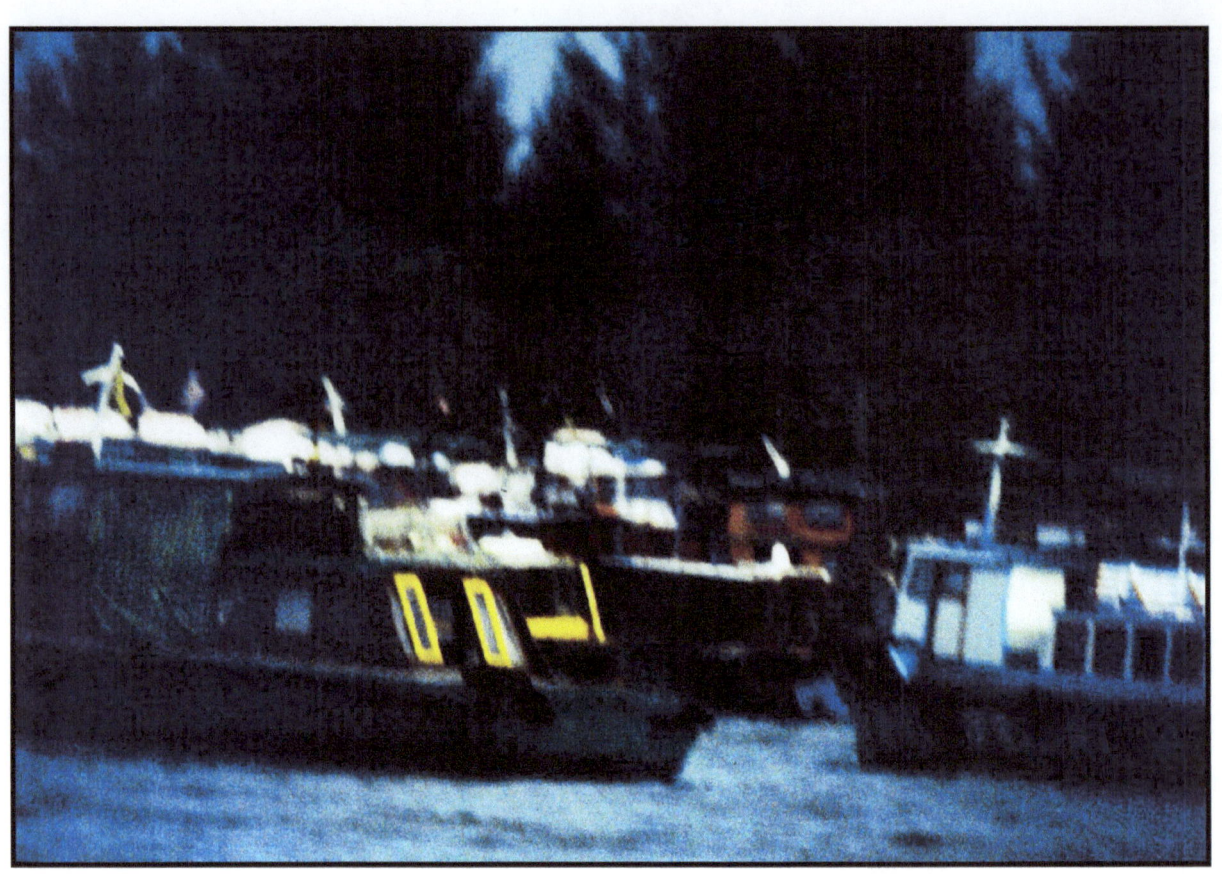

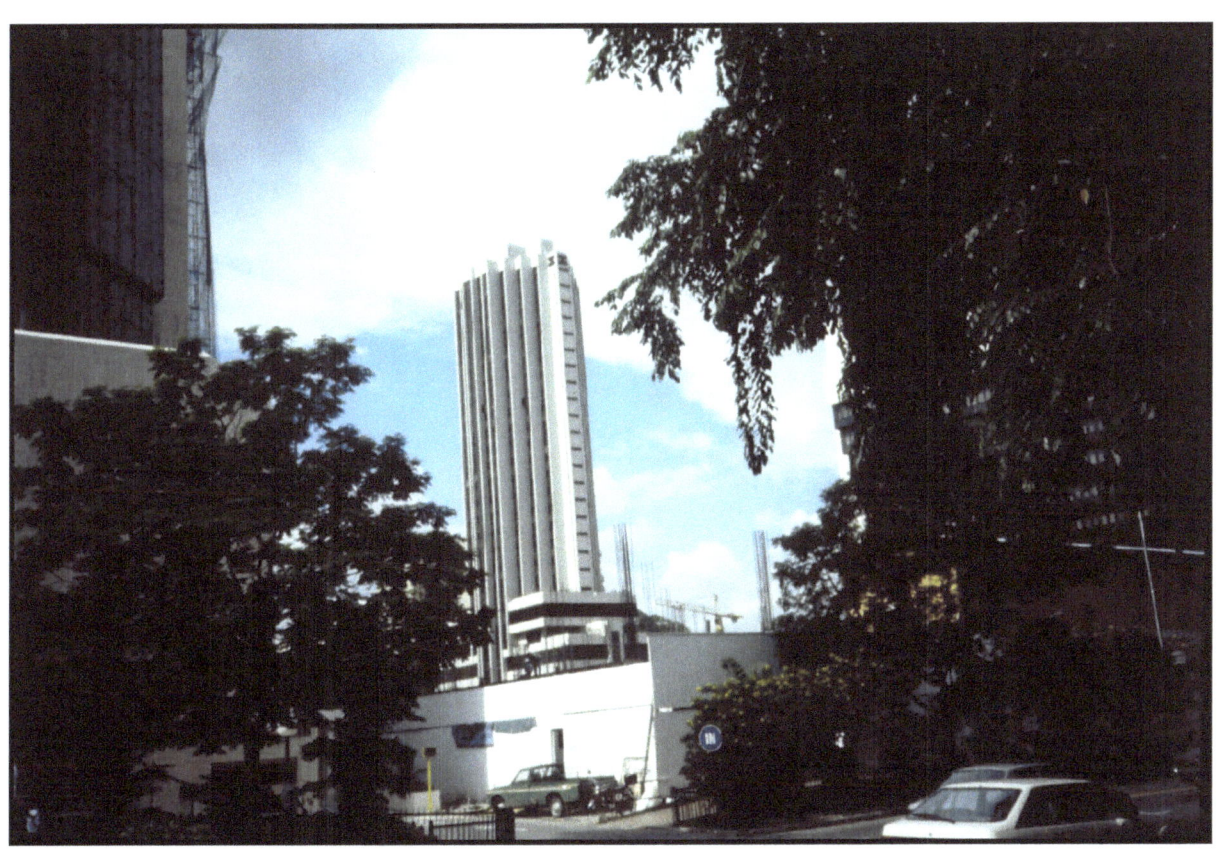

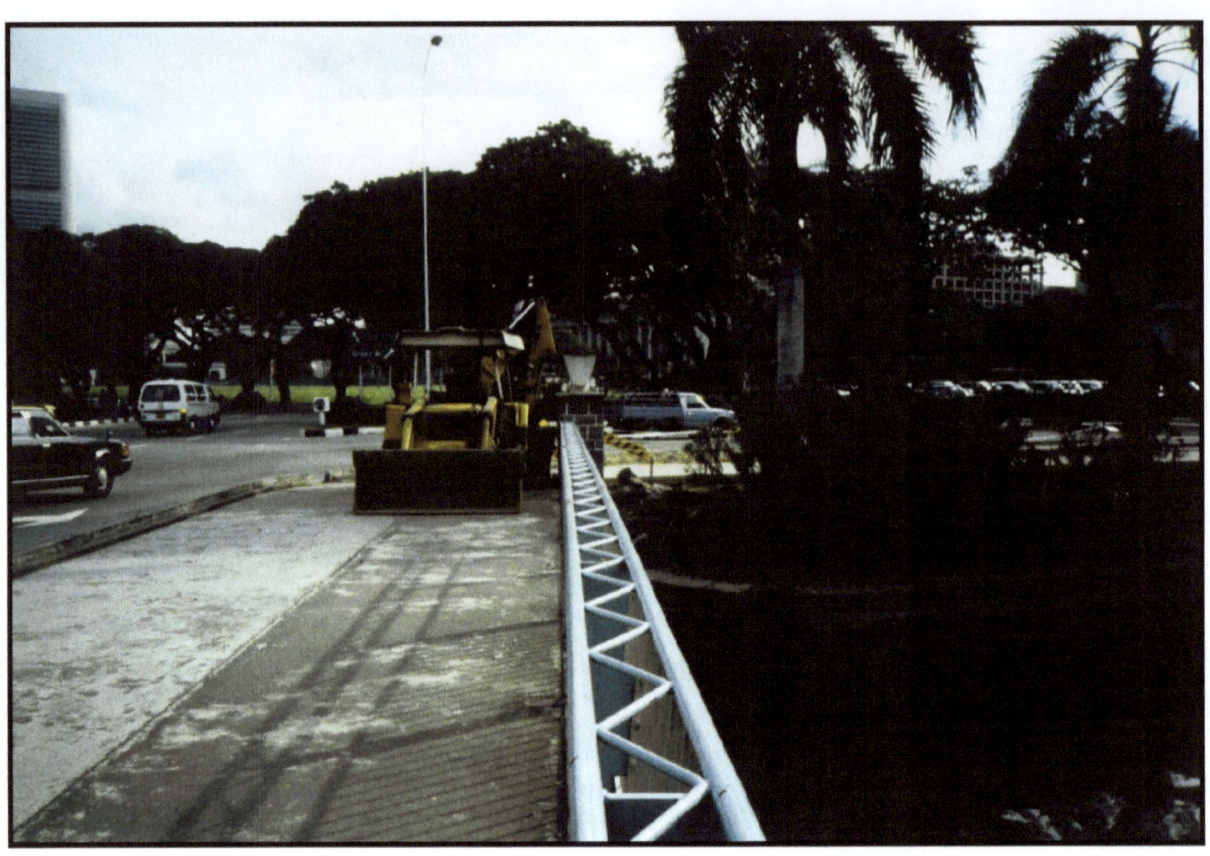

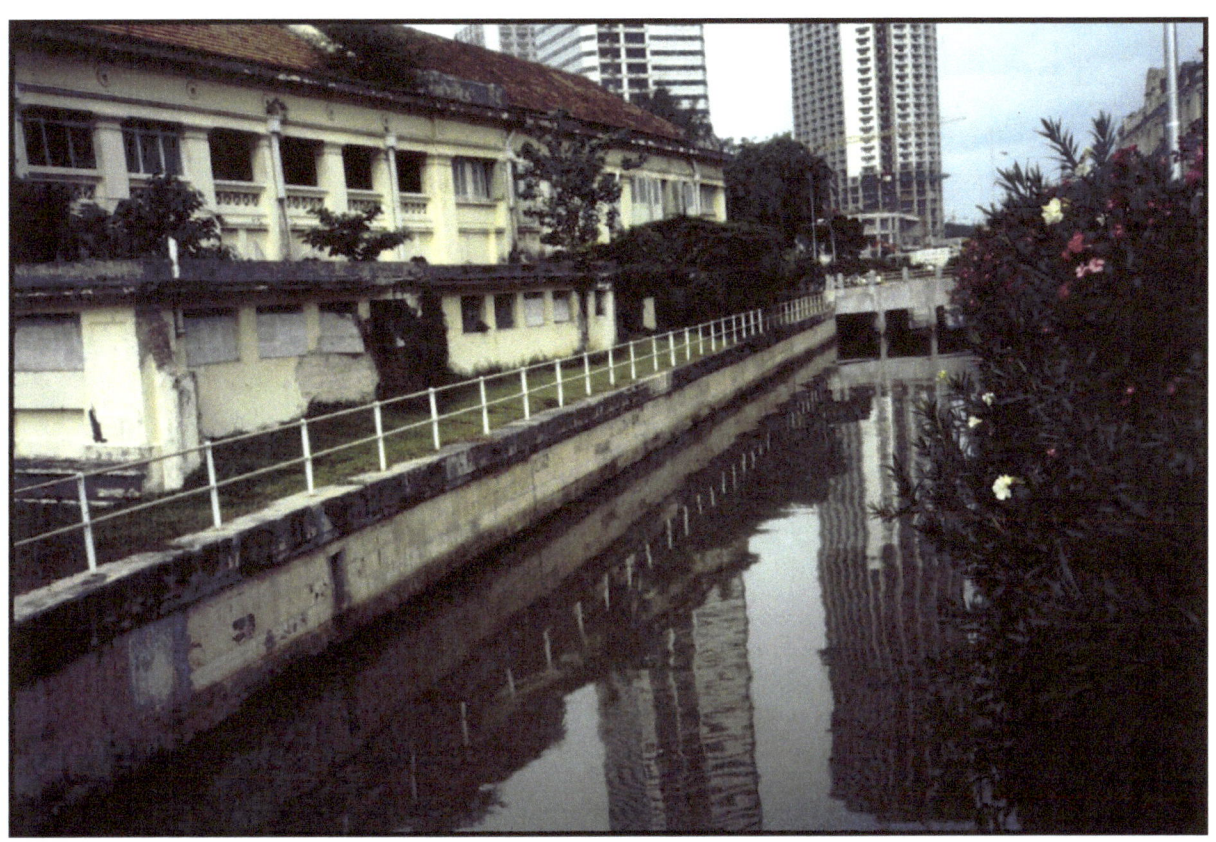

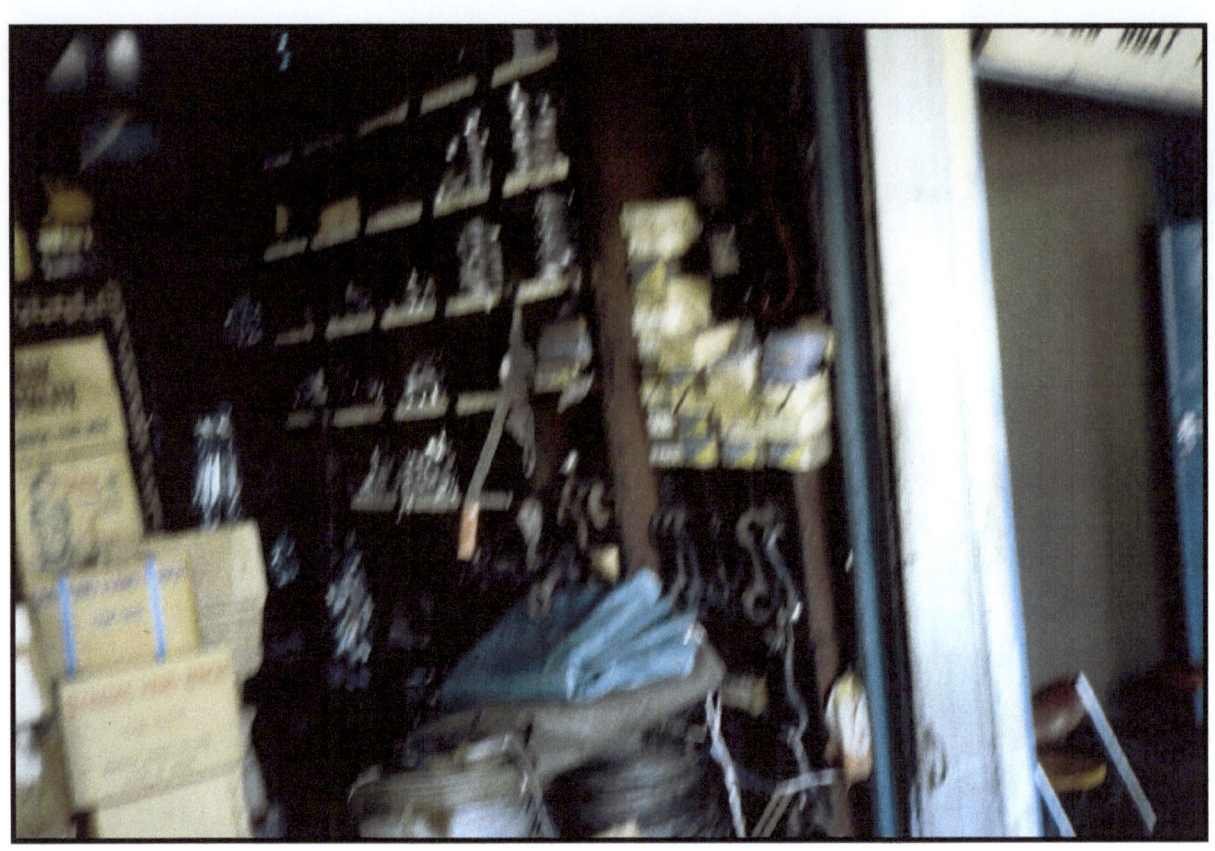

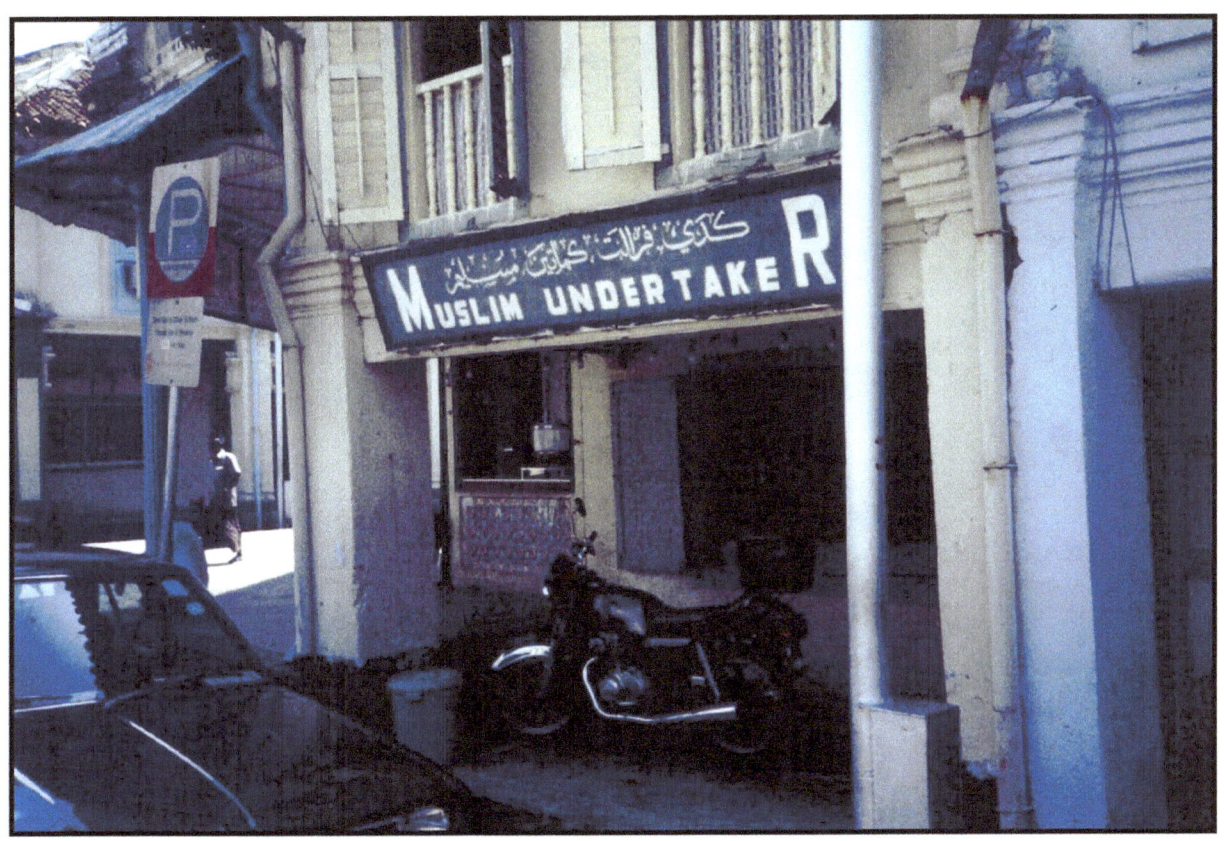

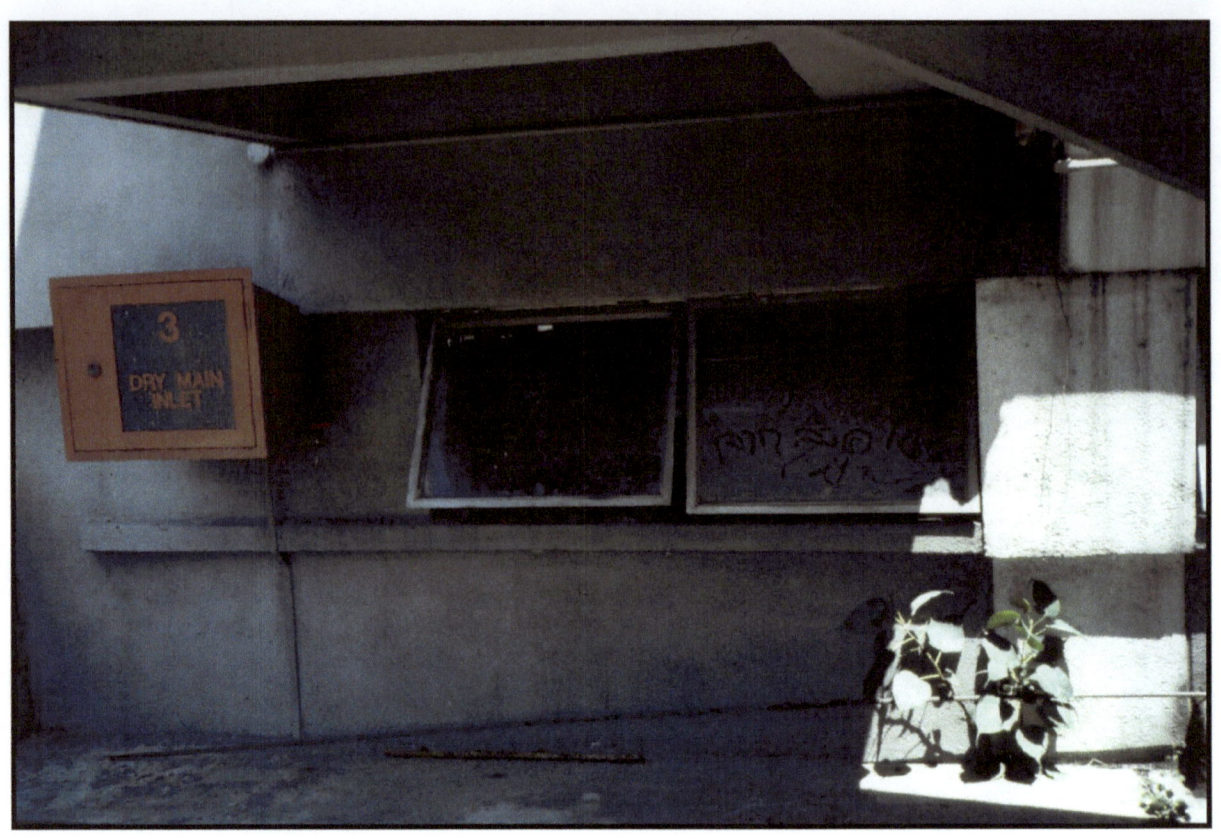

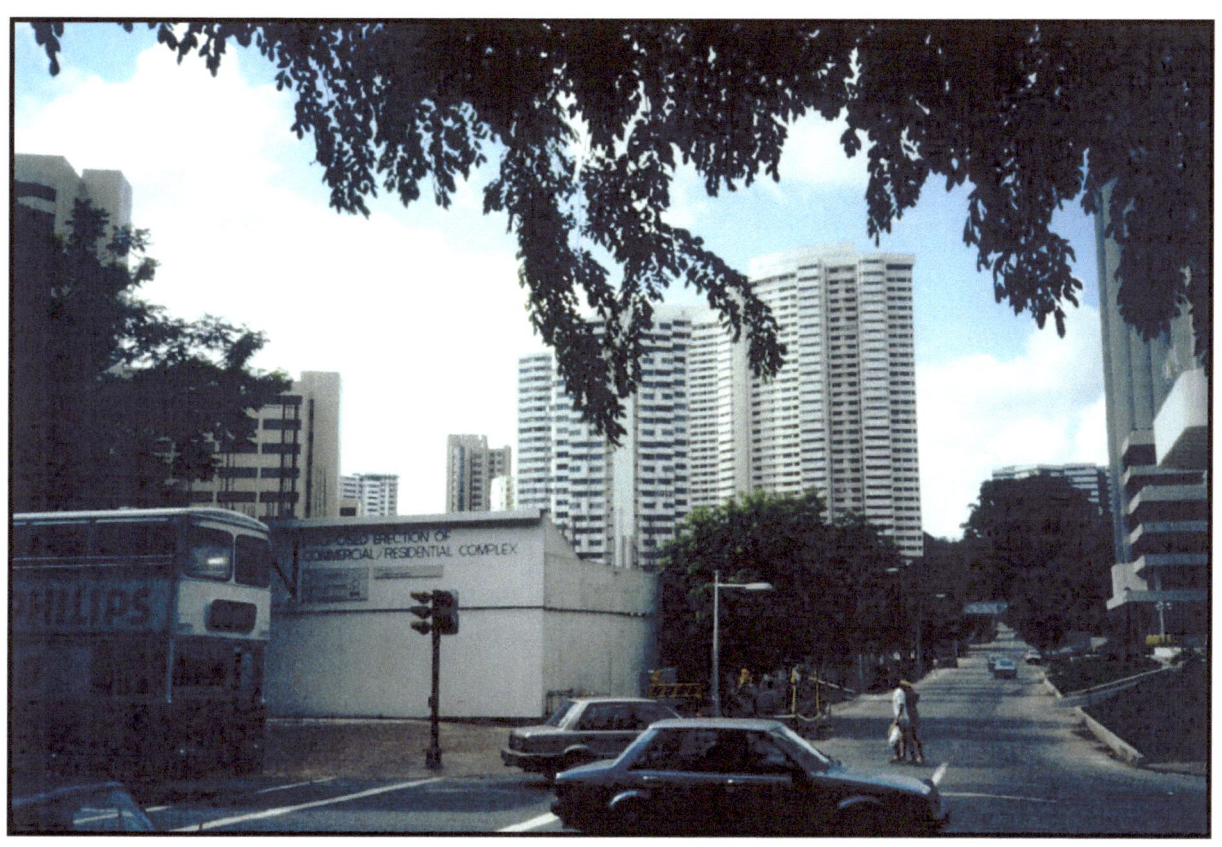

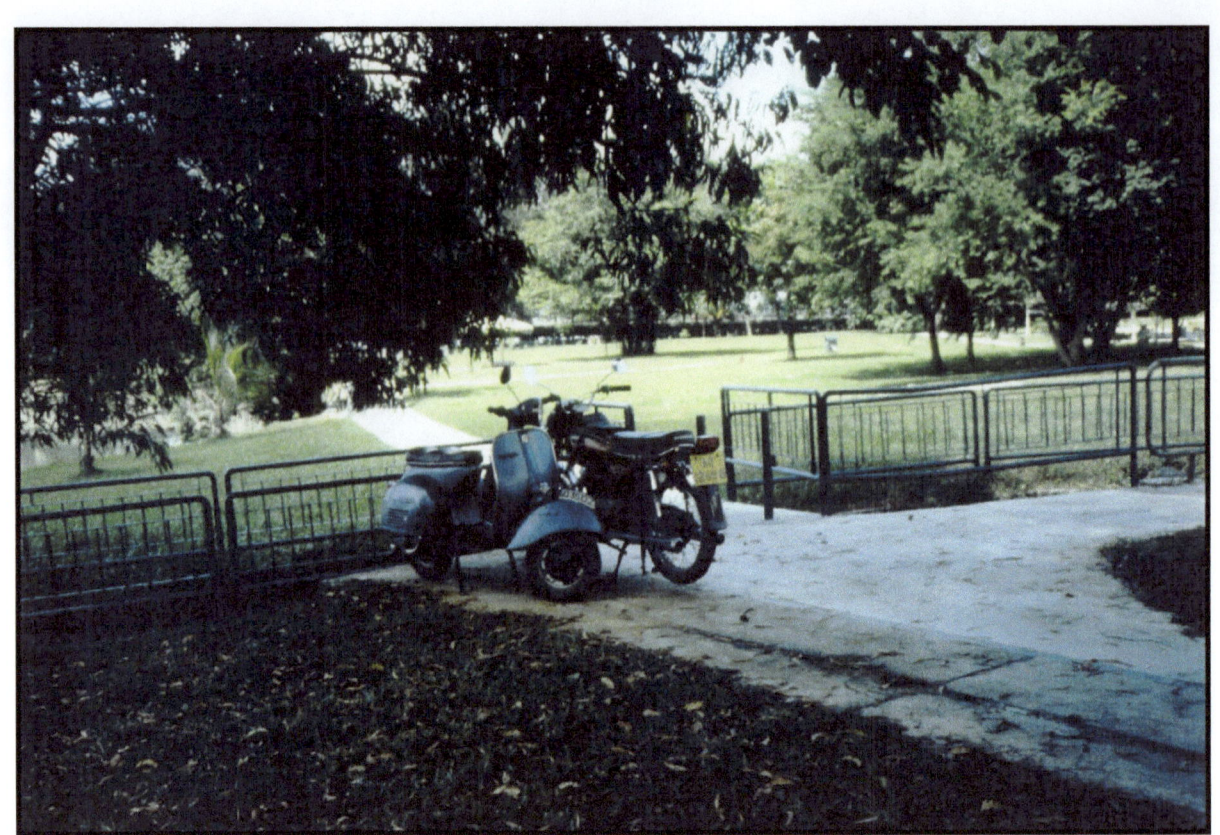

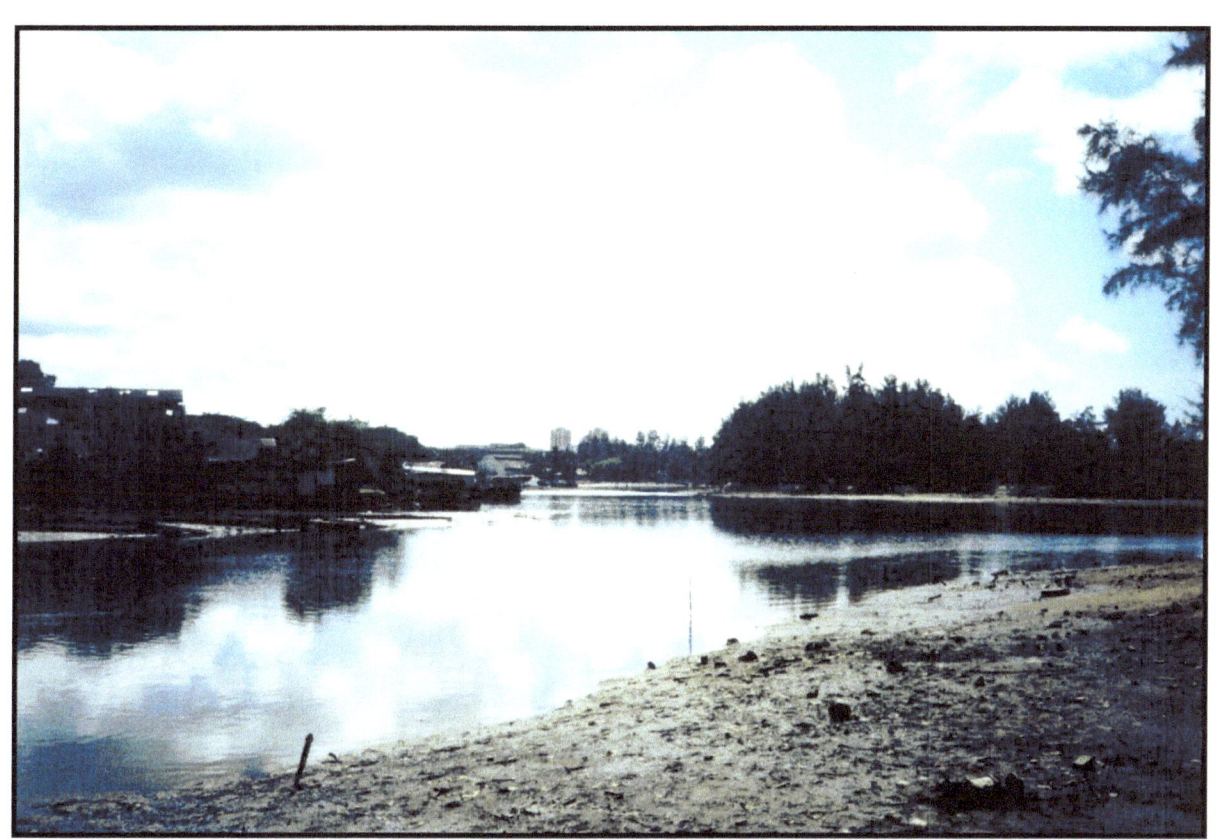

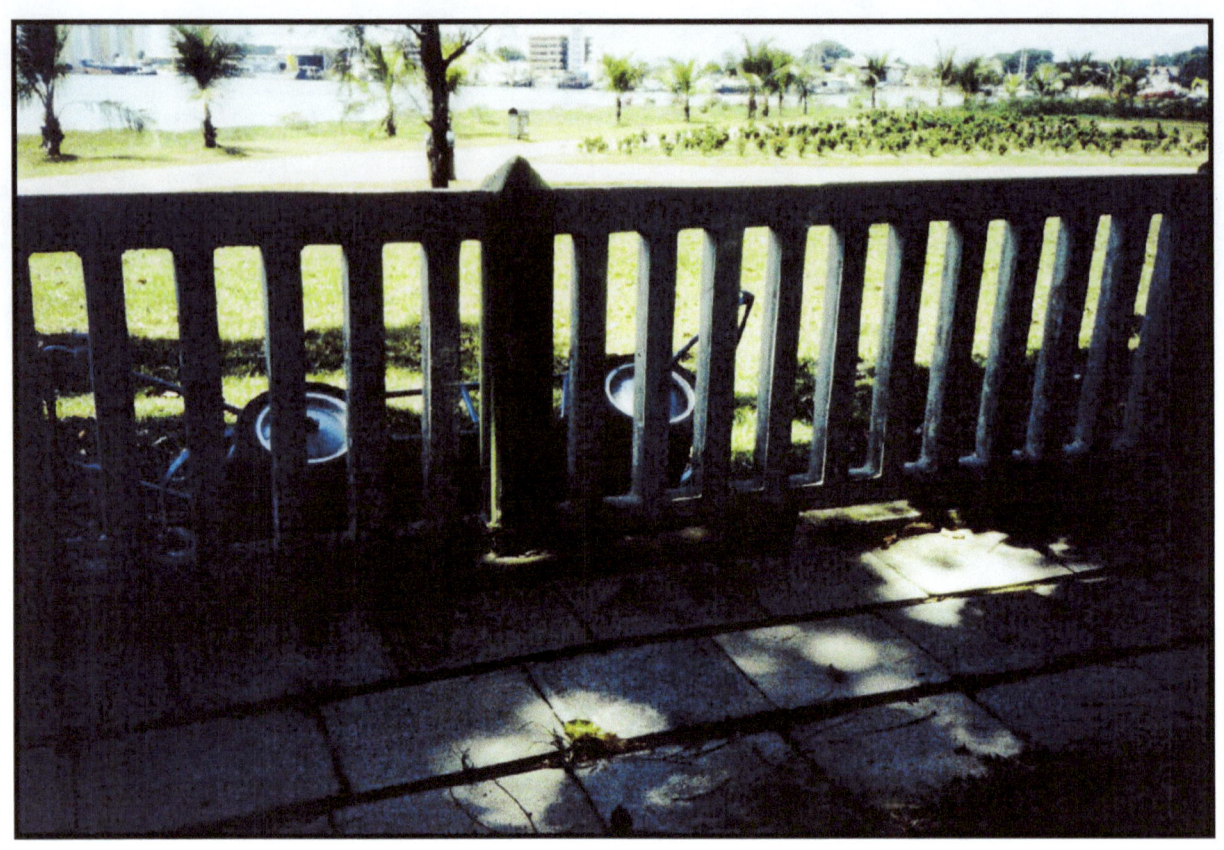

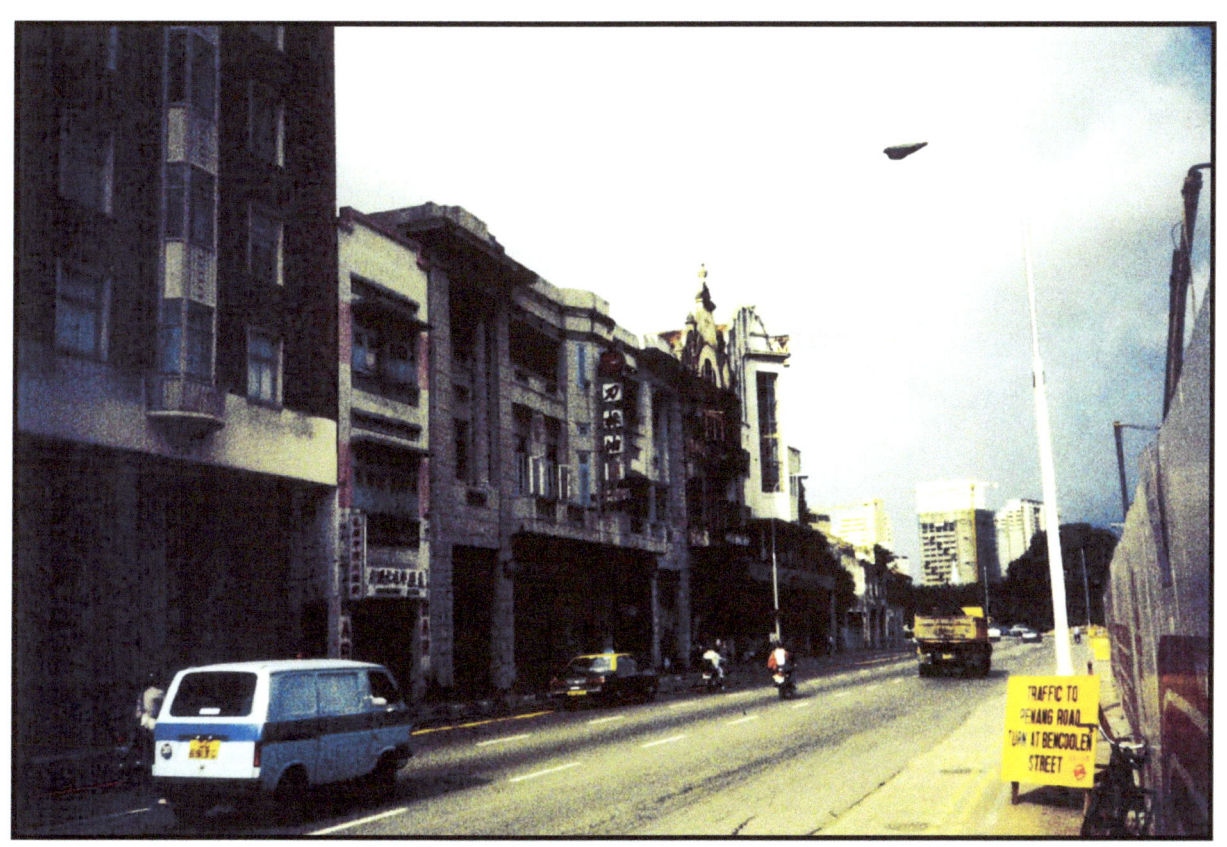

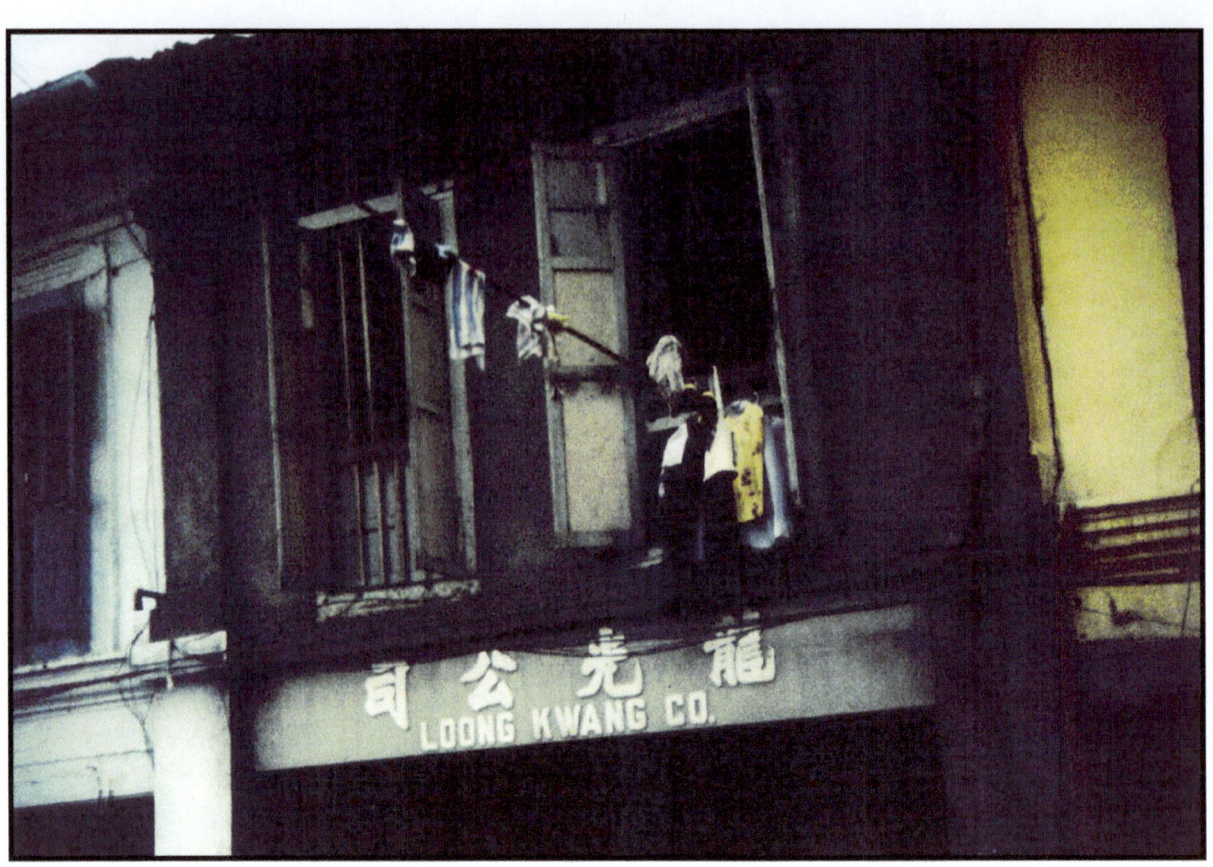

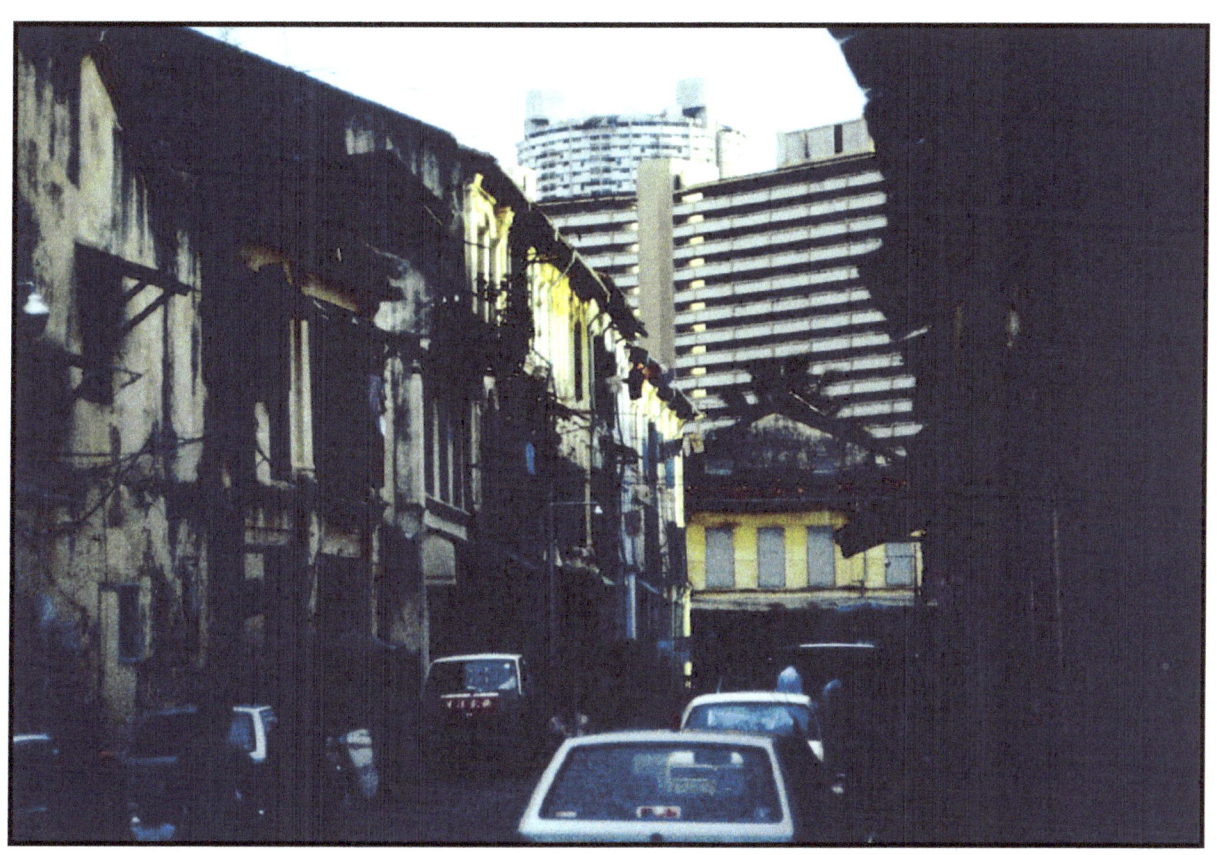

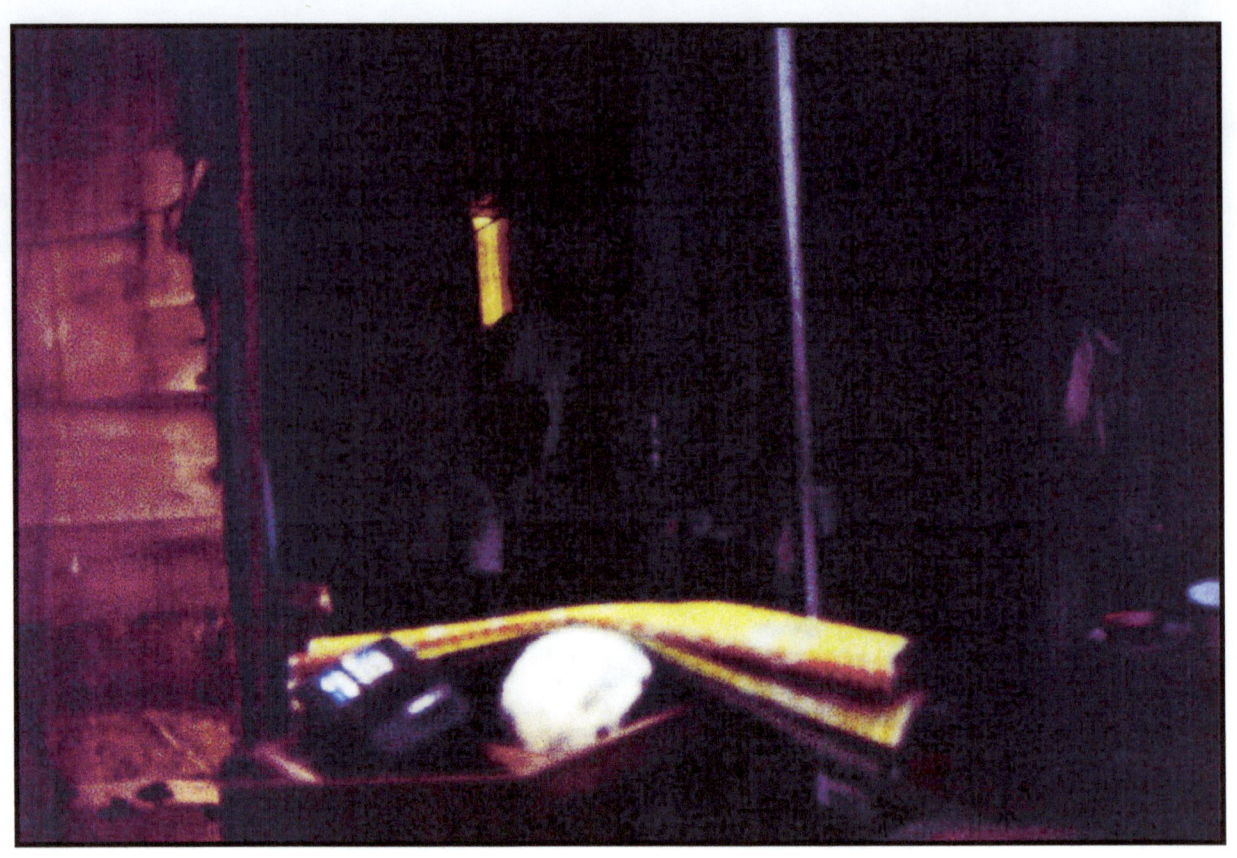

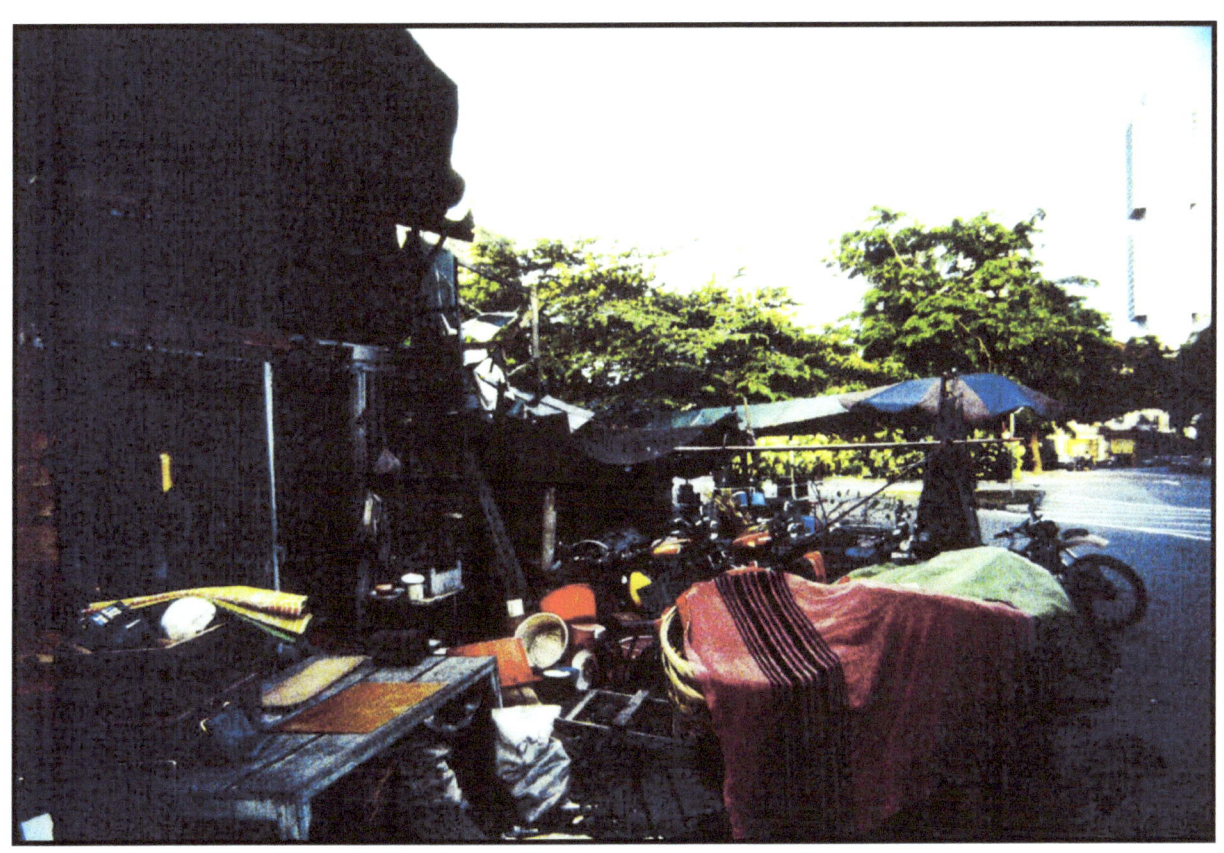

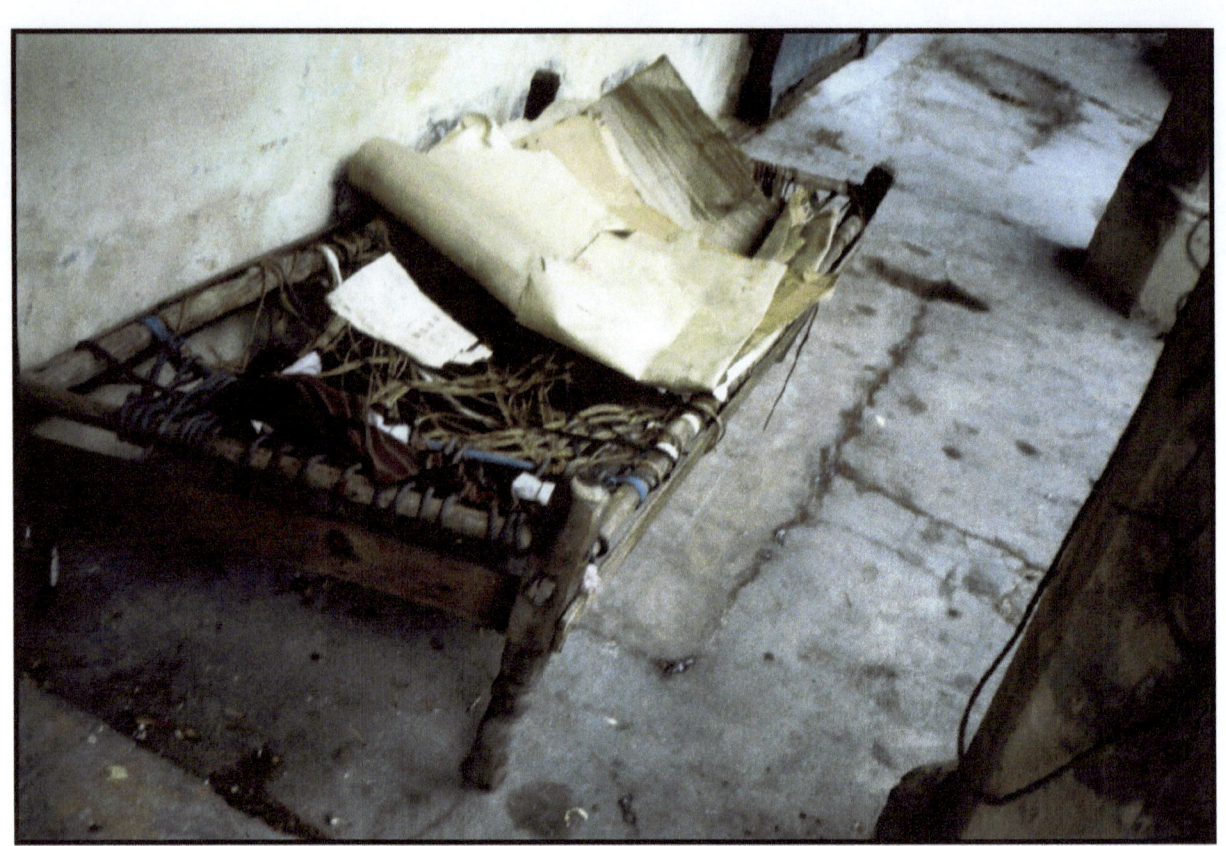

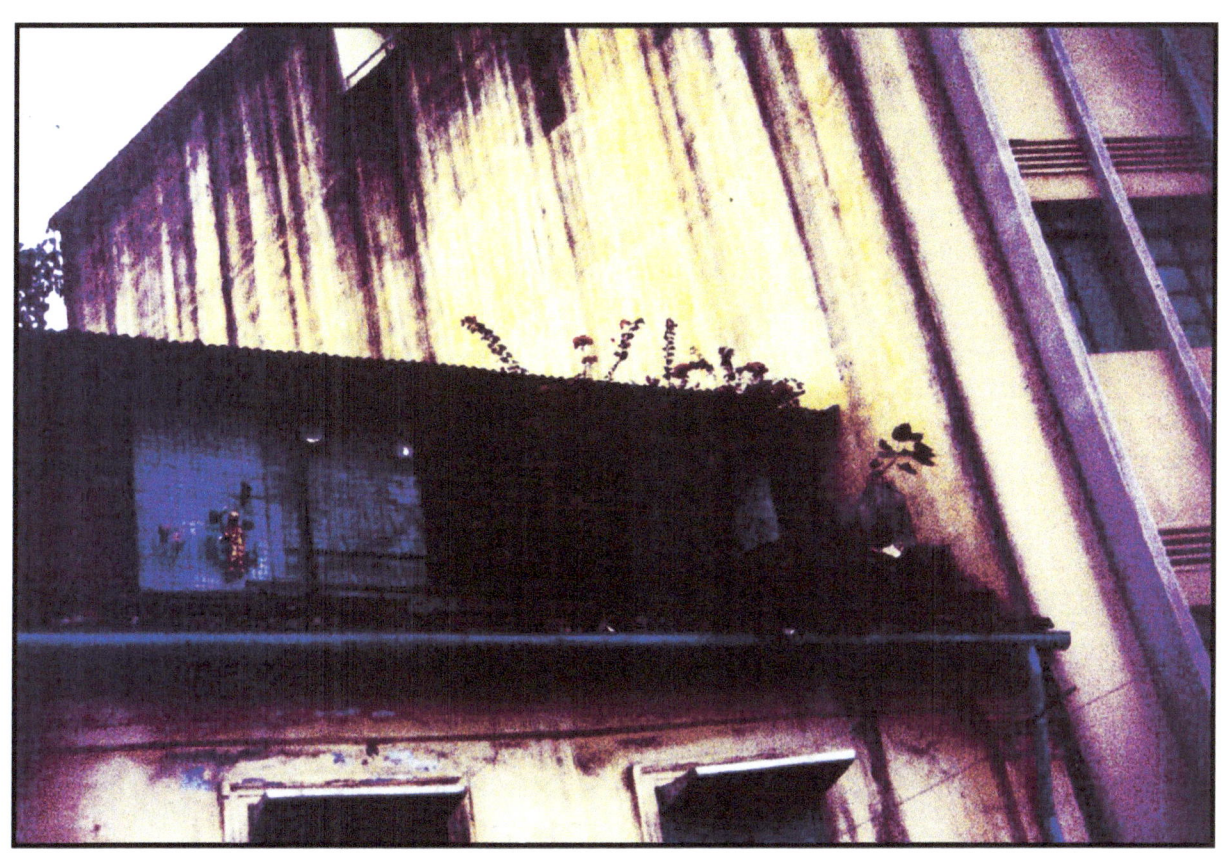

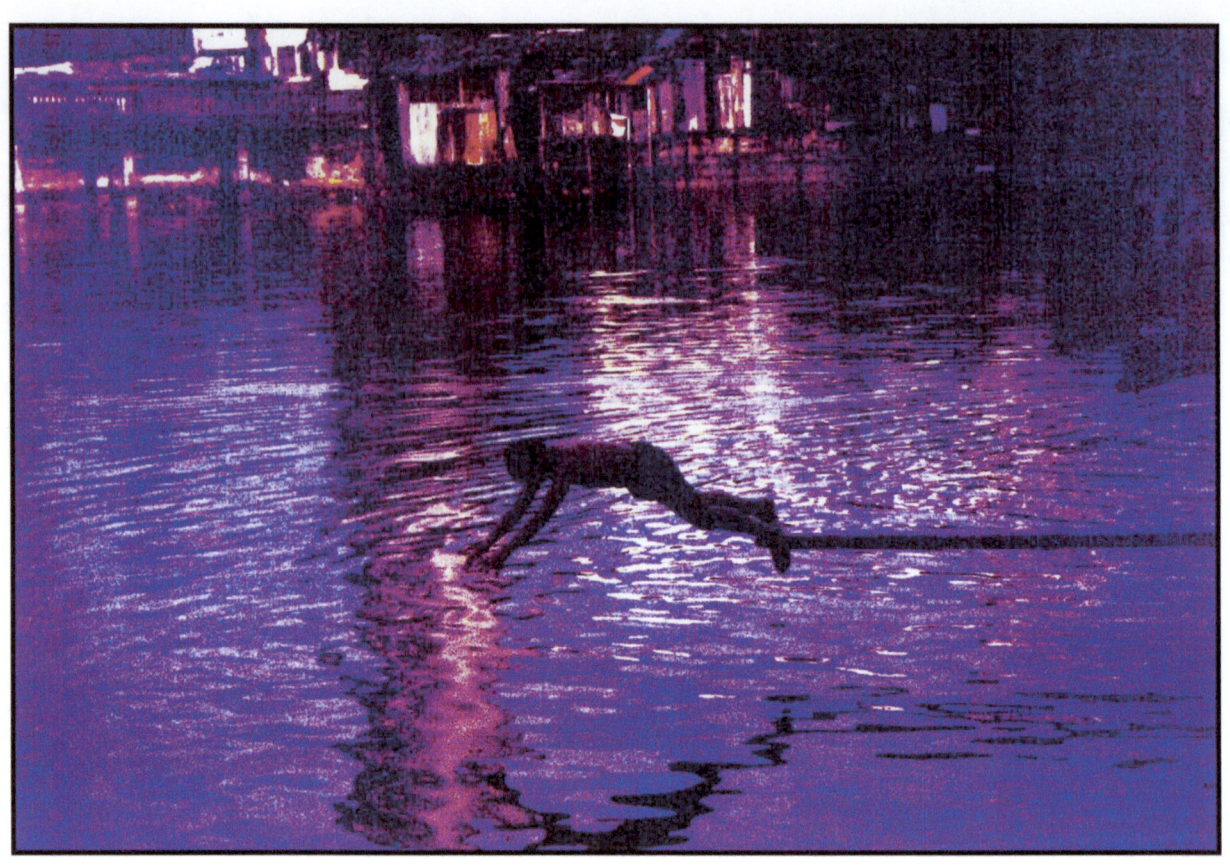

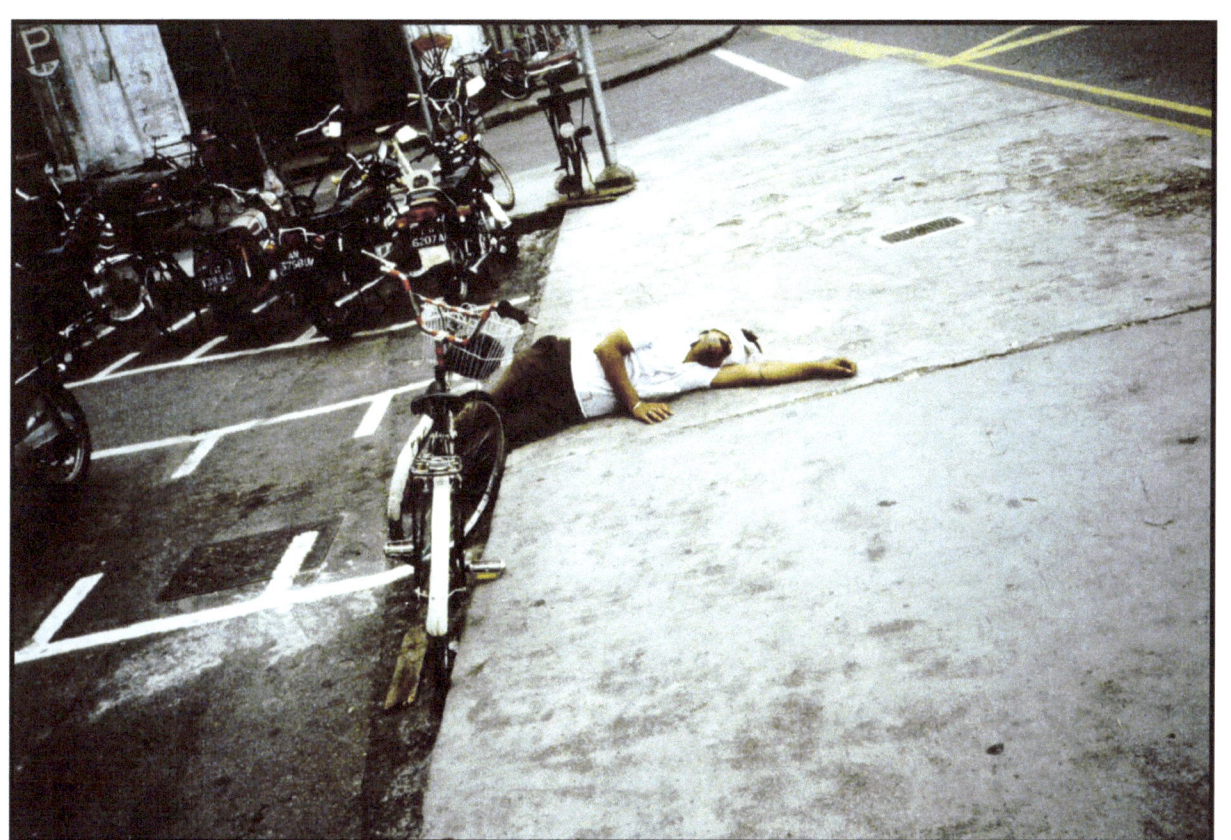

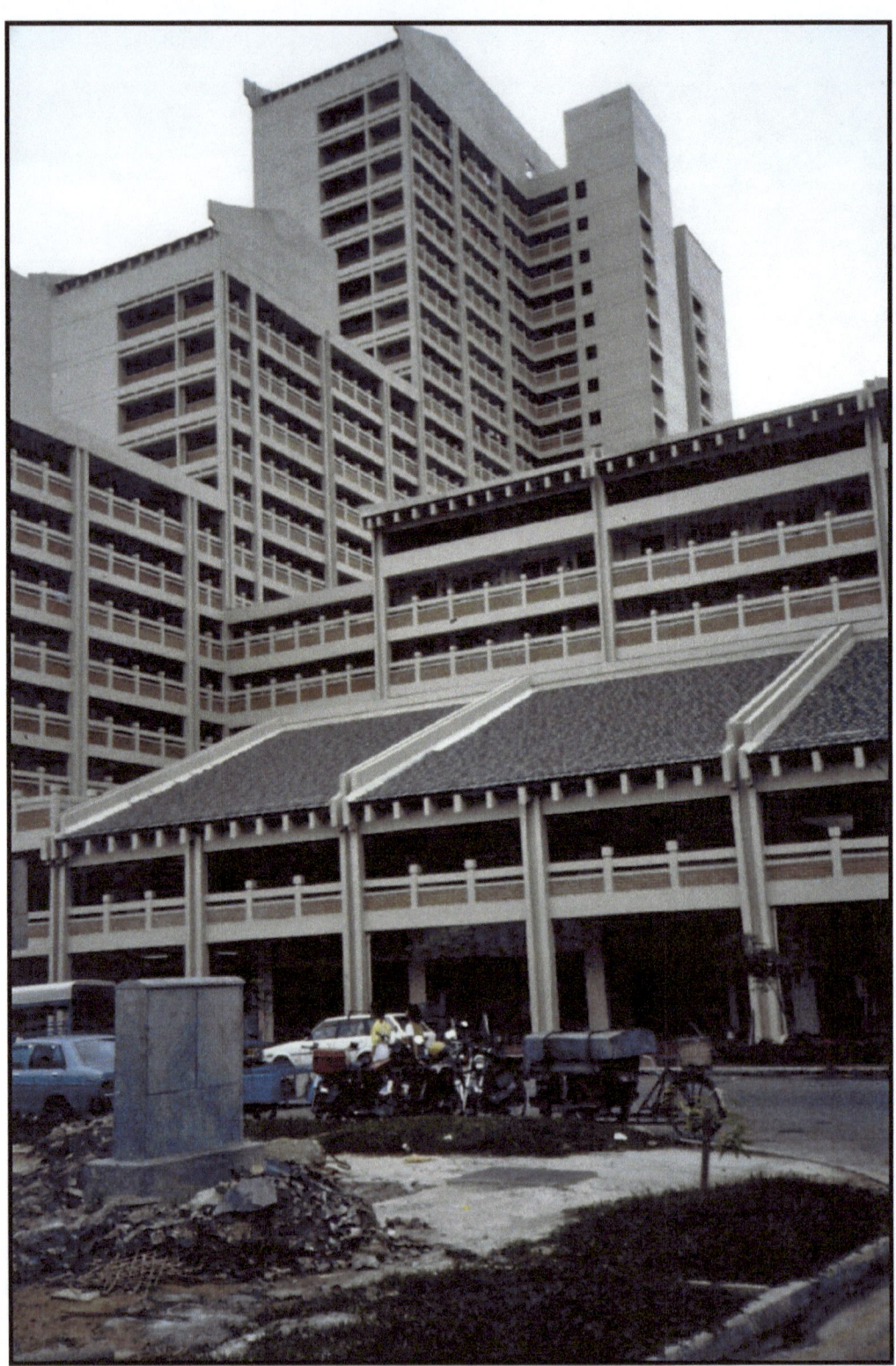

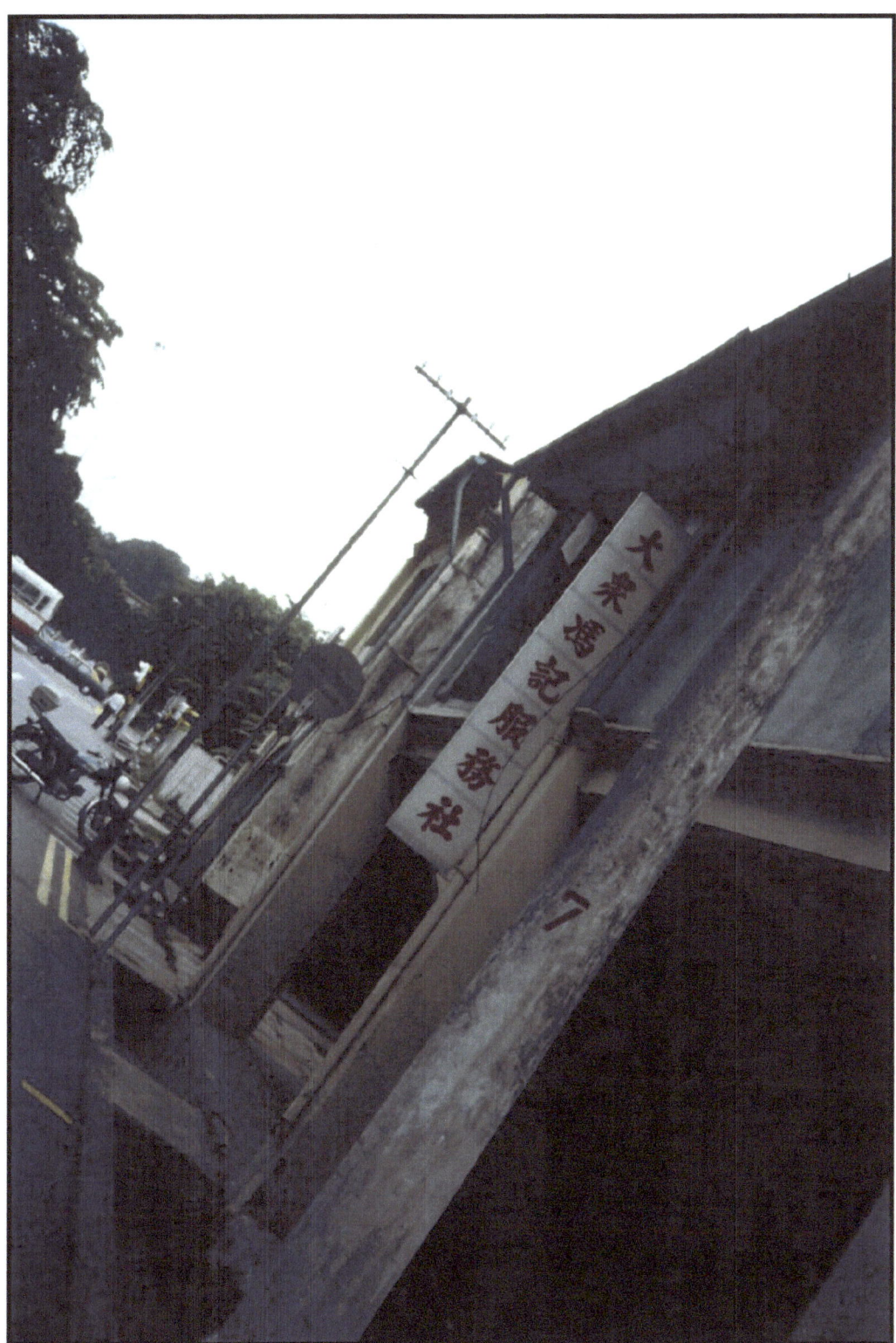

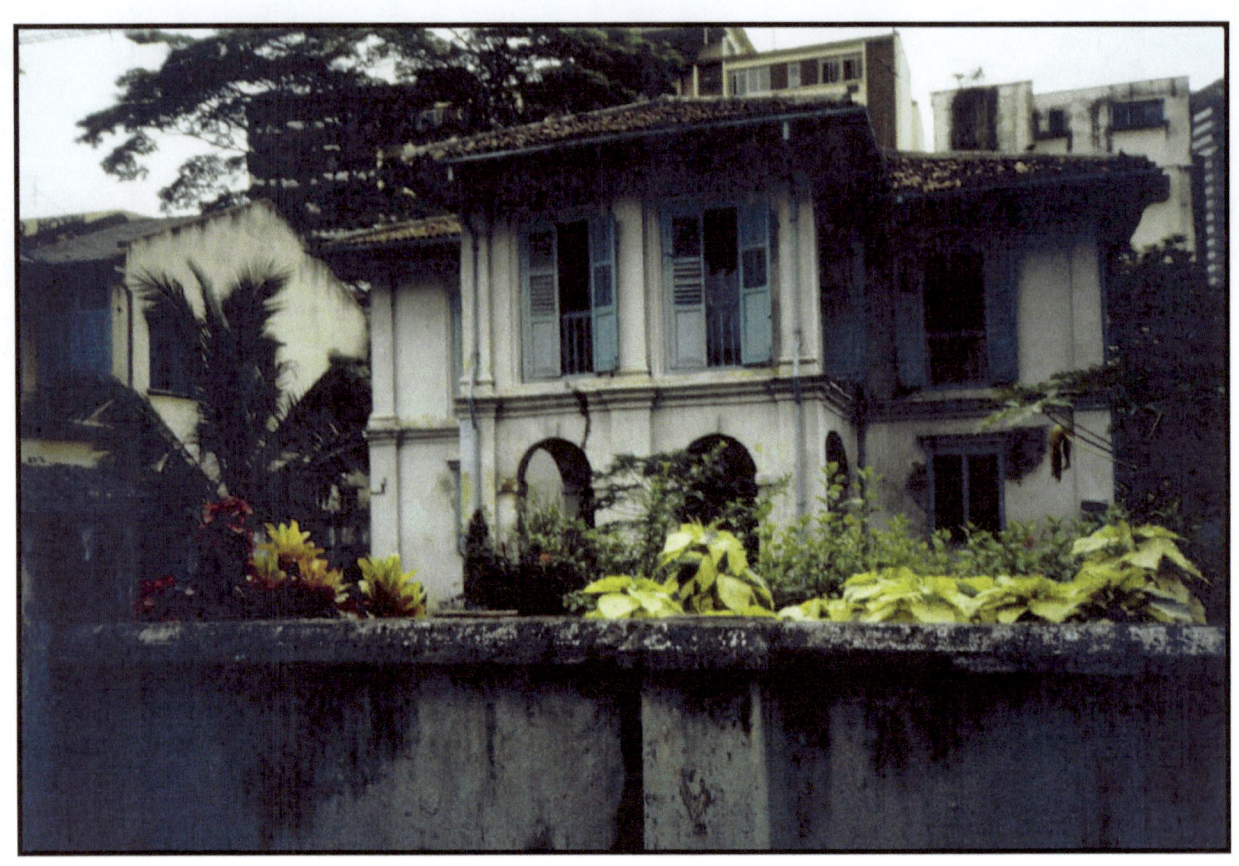

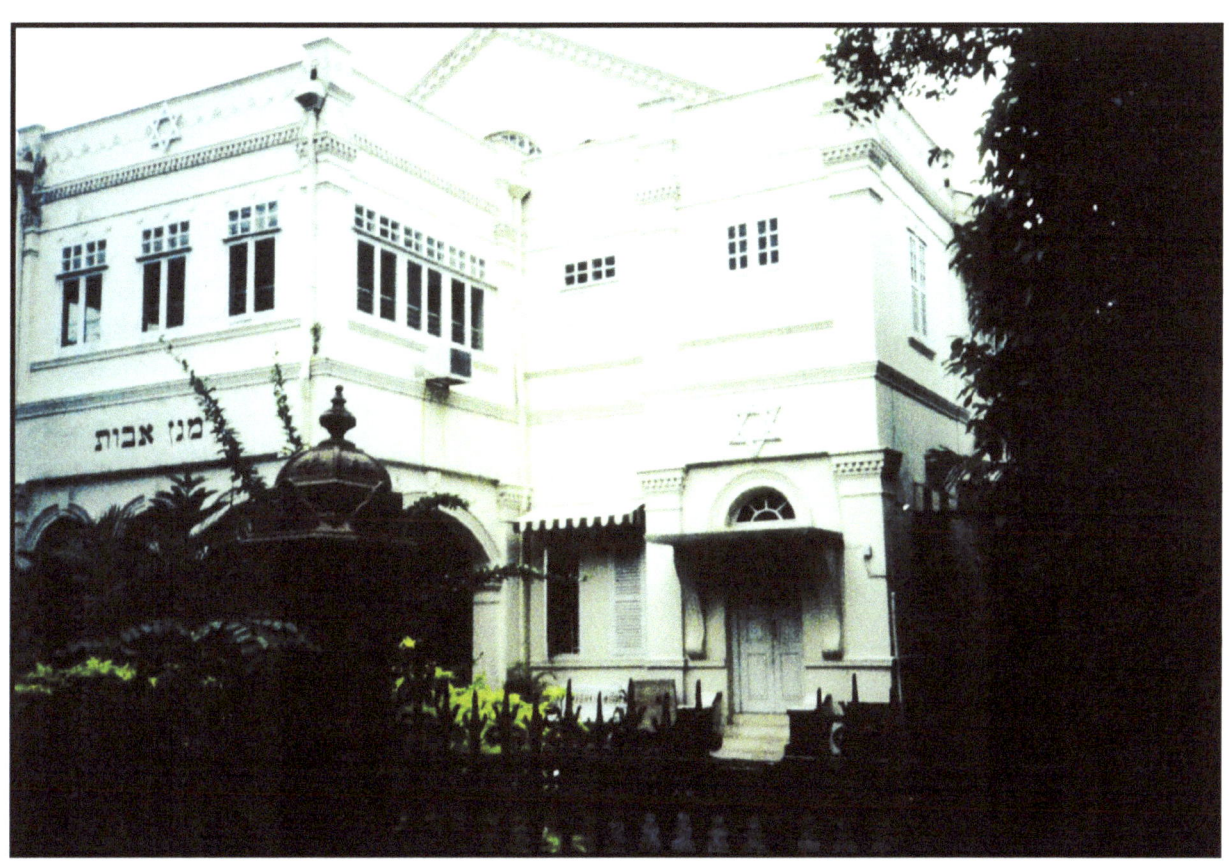

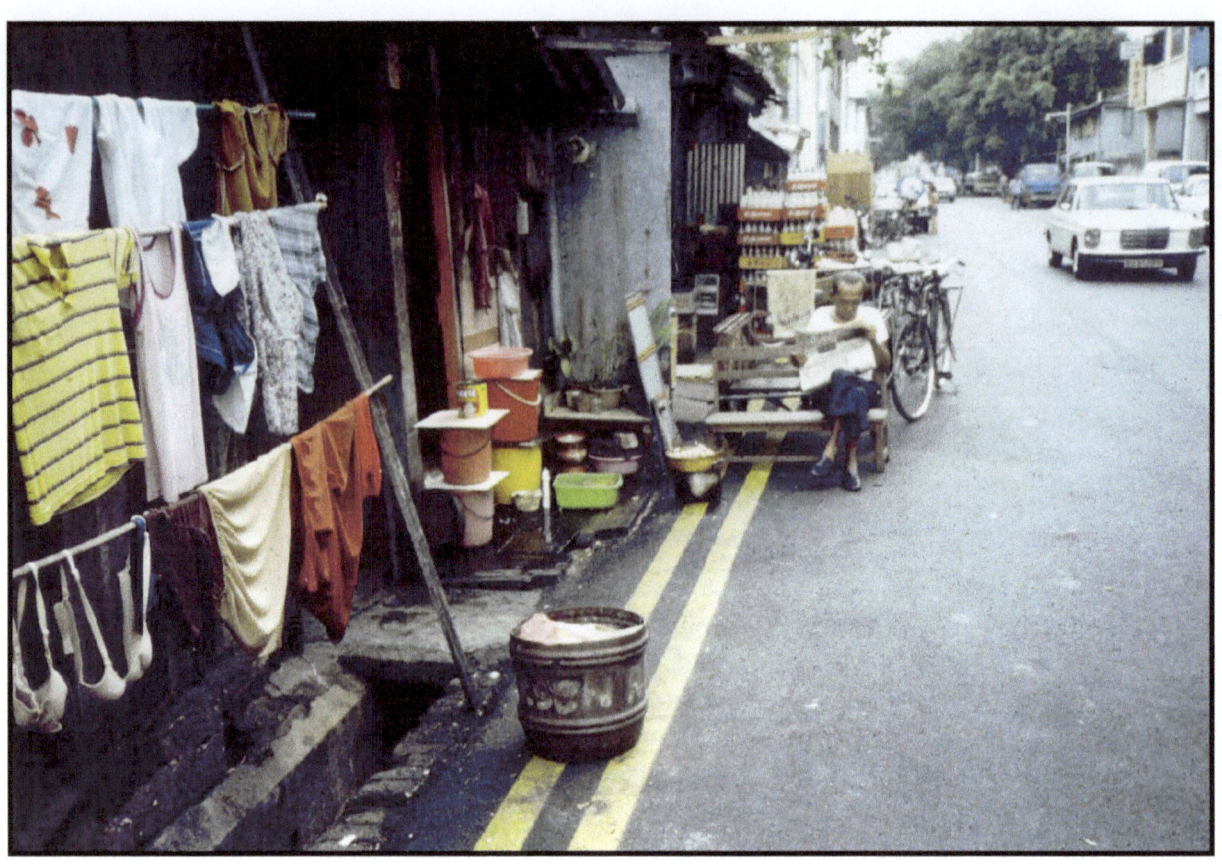

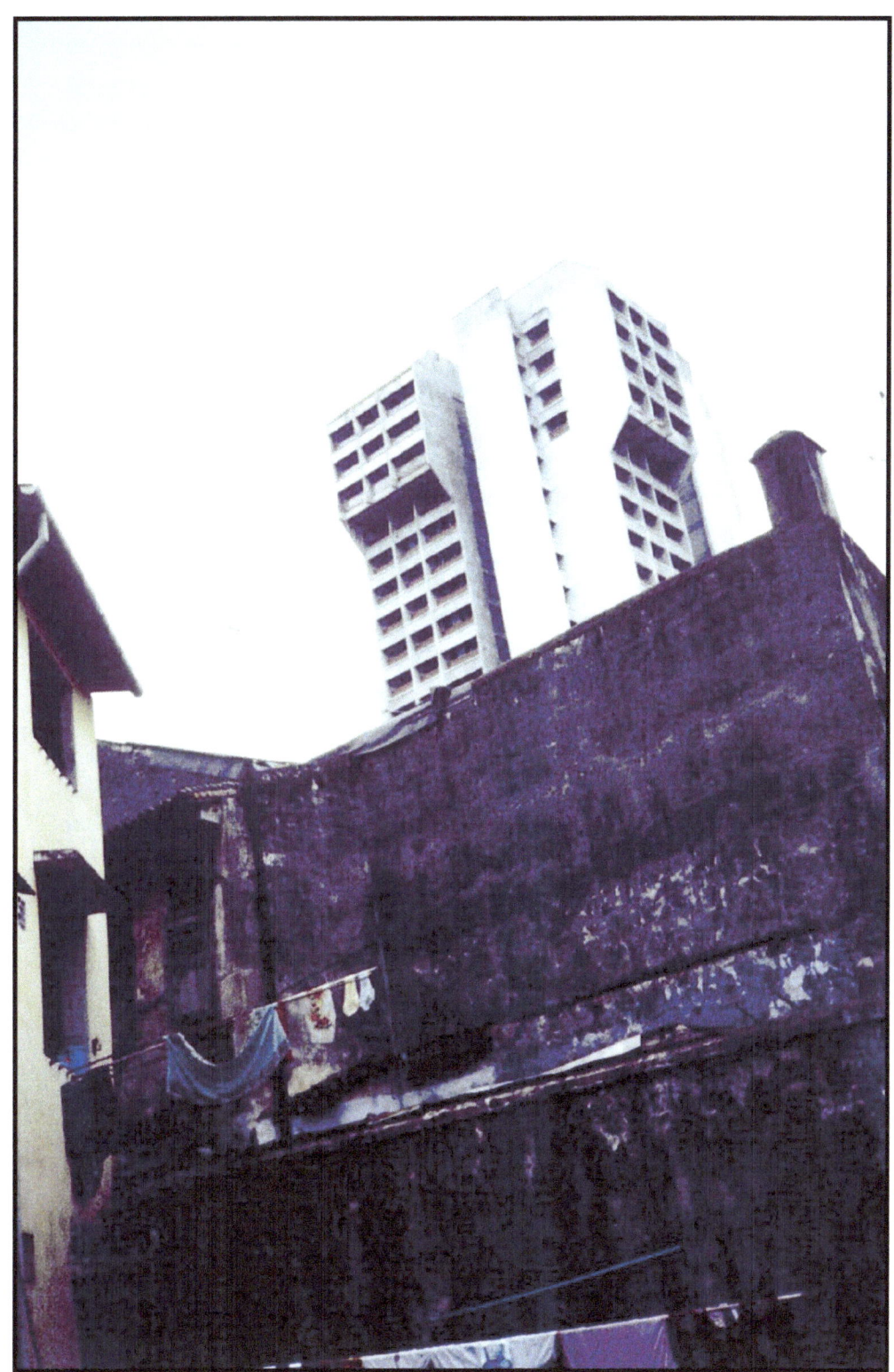

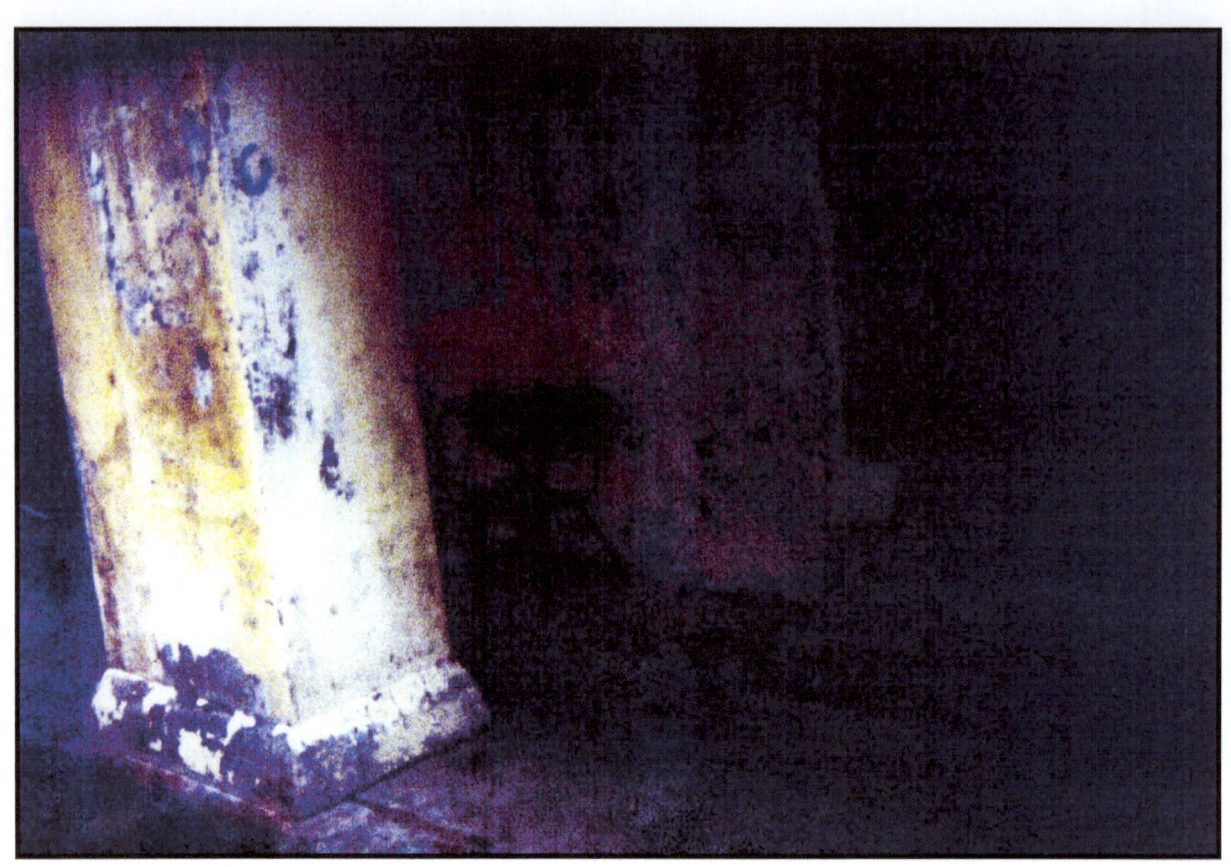

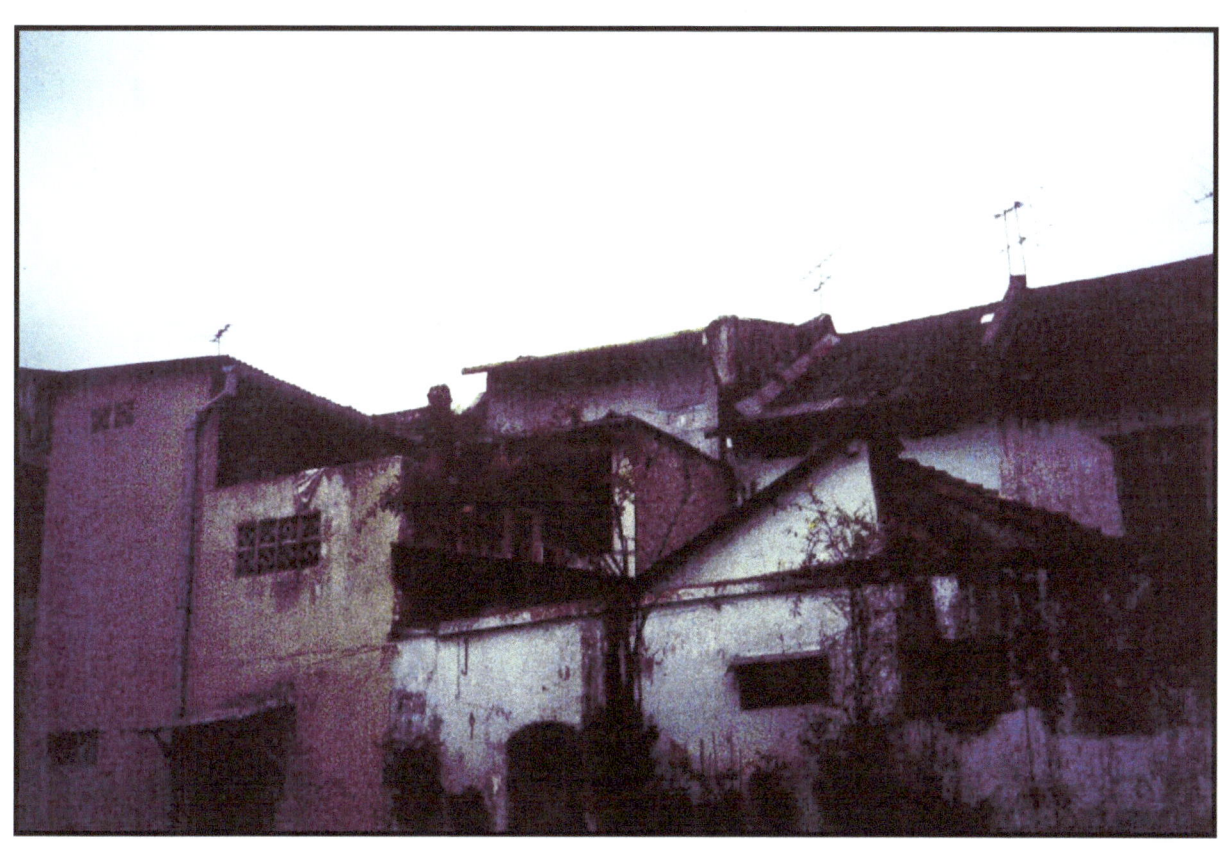

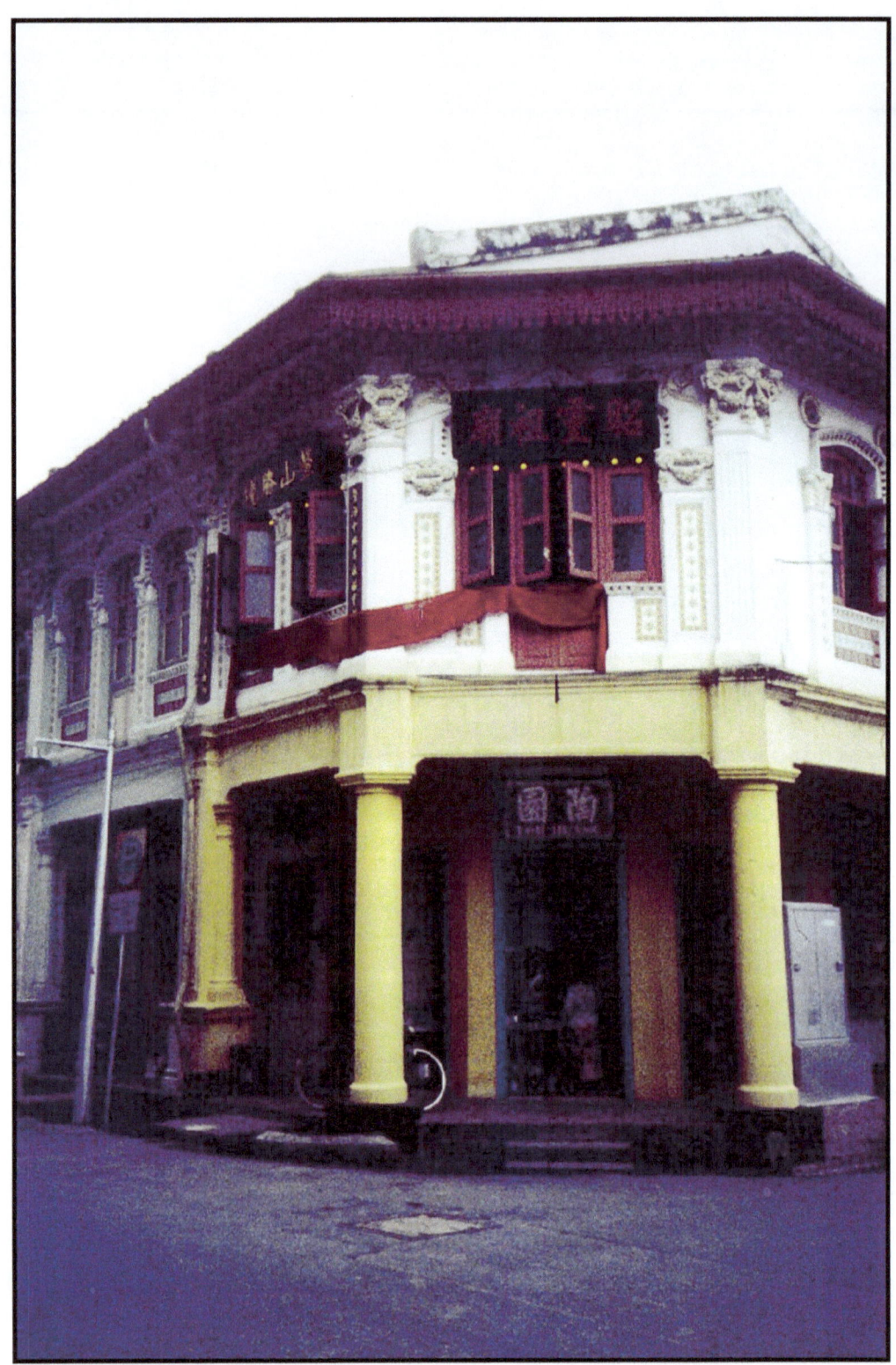

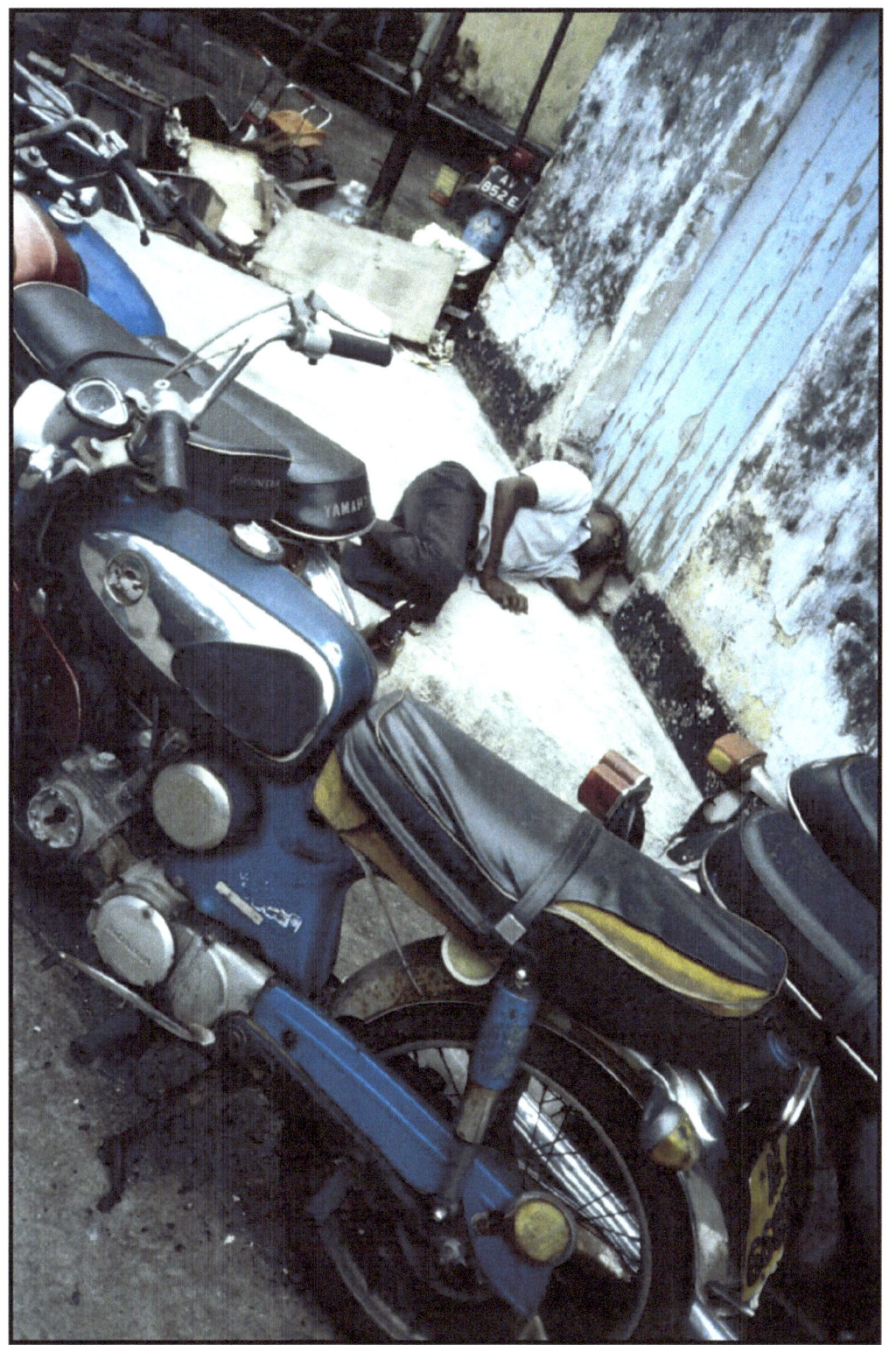

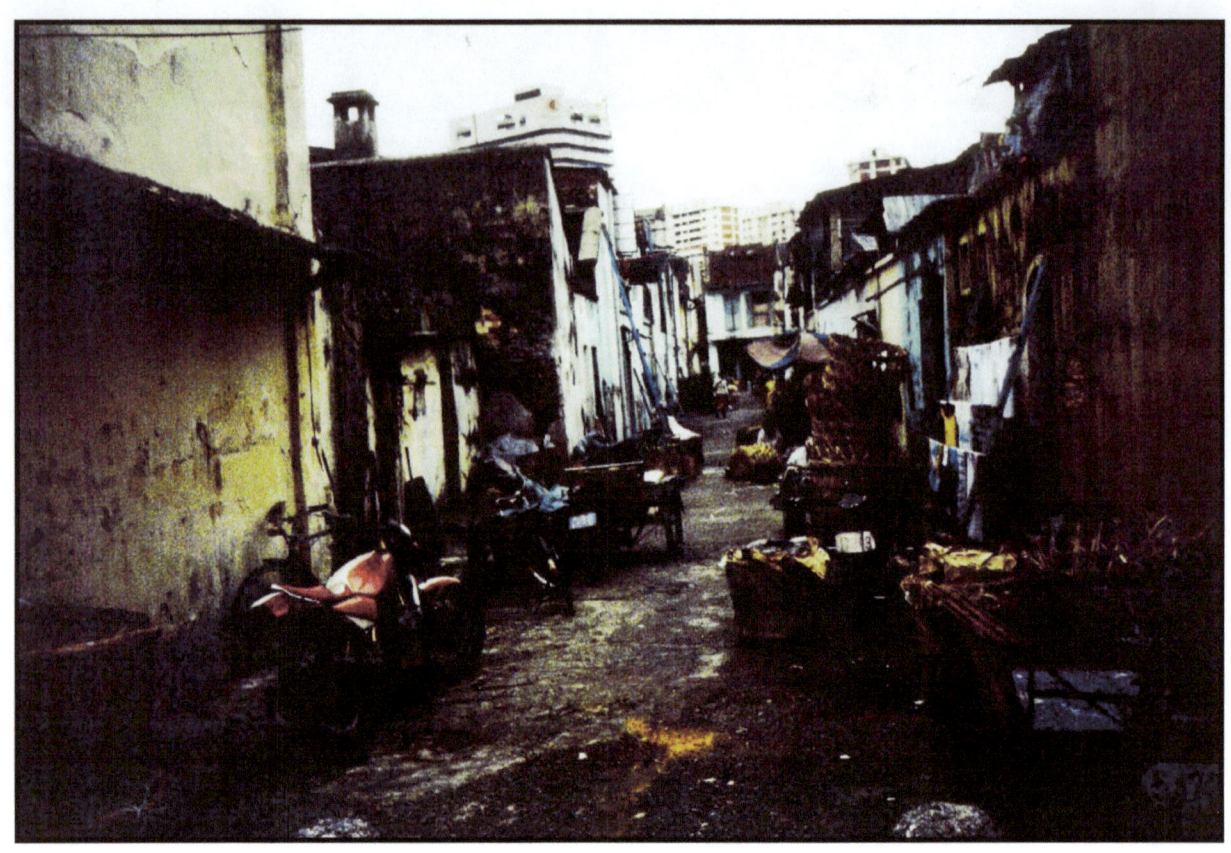

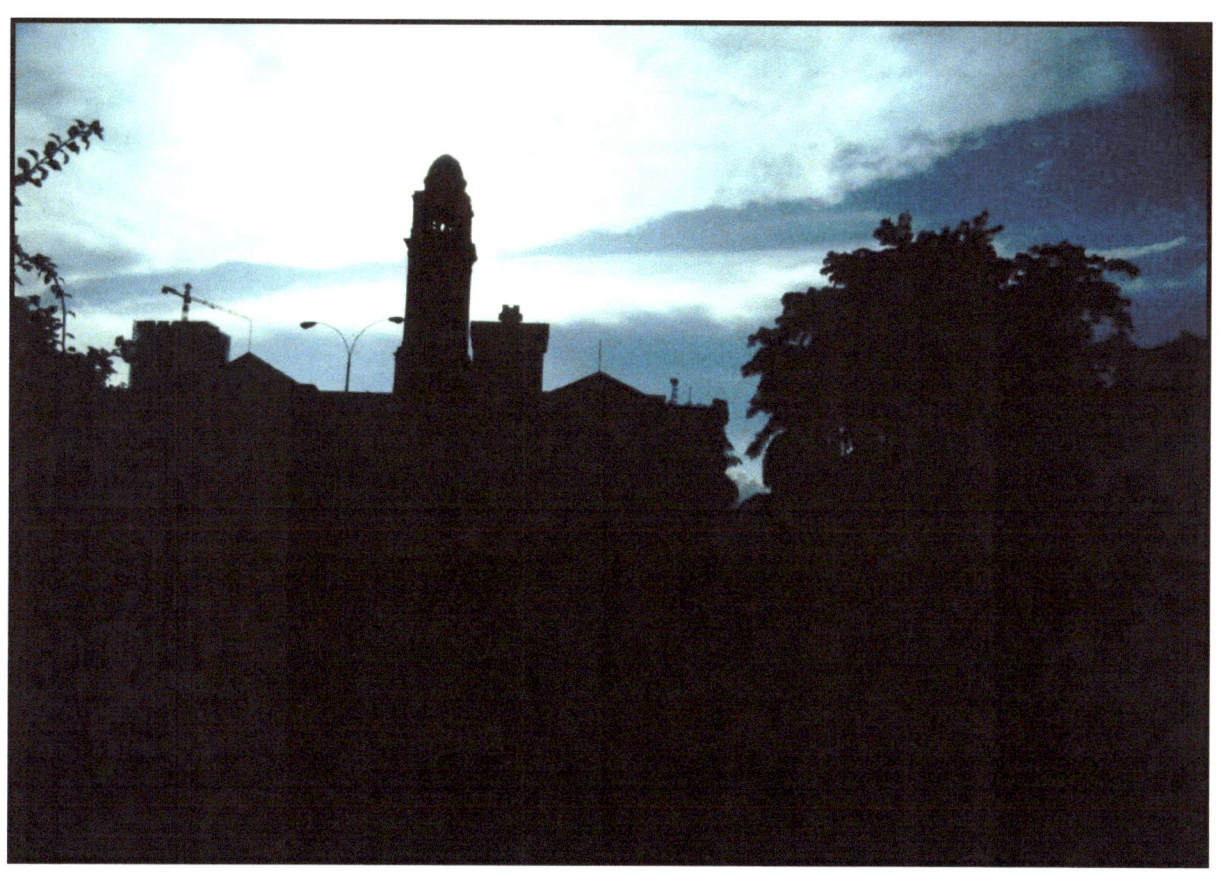

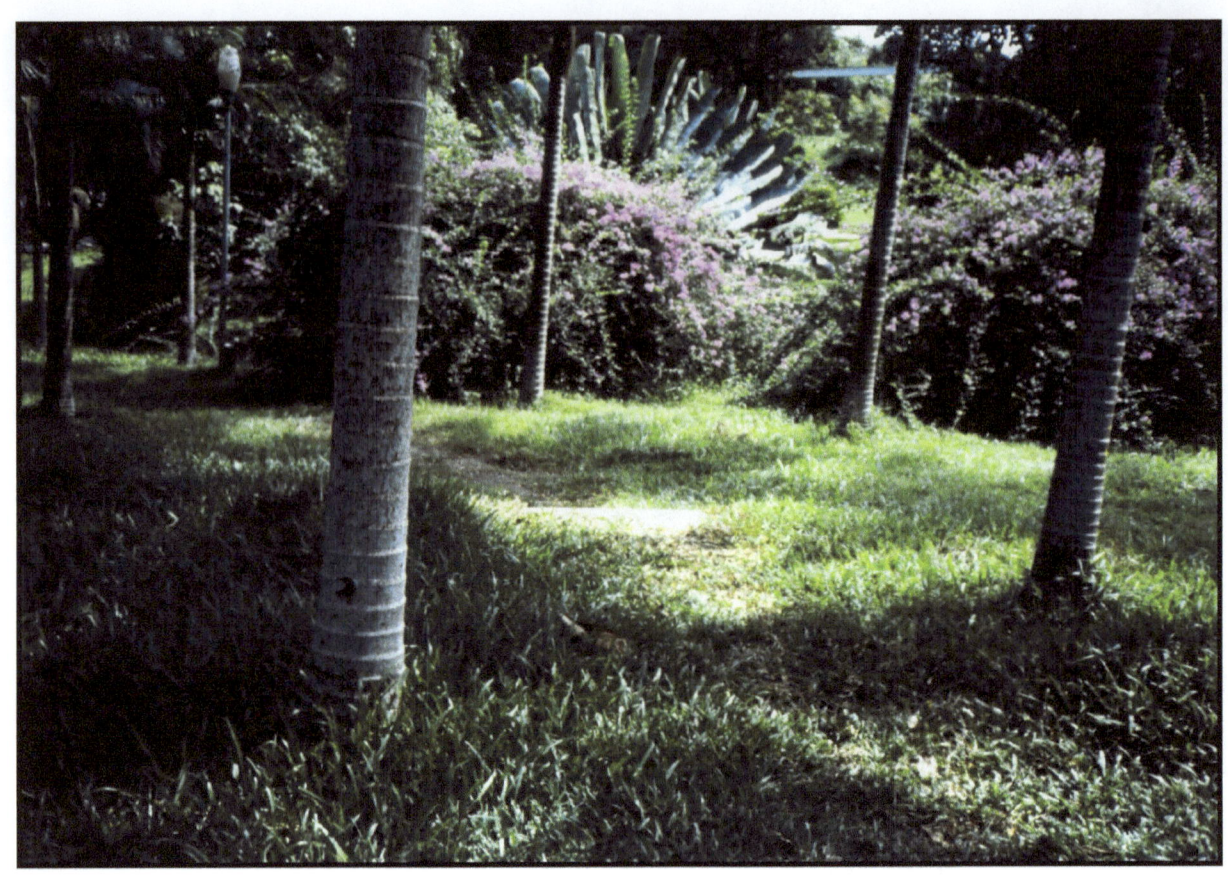

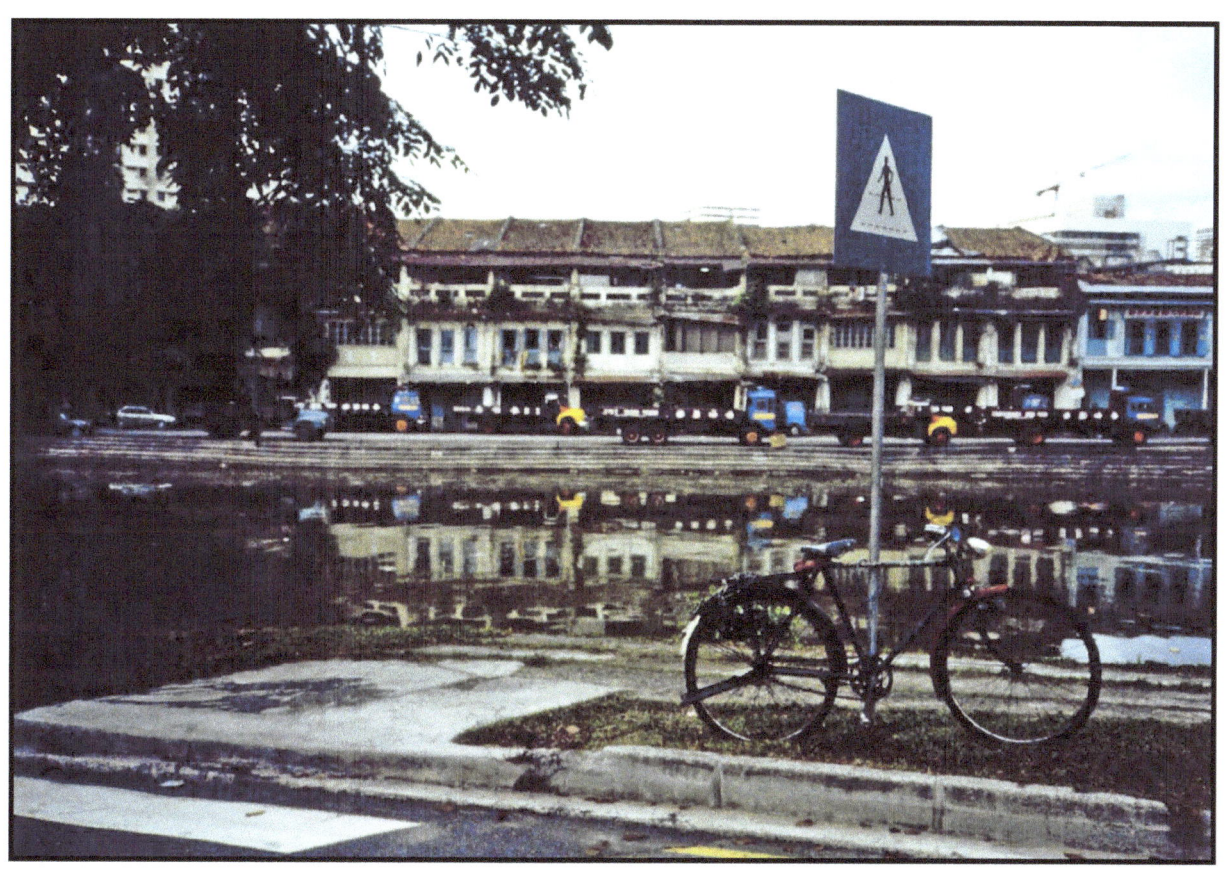

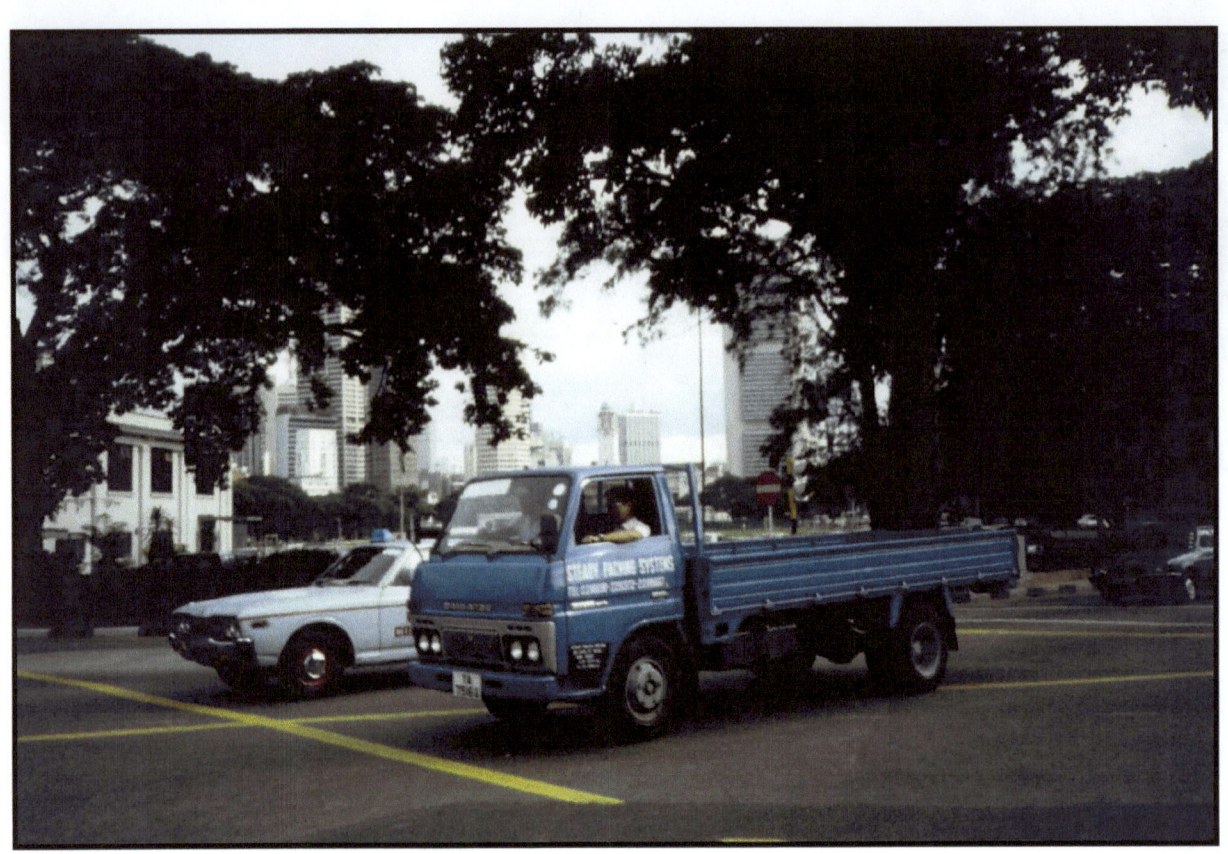

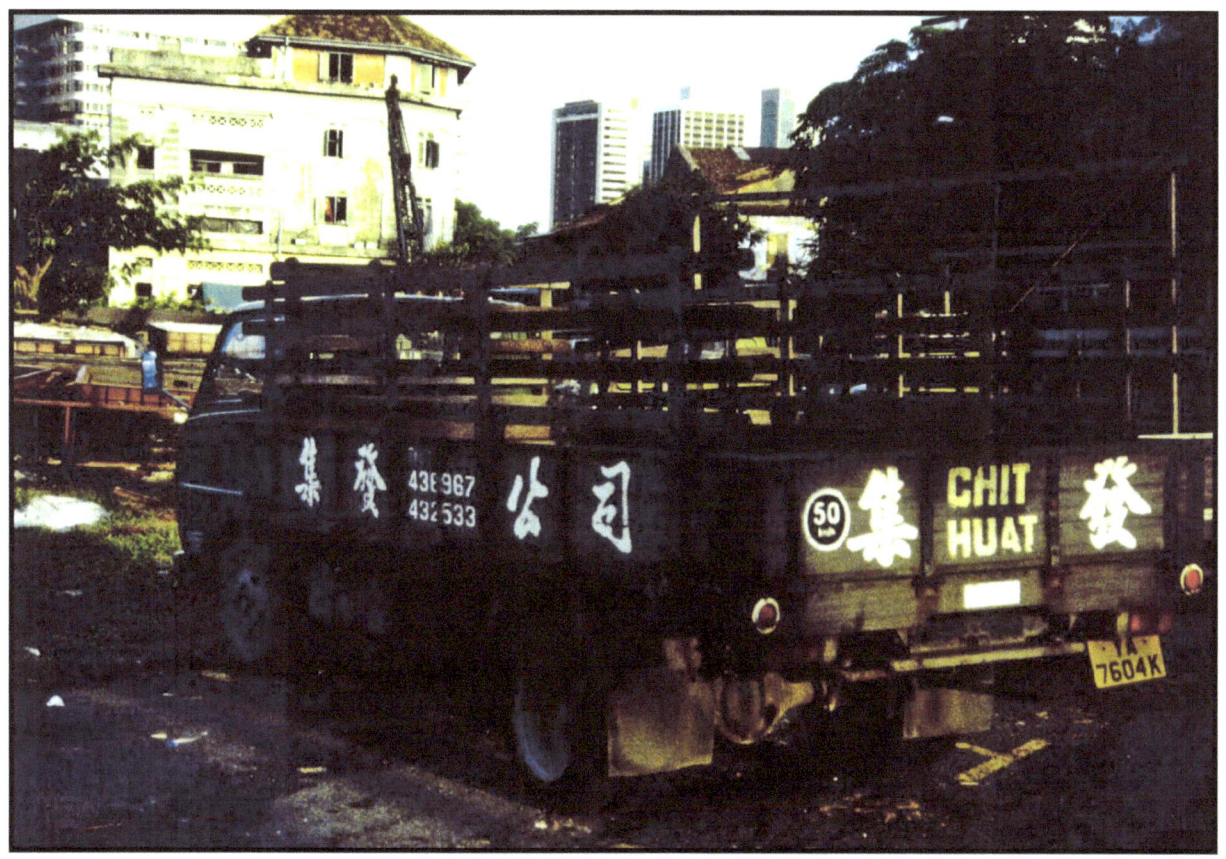

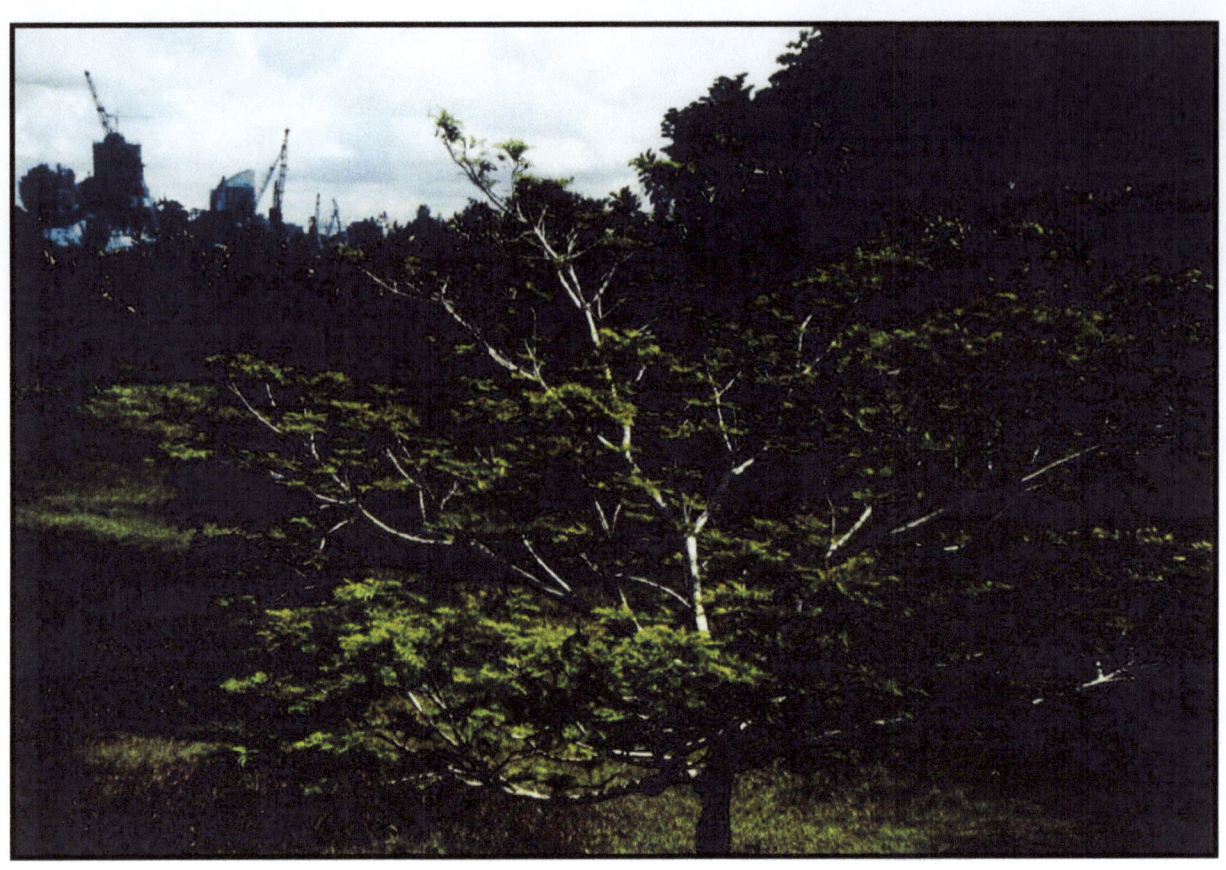

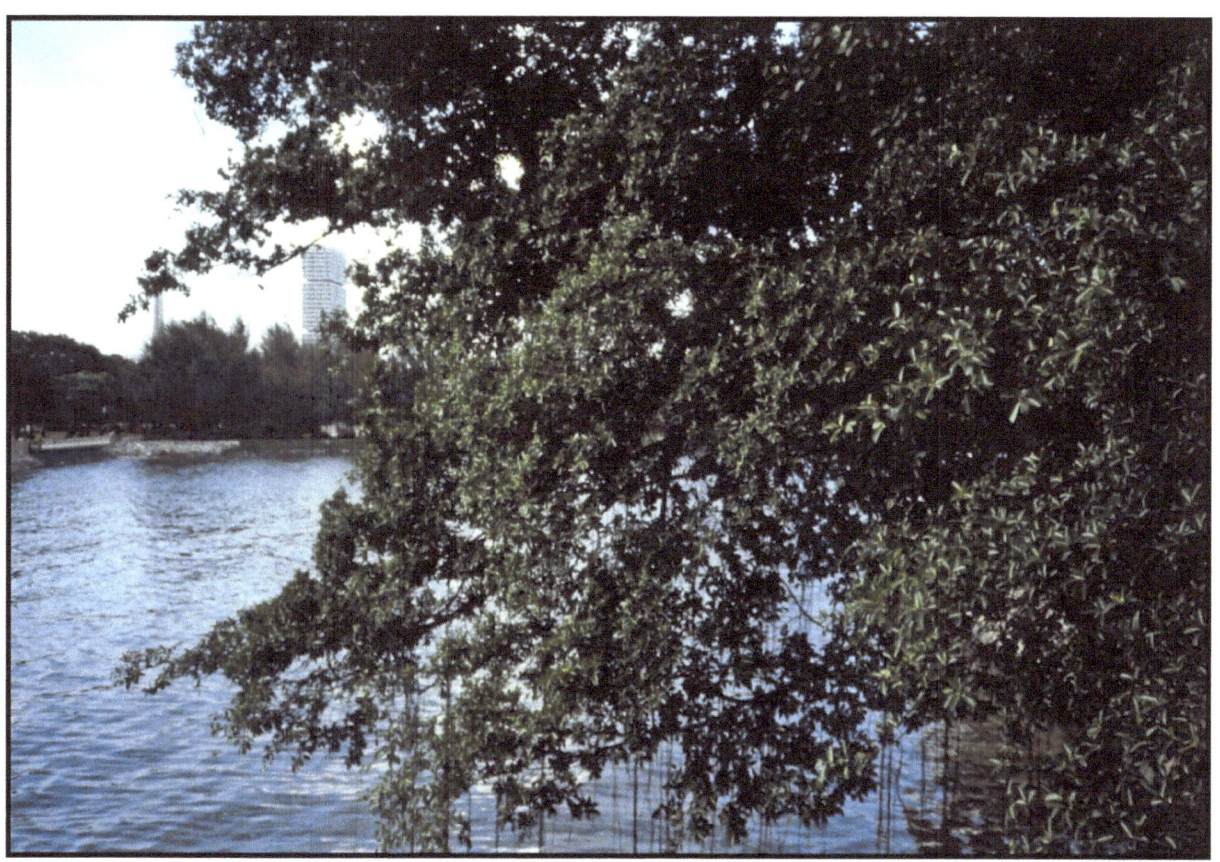

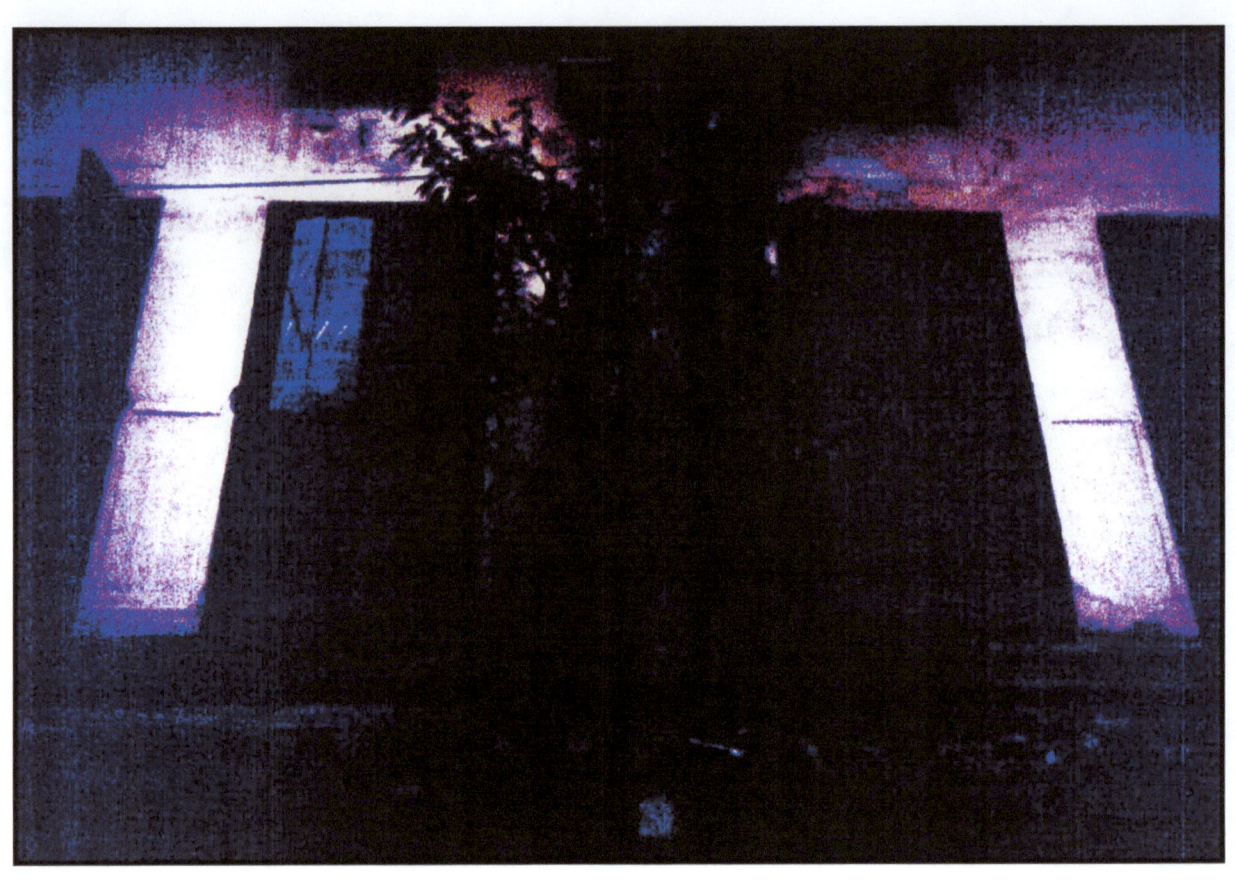

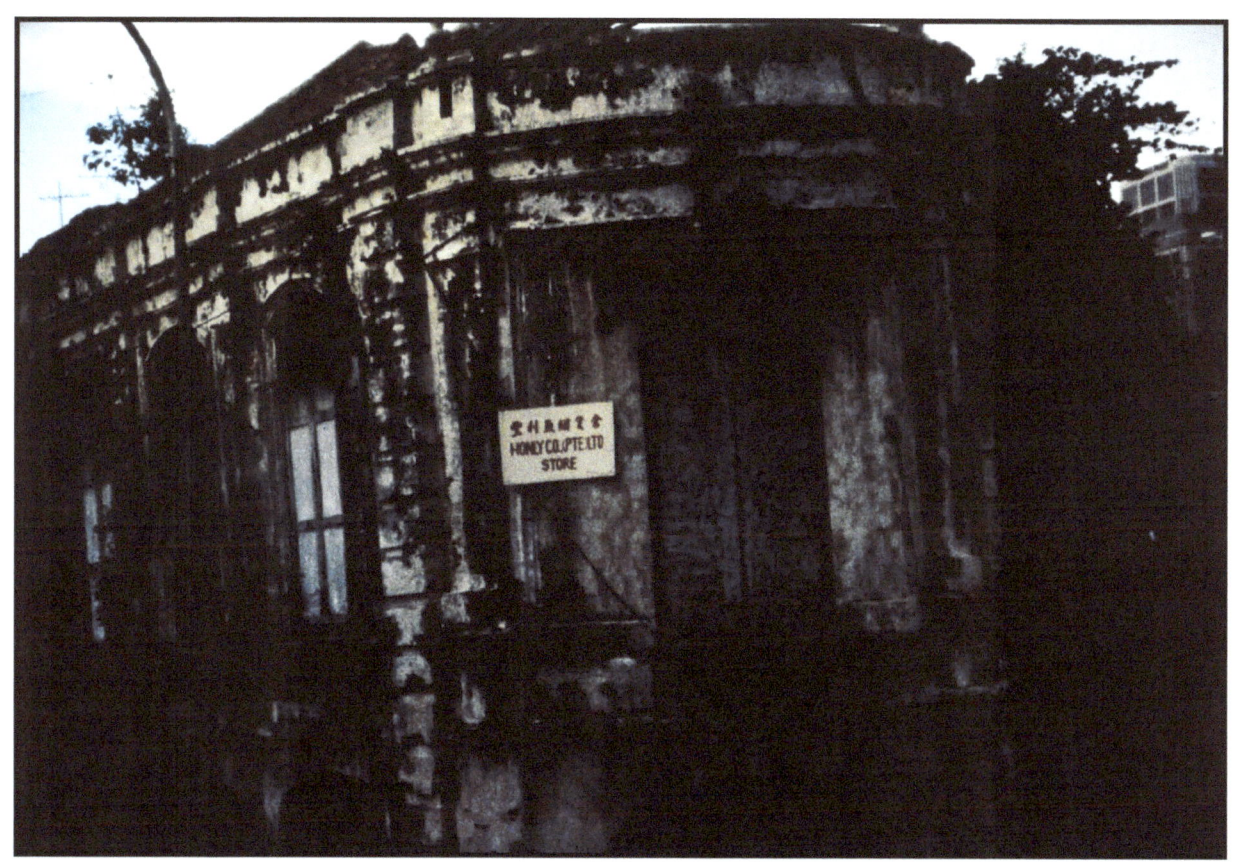

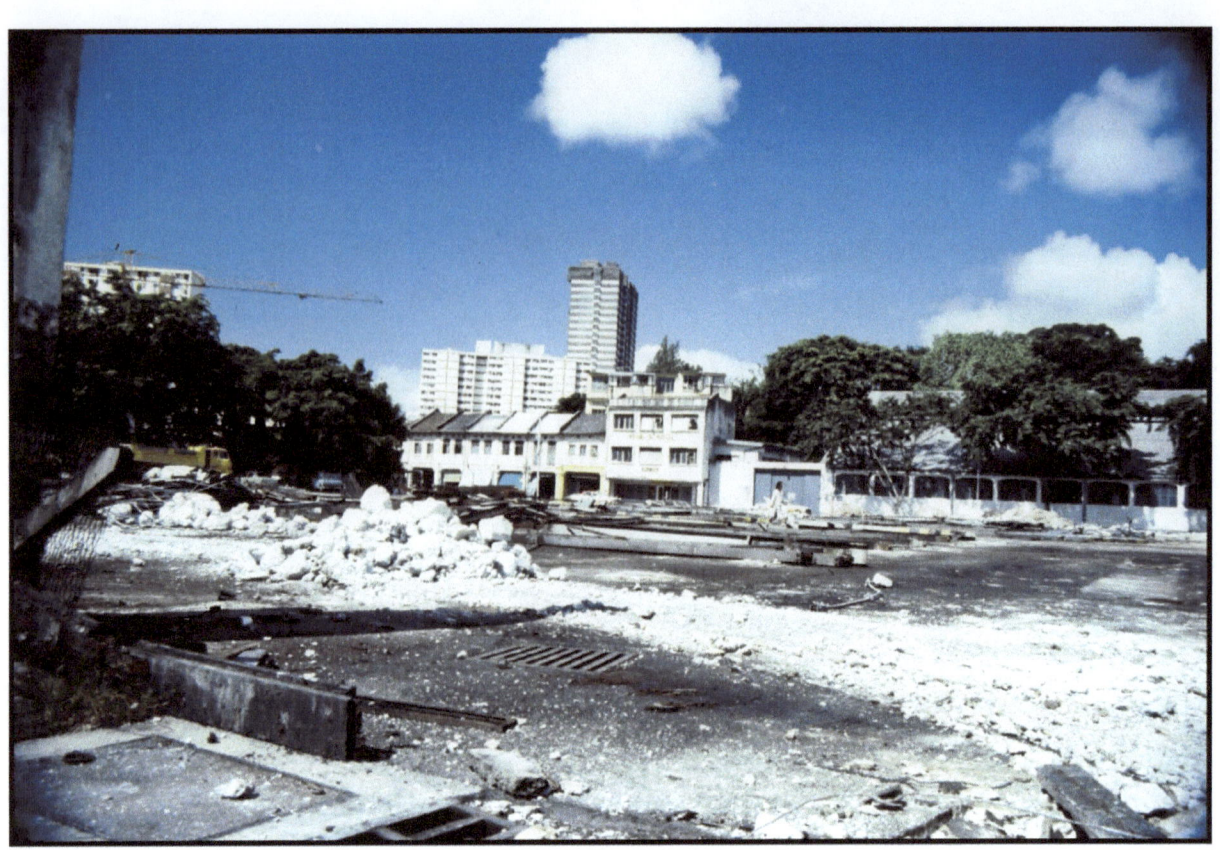

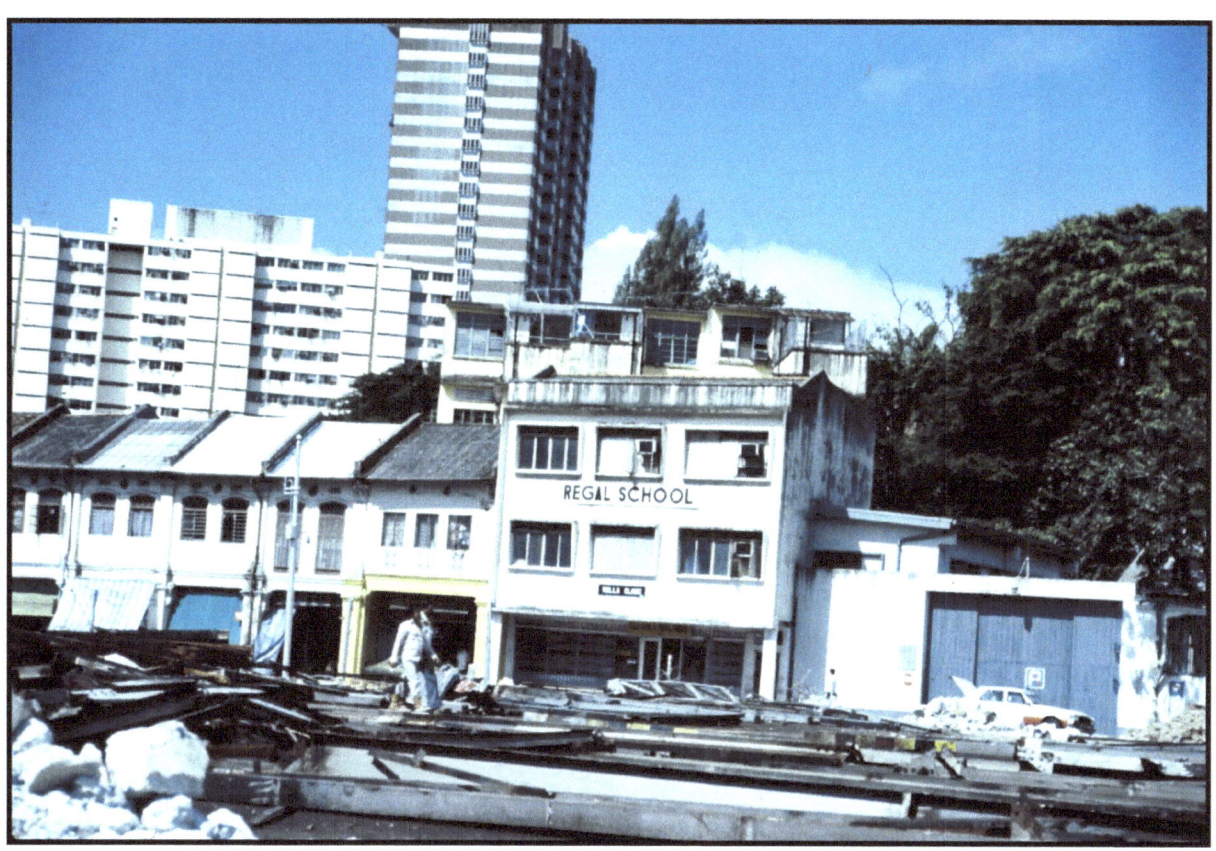

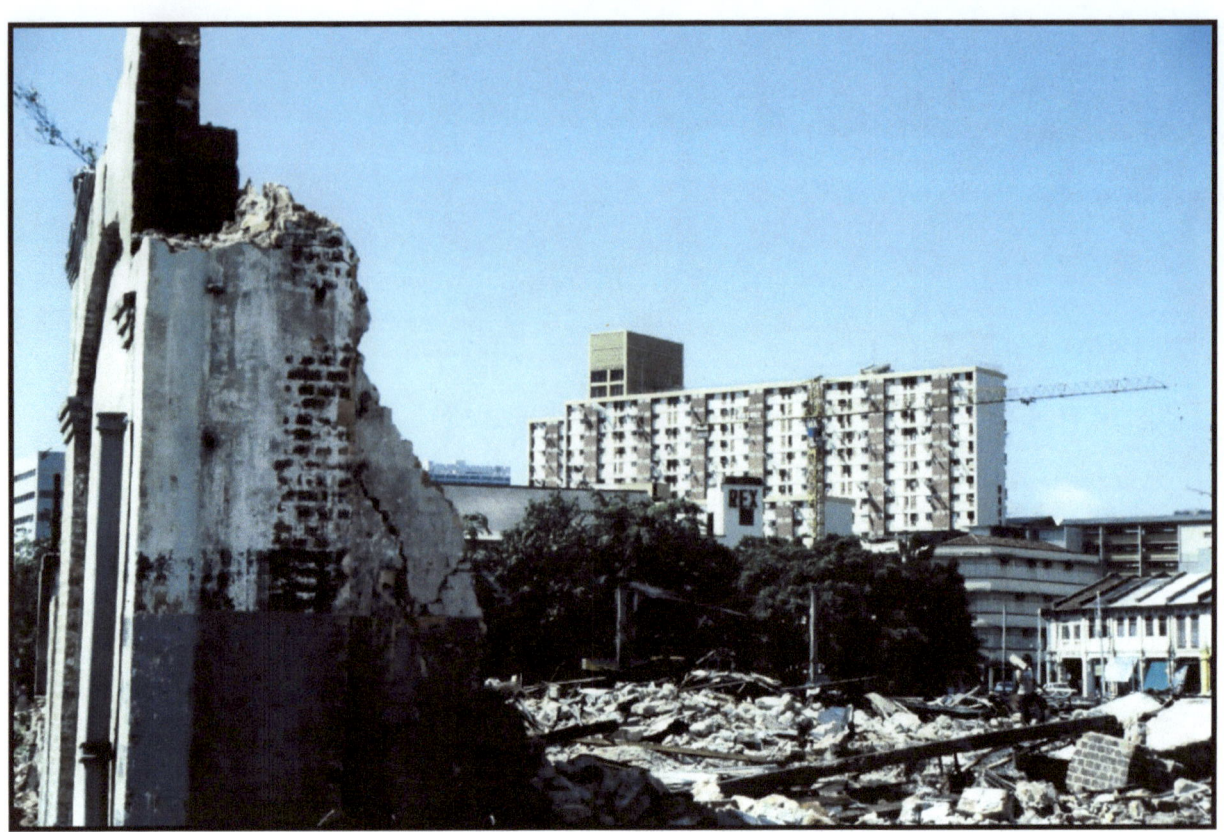

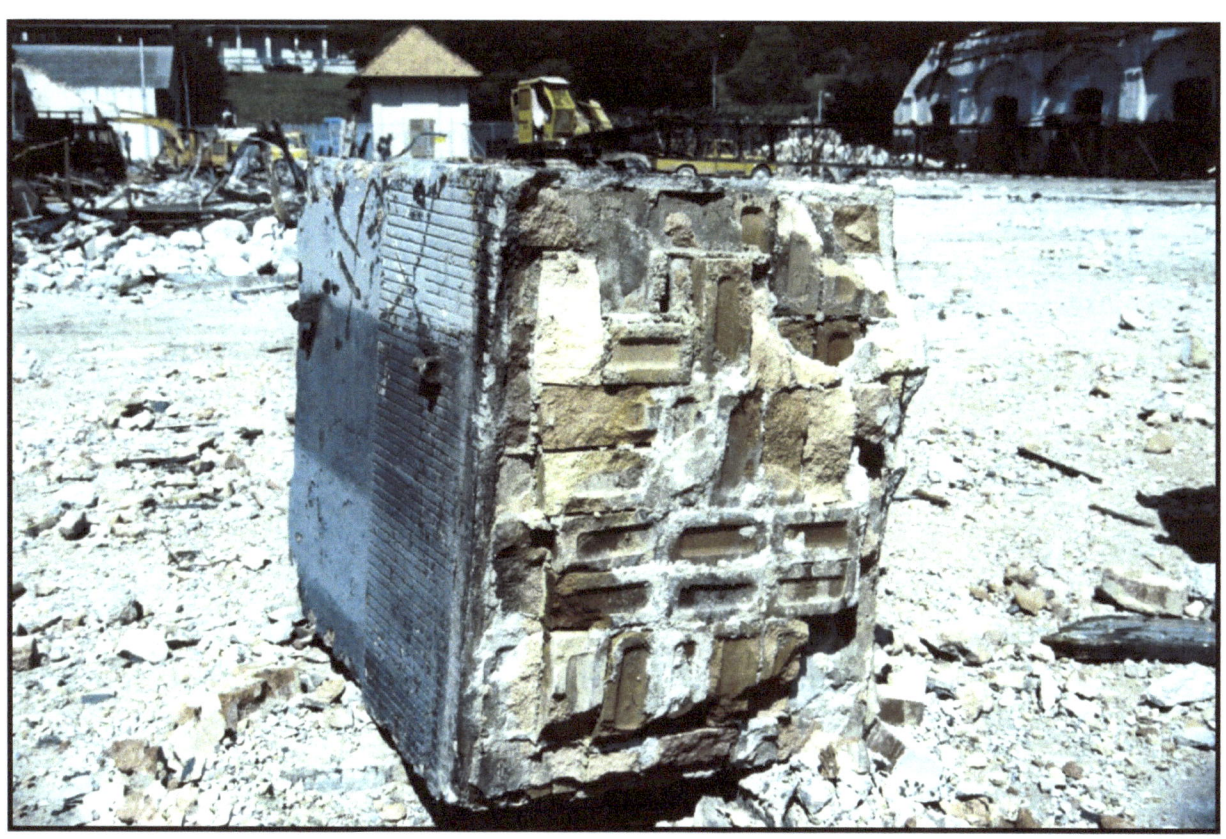

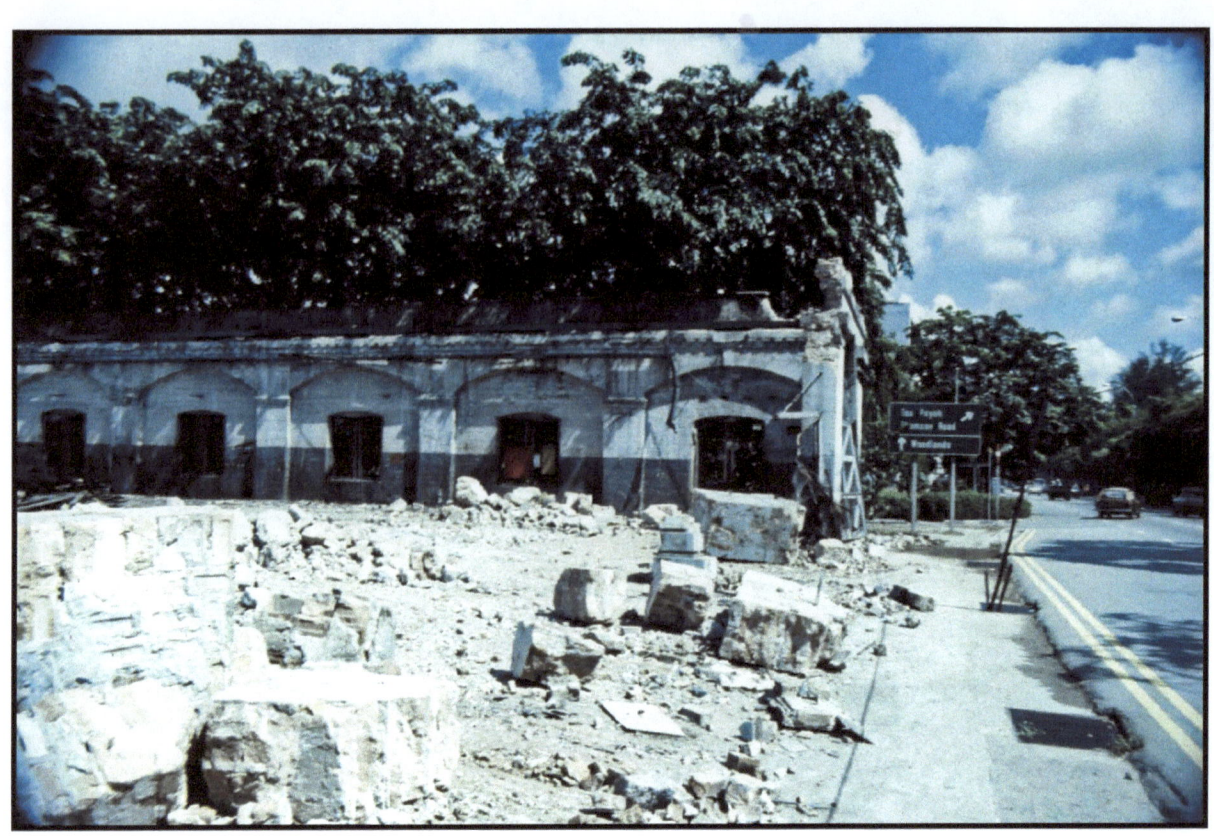

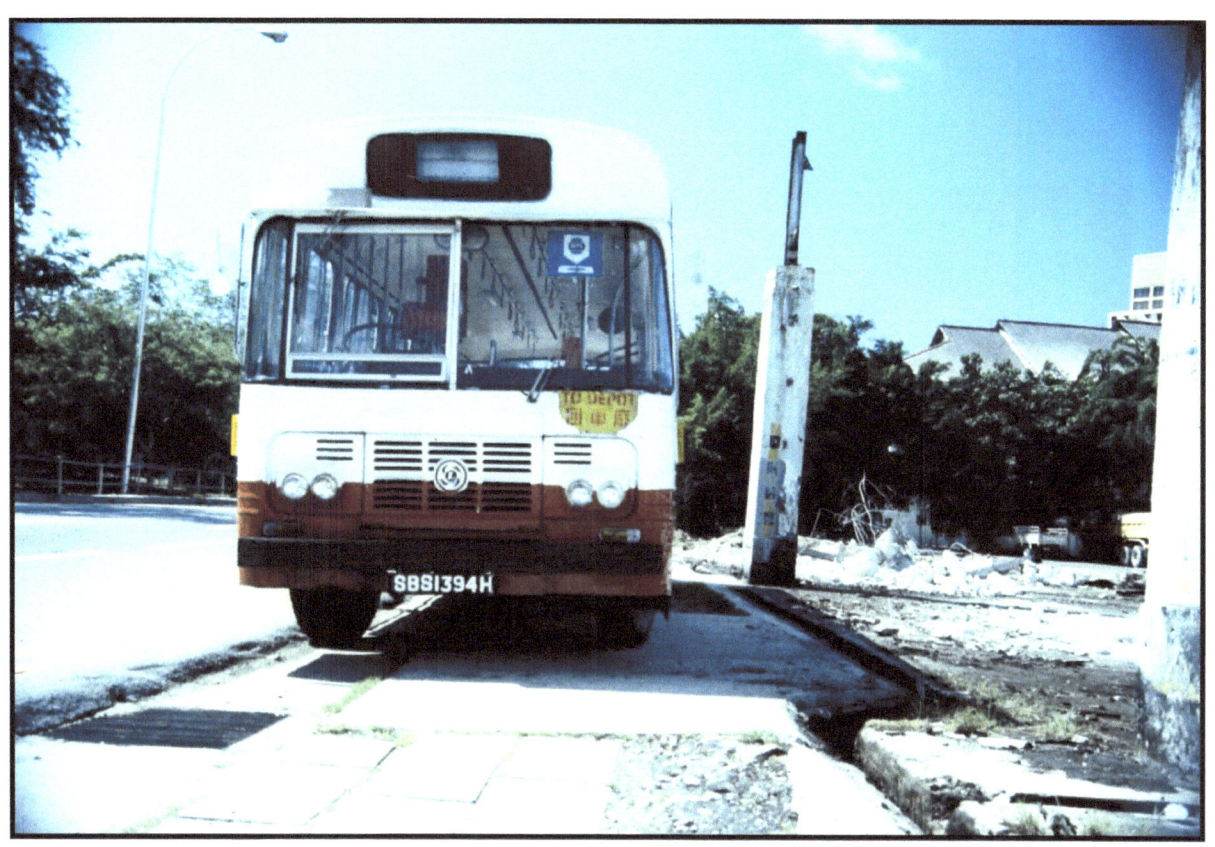

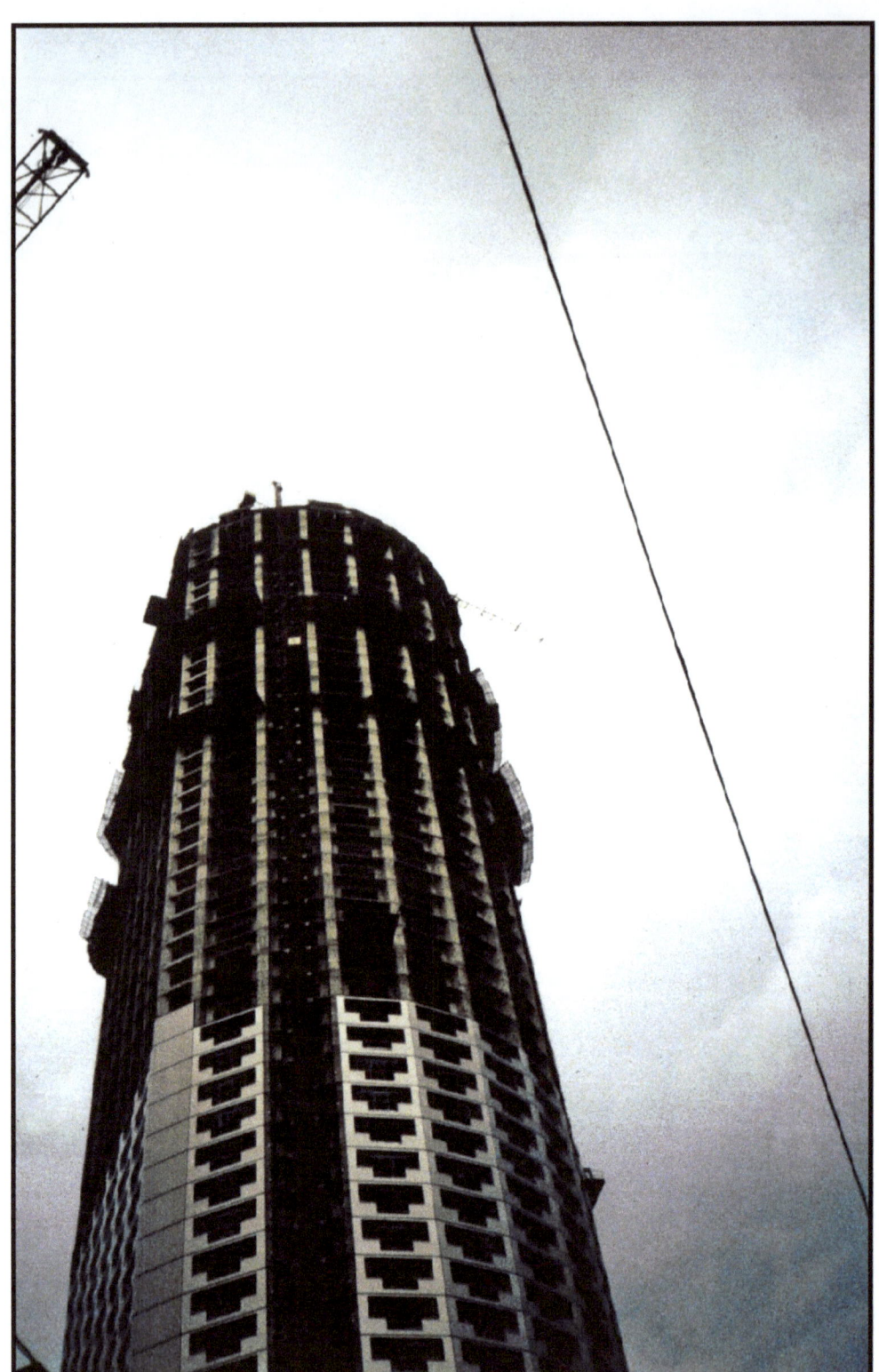

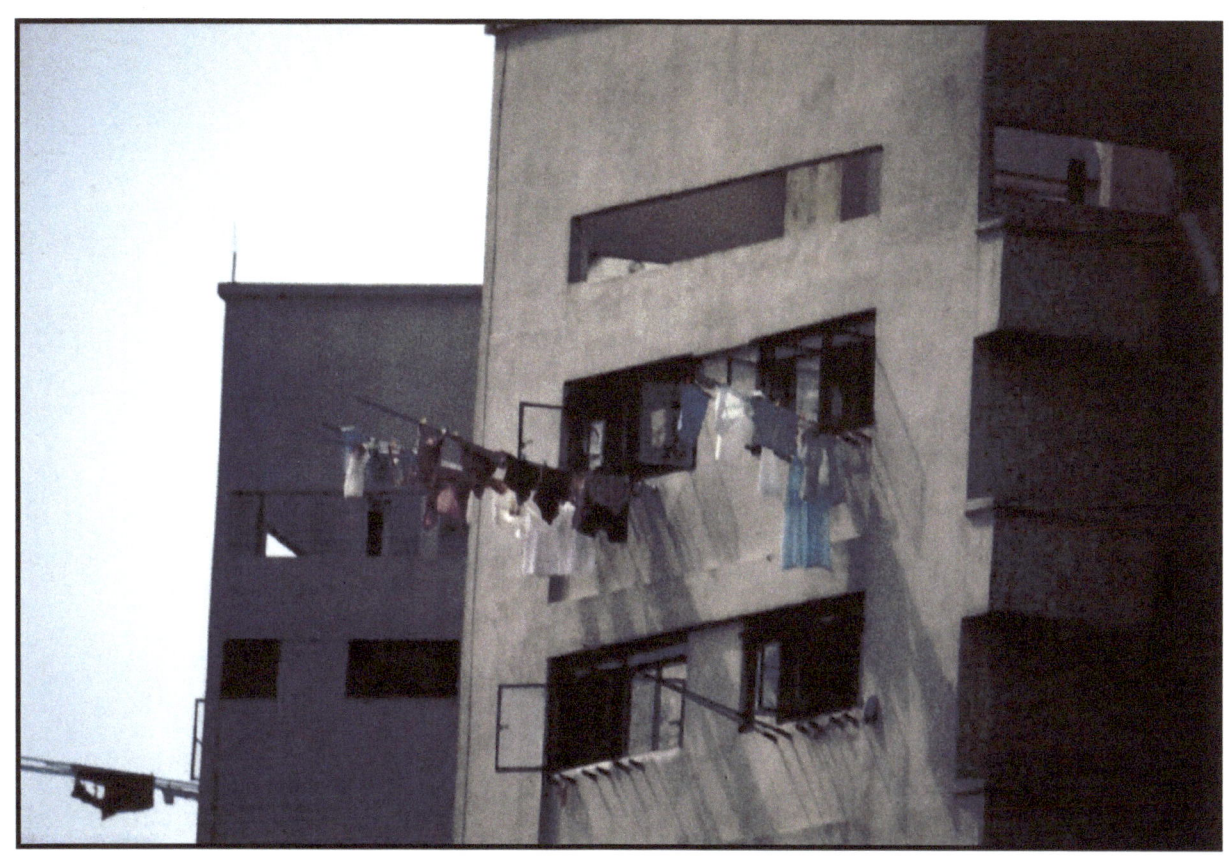

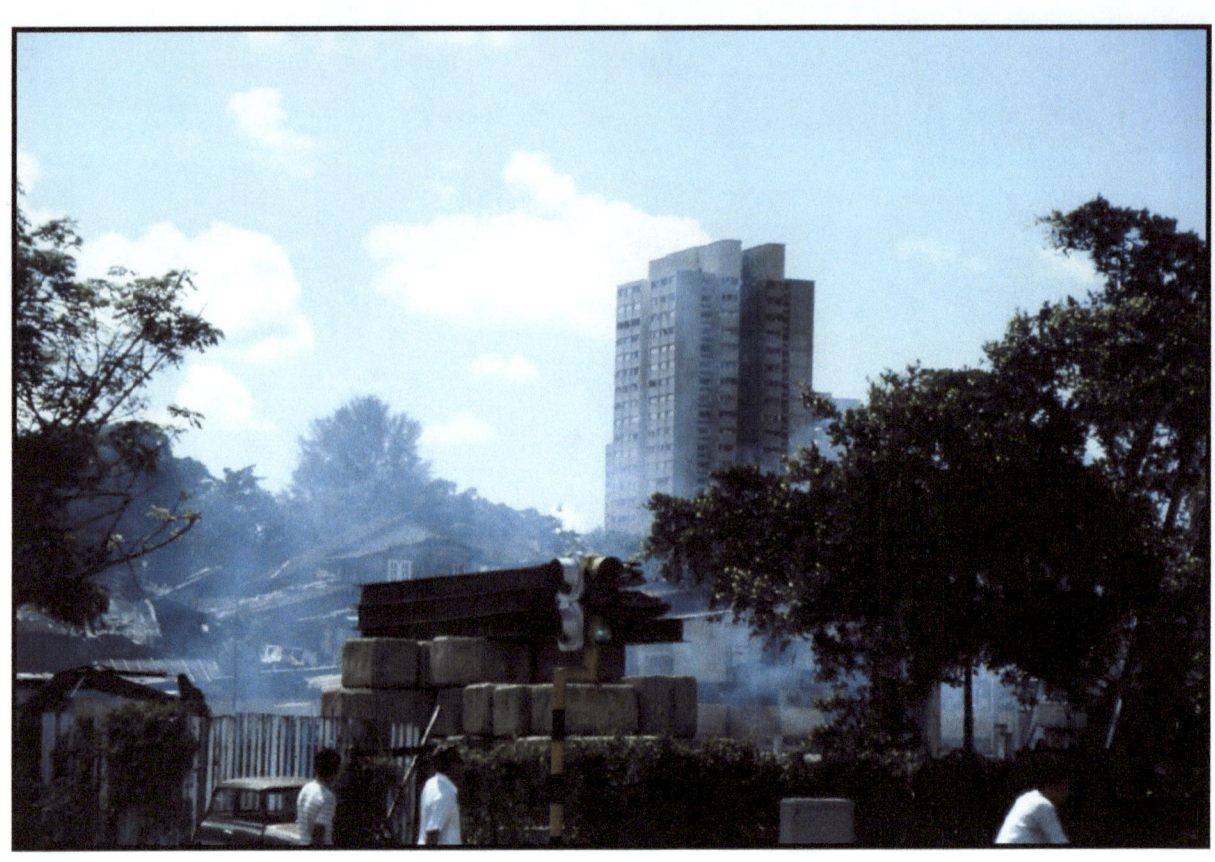

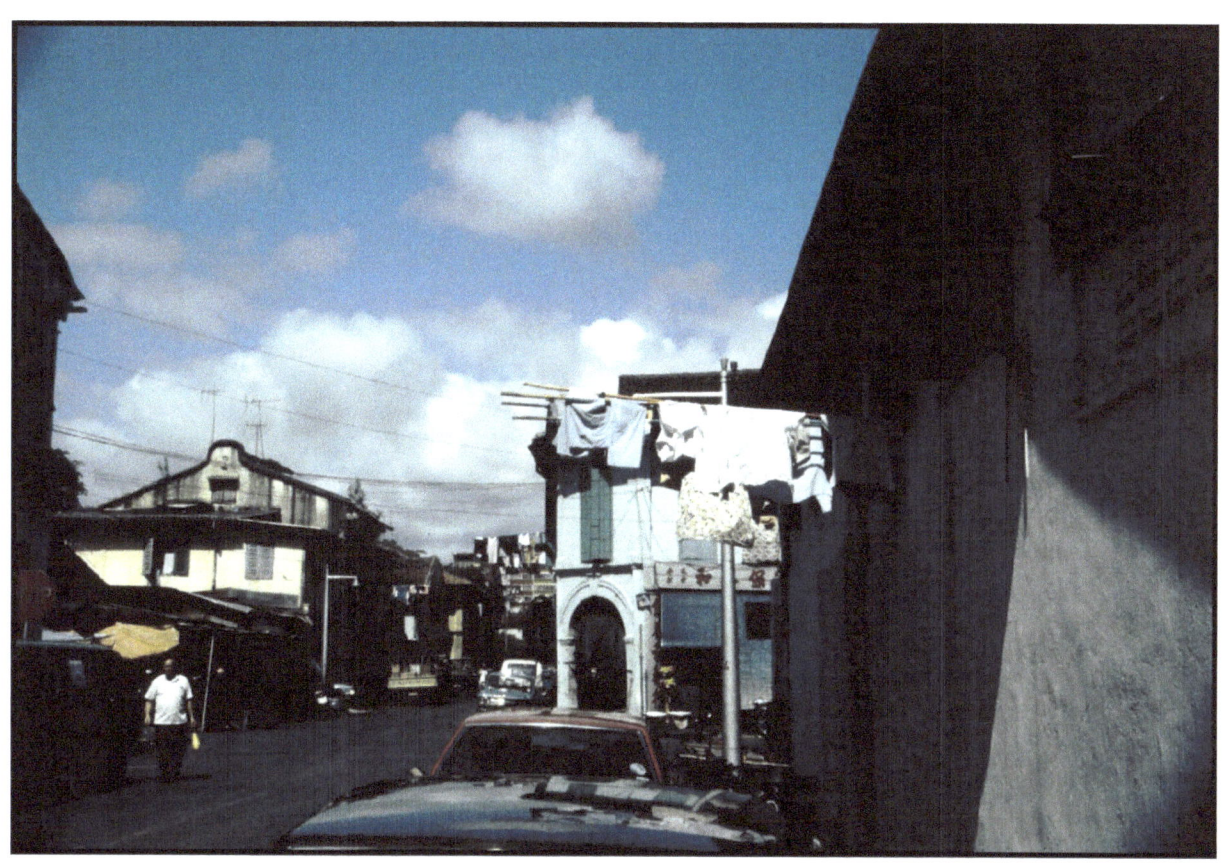

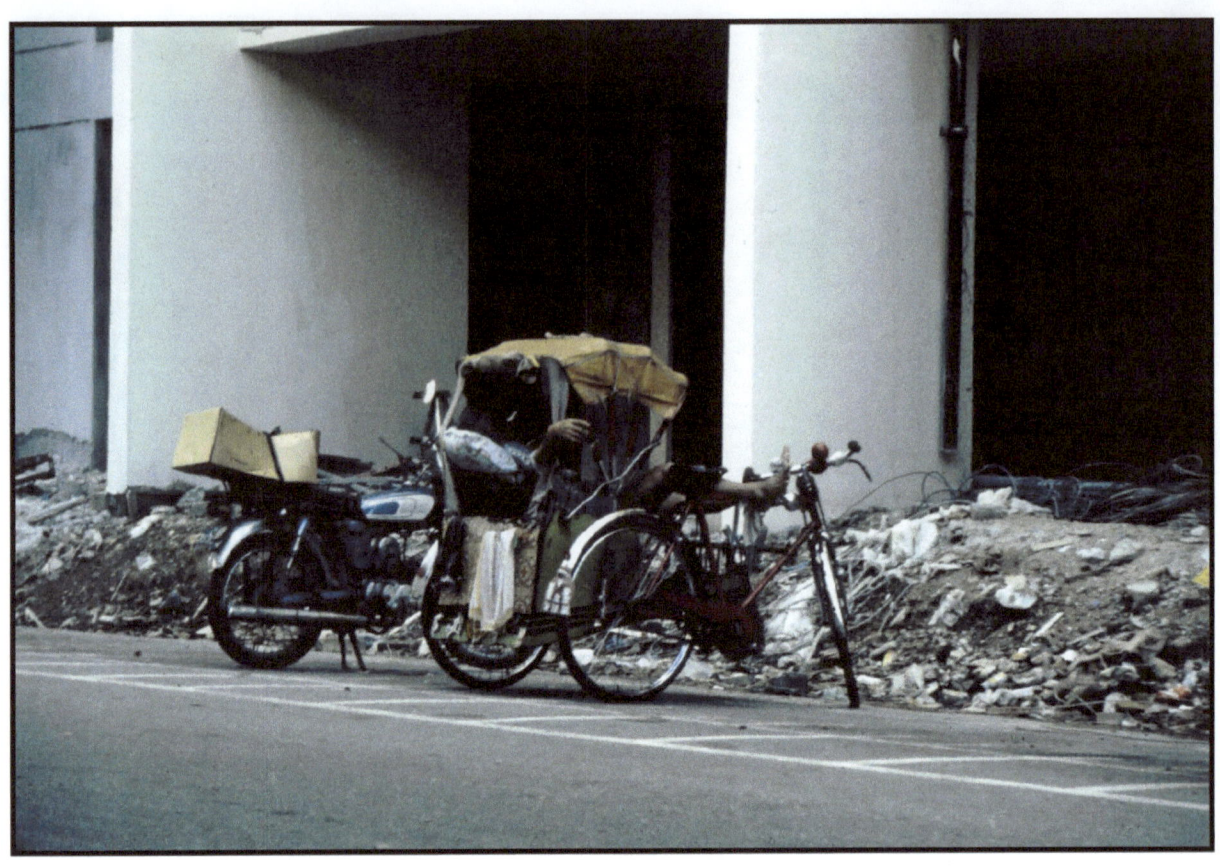

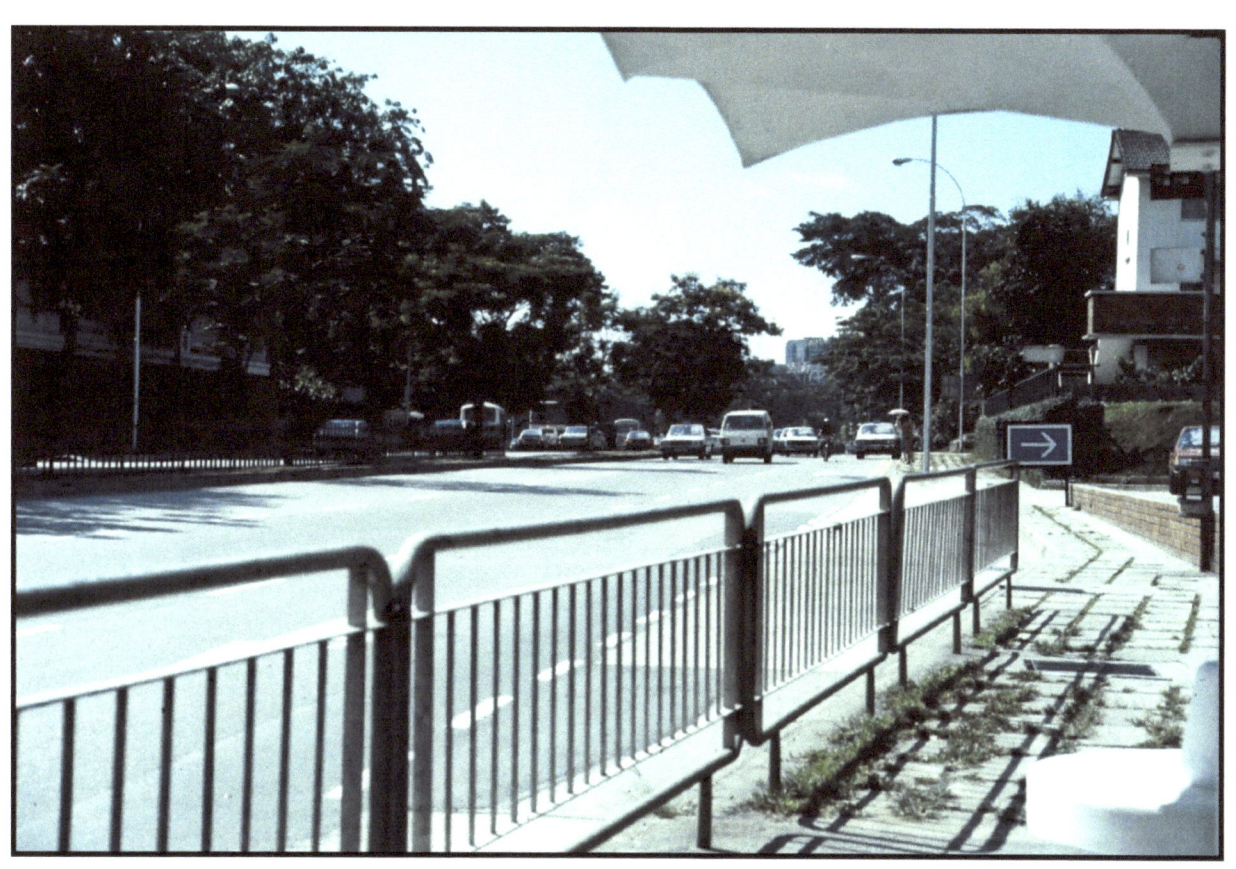

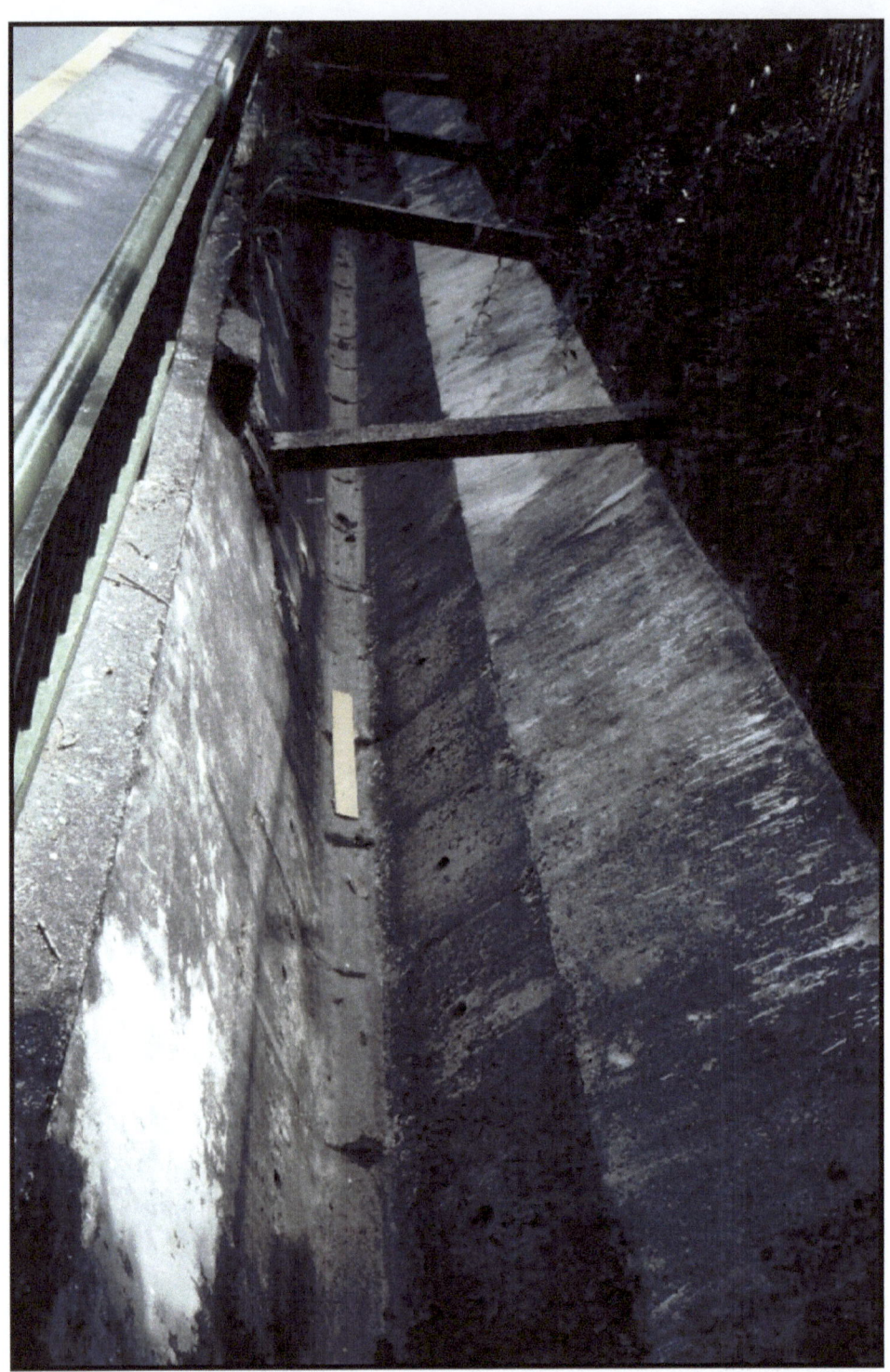

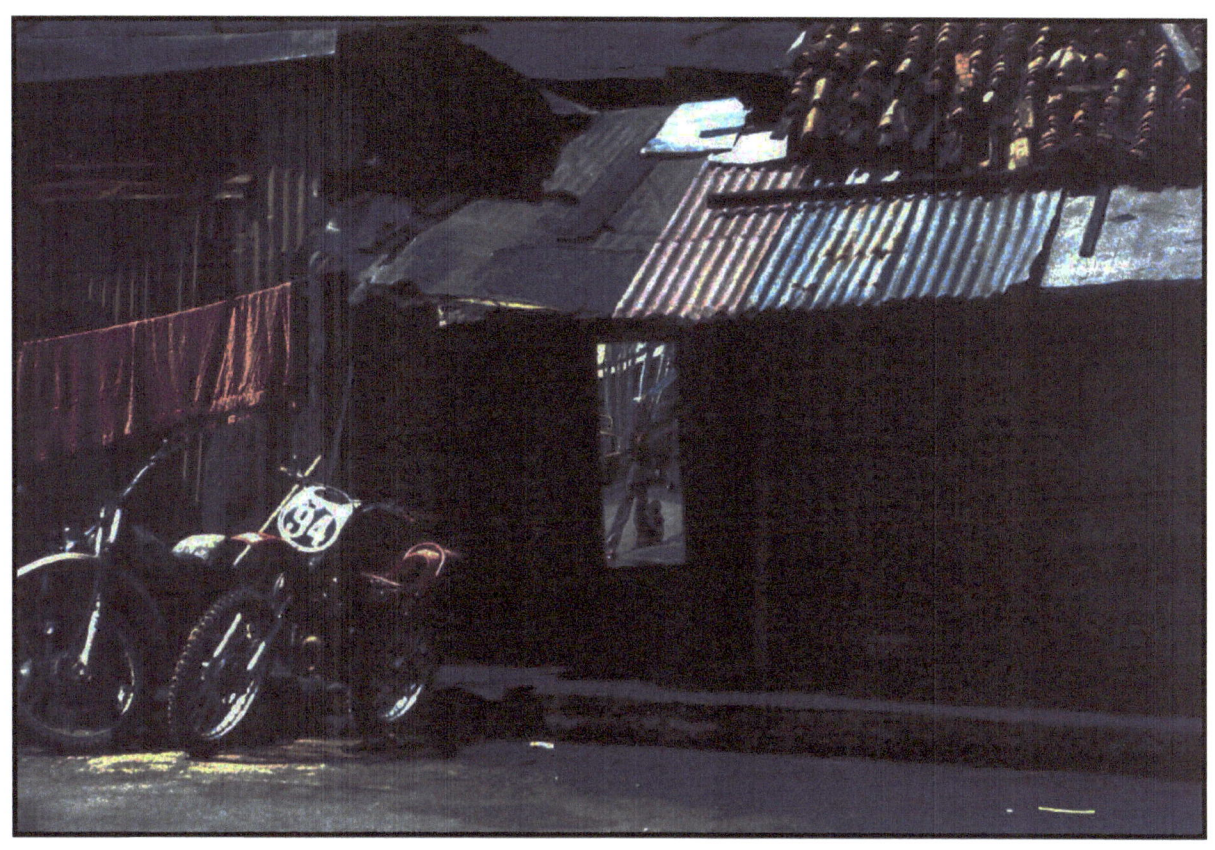

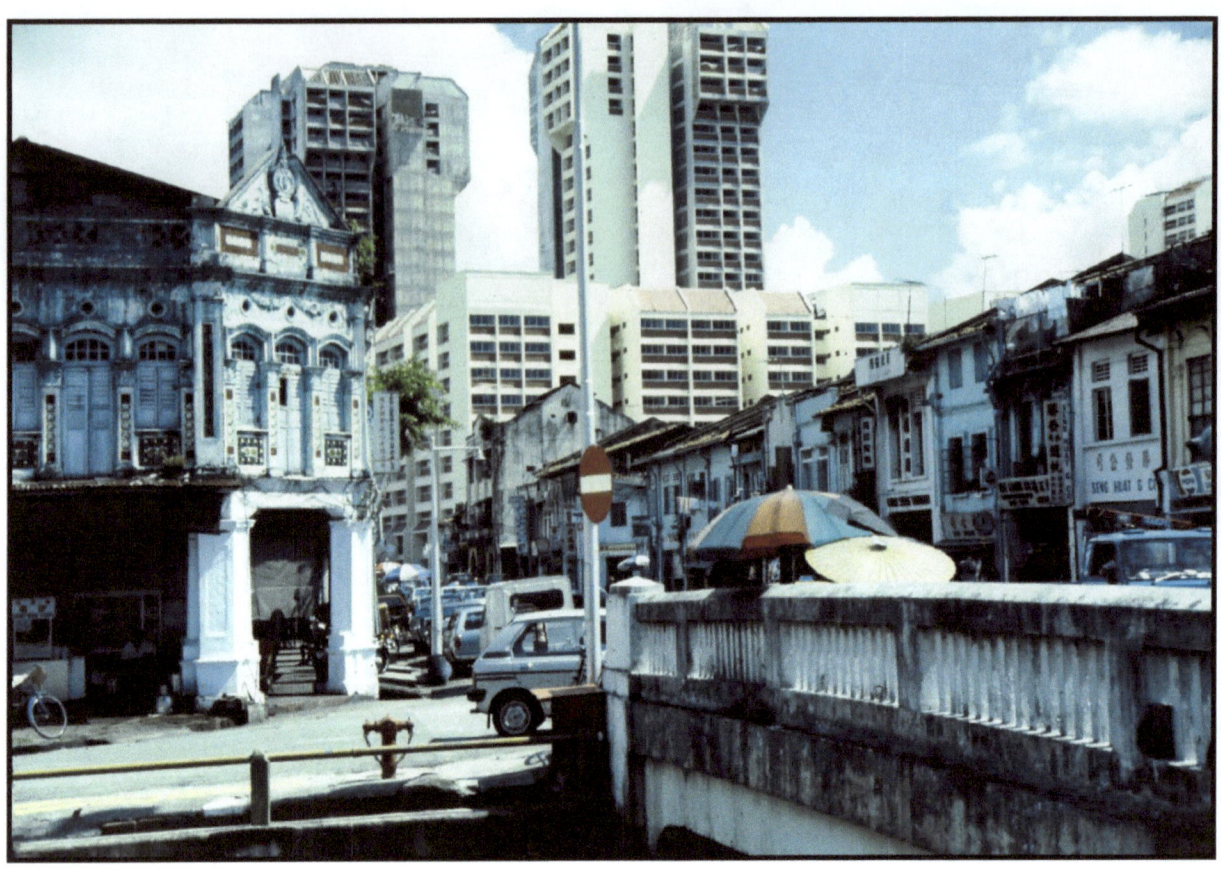

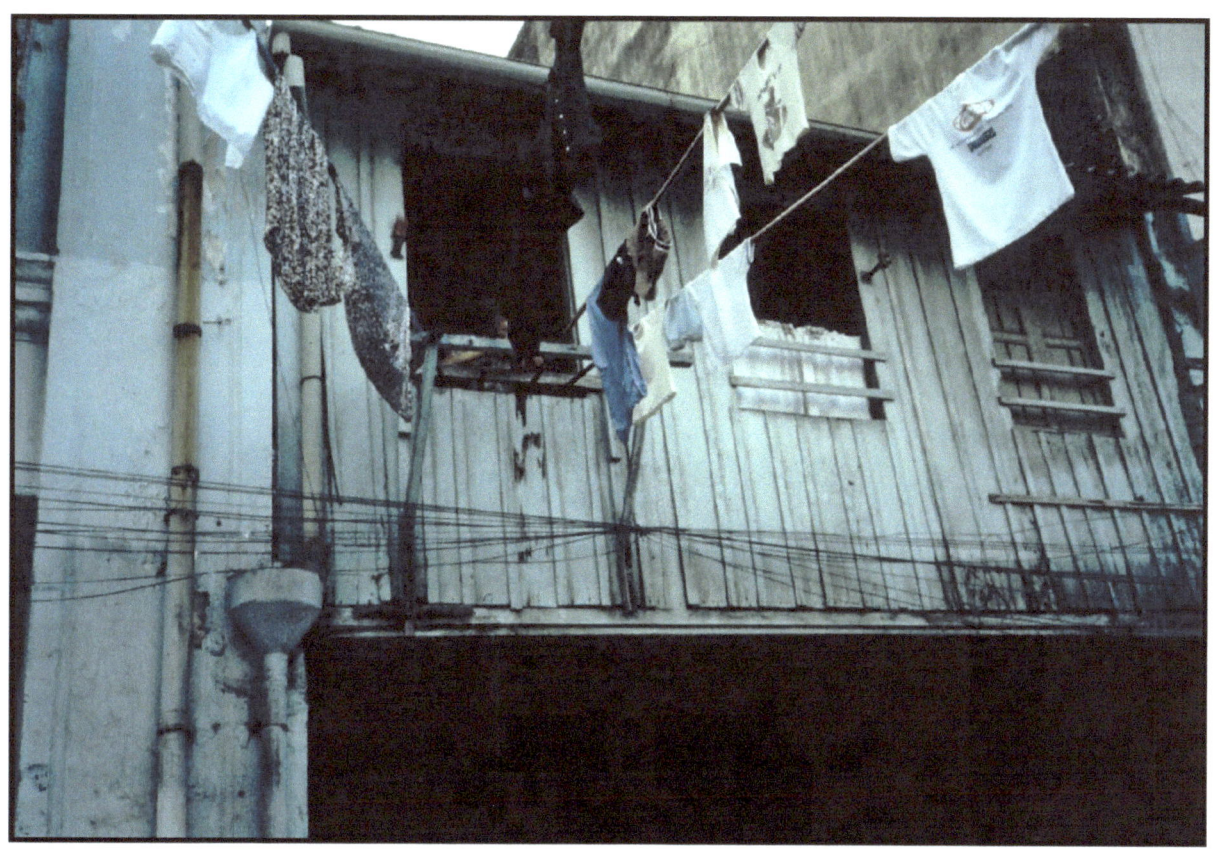

www.ingramcontent.com/pod-product-compliance
Lightning Source LLC
Chambersburg PA
CBHW051147220526
45473CB00003B/684